Training for Development

Dr. Rolf P. Lynton and Dr. Udai Pareek have been colleagues for almost three decades. They first worked together in Hyderabad, India, where Lynton was leader of the Ford Foundation team which helped start the Small Industry Extension Training Institute and Pareek was Director of Extension Education. This collaboration resulted in a reexamination of training in organizational settings and in the first extensive use of L-Groups (or T-Groups) in India. Later they both taught at the University of North Carolina (Lynton in the School of Public Health, Pareek in the Department of Psychology and both of them in the Carolina Population Center) where they wrote *Training for Development*. Their most recent collaboration was in Indonesia. They are founder members of the Society of Applied Behavioral Science in India, Pareek serving as the Society's President in 1986-87.

Rolf Lynton is now living and working in India again. His career includes a period as Professor of Public Health and of Preventive Medicine at the University of South Carolina where from 1974 to 1977 he was the founding Dean and Department Chairman. He has been Johns Hopkins University/USAID senior advisor working with the Ministry of Health and Family Welfare in India; Director of Aloka, an international training center for community development workers; and chairman of the International Society of Applied Social Scientists. Earlier he worked with the field research unit of the British Institute of Management, the European Youth Campaign, based in France, and the Harvard Business School. He has authored many books and papers, has worked as a consultant with many international agencies and is a professional member of the NTL Institute and of the Association for Creative Change.

Udai Pareek, author, researcher and consultant, lives in Jaipur, India, where he chairs the Scientific Advisory Council of the Indian Institute of Health Management Research. Until recently he was USAID Organization Development Advisor to the Ministry of Health in Indonesia. He has been Larsen and Toubro Professor of Organizational Behavior at the Indian Institute of Management in Ahmedabad. Pareek has worked in the fields of education, agriculture, small industry and public health. He has worked as a consultant with Indian and international organizations, has been a Fellow of the NTL Institute, and has served on the editorial boards of the *Administrative Quarterly, Psychologia, Group in Organization Studies* and other journals. He is editor of *Indian Psychological Abstracts* and of a new journal, *Human Resource Development*.

Both authors share current interests in systems change, institutional and organizational development, and human resource development.

Training for Development

Second Edition

ROLF P. LYNTON
and
UDAI PAREEK

Education is not for knowing more but for behaving differently.
—RUSKIN

The world owes all its onward impulse to men ill at ease.
—HAWTHORNE

KUMARIAN PRESS

630 Oakwood Avenue, Suite 119, West Hartford, Connecticut 06110-1529 USA

Cover design by Marilyn Penrod
Typeset by Macrographics, India

Printed in the United States of America
94 93 92 91 90 5 4 3 2 1

Second edition published simultaneously by Kumarian Press, Inc., for worldwide distribution exclusive of India and South Asia; and by Vistaar Publications, a division of Sage Publications India Private Ltd., for exclusive distribution in India and South Asia.

First edition published in 1967 by Richard D. Irwin, Inc., USA. Indian reprint edition published in 1973 by D. B. Taraporevala Sons & Co. Private Ltd., India, by arrangement with the original publisher. First paperback edition published in 1978 by Kumarian Press, Inc., inaugurating its Kumarian Press Library of Management for Development.

Library of Congress Cataloging in Publication Data

Lynton, Rolf P.
Training for development / Rolf P. Lynton and Udai Pareek. — 2nd ed.
p. cm. — (Kumarian Press library of management for development)
Includes index.
ISBN 0-931816-76-9. — ISBN 0-931816-86-6 (pbk.)
1. Employees—Training of. I. Pareek, Udai Narian, 1925–
II. Title.
HF5549.5.T7L9 1990
658.3'1243—dc20 89-7989
CIP

Originally to

STEPHEN M. COREY

and

FRITZ J. ROETHLISBERGER

from whose courage to develop themselves and others we have directly profited

and now, twenty years later, also to our colleagues in

THE INDIAN SOCIETY OF APPLIED BEHAVIORAL SCIENCE

and

THE INDONESIAN ASSOCIATION FOR APPLIED BEHAVIORAL SCIENCE

Preface to the Second Edition

He who wants to speak the truth must have one foot in the stirrup.

—*Turkish Proverb*

In The Twenty Years since this book was first published (1967) the training scene has changed; we want to reflect—and reflect upon—these changes in the new edition.

Most evident is the escalation of scale. Training and retraining is going on in many more institutions and in many more connections than before—in new technologies, of course, from computer operating and servicing to hang-gliding; also of women in management, woodsmen in social forestry, unemployed to be resettled, black youths, the physically handicapped, professional athletes, post–Vatican II clergy, program administrators, and armies in the space age. Prime Minister of India, Rajiv Gandhi, has instituted weeklong residential in-service training programs for all officers of the Indian Administrative Service, and also for Ministers; twenty-five institutions provide these programs to all parts of the subcontinent. In 1967 we noted that the membership of the American Society for Training and Development had grown from 15 in 1943 to over 5,000 twenty years later. India's STD, founded in 1969, now has 220 institutional and 1,700 individual members, and a second national network started in 1985 for Human Resources Development. With almost every mail we receive announcements of regular and new training programs; the dailies and weeklies, and television, advertise still more. Even small market towns have institutes for training in English and secretarial services, and everywhere are institutes for working with computers. The U.S. Agency for International Development earmarks $150 million a year for technical assistance to management training alone. The health services projects on which we are currently working envisage training for over 200,000 more nurses in Indonesia and 48,000 field staff in just four of India's twenty-five states. Training overall must have at least doubled in scale in these twenty years, in number of people going for training, size of training facilities and staff and costs of training. That would mean that the $10 billion spent on training in the U.S. in 1967 has now come close to $90 billion in today's currency and India's estimated $6 billion to then about $45 billion.

This is a massive enterprise, and its continuing escalation should be proof that training (or at least most of it) results in notably improved performances by individuals and organizations, indeed by whole sectors and governments. And this ought to be so most of all in developing countries, that is, in economies with the tightest budgets and the longest way to go. Training would then be a success story and its contribution real and tangible, justifying the expenditure on it to date and its trajectory into the future.

What evidence we see in this direction, however, continues to be slight and sporadic. Given the massive expenditure on training, surprisingly little determined effort is directed toward tracing it, let alone making training solid and reliable. Only here and there do we see instances where training has clearly resulted in improved performance at work; those in which improvements accord with predetermined goals which were planned into training programs furnish examples throughout this book. They point to the feasibility and promise of good training, but simultaneously reveal the vast reality of its absence. Most of the programs we have seen and know about make little or no difference to performance at work. Indeed their plans and designs were not really of a quality to improve praxis; yet they have been funded and continue to be funded.

Users of extramural programs, who are dissatisfied with one program, usually shop around for another for their participants; only rarely do they use more rigorous criteria in choosing one program over another. Hardly ever do they stop sending participants altogether. So training enterprises also go on and on. If one training program is discontinued, another usually takes its place. Only very rarely does a training establishment close its doors. One large Indian company was such an exception.

Once in the forefront of the training movement, this company discontinued all management training and closed its department. Now it selects and promotes managers strictly on the basis of their past performance with the company or, if such personnel are new, during limited probationary periods; training and educational qualifications no longer count in promotion. In the U.S., dissatisfaction with what new graduates of colleges and universities know and can do has led large companies and associations to set up their own institutions to such an extent that funding of these "proprietary institutions of higher education" now exceeds funding for state universities. But direct control over preparatory work does not guarantee the outcome either and, furthermore, is fraught with intrinsic pitfalls which we will consider from various angles in this book.

As things are, dissatisfaction with training and the scale of training efforts are both increasing, side by side, but training seems unaffected by its partner. Like a juggernaut, training just rolls on.

We are dissatisfied with most training and hope this book will encourage trainers to come to grips early and properly with the large tasks and large problems that confront the field. By indicating useful "holds" in the field, we hope to provoke colleagues everywhere to join in the very necessary struggling that lies ahead. We see and use seven.

Hold One: Training Strategy

Training as we see it has become increasingly reified and this invites the first throw. Training is presented more and more as though it were an activity to be set well apart from the demands and activities of every day, at its purest and most desirable when cloistered off somewhere and guided by a quasi-priestly caste of trainers. Such training can have important specialized uses, but it plays a minor role in the field as a whole. Major developments in the past twenty years have been in quite the opposite direction. The most extensive and far–reaching learning has proceeded with no trainers at all or with trainers involved only marginally and at some distance.

Large numbers of people around the world have learned, without training, to exercise regularly or to control the size of their families, to eat more wisely and other useful habits. If some learning was required, they organized and paid for it themselves. If they made a program of it, e.g., by joining television classes, they engaged in what trainers call distance learning. We include this type of learning in the set of training modalities added to chapter 3, "Training Strategy." Such self-directed activities are of course "distant" only from trainers; the learner/actors could not be closer nor more involved.

Trainers and funders have meanwhile become quite inordinately preoccupied with curriculum content, program design, training methods and materials, and other details—anything, it seems, rather than face such broader basic issues as purpose, options for achieving it, and a good fit with the wider organizational and social contexts that must first support the training and then the developments training is expected to promote. This premature, misplaced preoccupation reduces to chance any relevance and usefulness training may have. All that it guarantees is high entertainment value.

For us, training as circus is an extreme perversion. We see a growing army of technique-happy trainers trapped in it, with folders full of preplanned programs and ready access to masses of standard exercises, simulations and games. These aids have become powerful seducers away from thoughtful attention, painstaking designing, and honest appraisal. In developing countries, where tasks are always urgent, trainers scarce, often inexperienced, and lonely, and administrators harried and looking for sure, incontrovertible outcomes, neat schedules and printed exercises are highly attractive. Imported designs even satisfy that newly prominent requirement of involving participants *actively*. So all parties enjoy them—

which would be fine if the training also promoted the very purpose behind the design, namely, the required learning. Instead, in the ease and fun and certainties, the means all too readily become ends and spin off into orbits independent of purpose. In many programs numerous topics are lightly and briefly touched, then dropped as though unimportant. More and more information is displayed—formica boards, overhead projectors, and photocopies make display so easy. We are particularly distressed by the apparently ubiquitous one– or two-day workshops in management, supervision, community involvement, and other people-centered topics. They are highly advertised, and even at fees of $200 and more per day (plus travel and living) attract an apparently unending stream of participants backed by organizations. If such short programs affect participants at all (and enrollment lists show that many participants repeatedly attend programs with similar titles), they are far more likely to strengthen the participants' defenses against human understanding and encounters than to lead to useful learning.

Greater emphasis on strategy is our response to these imbalances and perversions. Besides expanding the chapter on strategy we have also advanced its placement in the book (now chapter 3). It now precedes even the broad overview of the training process.

Hold Two: Evaluation

Better evaluation could check the perversions, ineffectiveness, and excessive costs of many training programs. The clients of training, work organizations and public funders, are in the best position to take hold of training from that angle and can be coached to do so effectively. The two most telling moves for measuring the effectiveness of training are first, to help them institute work-based evaluation well after participants have returned from training, and second, to establish the *total* cost of training instead of only the direct training costs or fee payments. Total training costs would include the participants' ongoing salaries as well as their travel, stay and meals and also the costs of replacing them, extra organizational costs, and overheads during training. Such realistic costing yields figures at least twice those now commonly used and can translate quite quickly into client insistence on more effective training.

In our opinion, evaluation has moved in the same miserly direction as training in general: increasingly elaborate technologies for asking minor questions, leading by incestuous processes to self-satisfaction for trainers. Program directors and trainers design the questions, collect data, hold conferences, and talk and report to each other on what worked well and what worked less well within the confines of the training program; or even less indicative, they record and report the end-of-course enthusiasm of participants, before they returned to their daily work. This protection of the providers of training from the views of the participants, colleagues, supervisors, and employers back at work is greatest when all the costs of training, even the participants' travel and per diem, are covered in the budget of the training institution and when mere course attendance counts toward promotion. Thus no one's actual performance needs to be taken into account, neither the trainers' nor participants'.

These extreme conditions are true of many government agencies in developing countries, which fund training institutions to pay all costs and often give stipends directly to participants. Happily, many of these countries are now sufficiently far along in staffing their civil service following independence to be able to look training far more critically and to insist more and more on adequate value for training funds.

Properly used, evaluation can be a second promising hold on training, alternating with a firmer grip on strategy. Hence we have expanded this topic into a full chapter (11).

Holds Three through Seven: Training for Action

The most far-reaching changes in this book stem from our broader understanding of action and its requirements, and therefore of the contribution training can make to action and the contexts training needs to take into account and deal with. This has led us to identify five more holds on training which are also promising. First, in trying, separately and together, to understand better why training continues to be so unreliable and often quite ineffective as a means for improving work performance, we have learned to give much more weight to *organizational readiness and support* for improvement (Hold 3). Where these are lacking or deficient, training makes little or no difference, certainly not for long, except to increase the frustration of the best participants and to stimulate them to leave for situations where competence is valued more. In this larger picture the quality of training itself is secondary. Moreover, more is known about how to achieve it than how to assess organizational readiness and support and, beyond assessing, to ensure them.

This shift in our emphasis is evident in many places in this new edition. Besides broadening our perspective on training strategy, we now also advocate *widening the trainer's role* (Hold 4) to include consultation with participant organizations, especially to match participant selection with organizational change strategies, and to ensure organizational support for improved performance subsequent to training (chapter 10). While we are aware that effective training depends greatly on corresponding organizational developments, the reverse is also true: organizational development, by creating new settings of clearly identifiable people in affected positions. This recognition tends to blur the distinctions between training and organizational consultation, and between training and follow-up activities. Increasing numbers of training staff will also have to become competent in these related roles and more familiar with and credible in work settings. The inclusion of more administrators, line managers and field staff in training faculties can facilitate building these bridges, whereby training and practice can reinforce each other much more than they commonly do now.

This broader perspective has led us to two other changes in this second edition. A new chapter (12) on *developing training systems* (Hold 5) introduces part 3. In it we have mapped a wider variety of training resources which can be brought to bear on a training task and additional ways in which these can be interrelated and further developed. Training centers and institutes are not the only or major part of such a system; in our experience this realization itself can provoke these establishments into taking a fresh and more effective position. In line with this broader perspective, the chapter on *"action research"* (14) has been expanded and better integrated (Hold 6). All trainers need to undertake action research, both for its approach and as an activity, and certainly "to stay honest." Throughout the book examples from our own practice, many from Indonesia where we worked together once again, ground the new generalizations and make them concrete. Training depends for its further development on action research.

The broadest context to take into account in training is the cultural one—promising hold number seven. In the light of our experiences in Indonesia, we have added a chapter on this aspect and placed it early (2) in the book. It is not merely descriptive. Besides urging *sensitivity to local cultural contexts,* it is prescriptive in just one respect: to engage actively with the cultural environment relevant to the task in the expectation that organizational development and the training of people are channels for also *developing the culture*. This realization is similar to that recorded only twenty or thirty years ago, namely, that organizations need not regard their environments as fixed, to be taken into account and adjusted to, but rather to be actively interacted with for mutual adjustment and development in tandem. As this realization widens to now encompass the cultural context, it has very practical consequences for training and its organization.

Concepts and Words Updated

Our practical experiences with "taking hold" of training over the years—through stretching the perceptions of it by clients and, when possible, by trainers and through pushing forward more precise, exacting measures for its effectiveness and economy—stretch the language we need to use beyond what is in common use in and about training. All the particular Holds recommended in the previous pages interrelate training more directly and actively with wider, "system" contexts than the earlier book did: with participants, including in that term the increasingly large number of independently motivated learners using varieties of public media and self-study; with work organizations and public funders of training and development; and, wider still, with broad cultural dimensions which training has to reflect if it is to be effective but which it also in turn shapes. The earlier edition had this broad framework, too, but to a much lesser extent than this, whereas now we shift the focus from training activities *per se* to the systemic interconnections and hold it there. This calls for systems language, and we will use as much of it as will clarify our purpose—as craftspeople at work, in short, not as discussants in the ongoing elaboration of systems science itself.

One particular use to which we put the word "systems" throughout the book may be awkward and we have searched unsuccessfully for something as appropriate and also less liable to appear too large or too small. By training "system" we mean the whole range of training resources to which any particular set of work organizations and participants have access to meet their needs—or could have access if they knew of their existence and if the resources were organized enough in actuality. Theoretically the work "institution" could be a useful substitute, in the sociologists' sense of family or governance as social institutions. But in the training field "institution" too readily evokes an image of buildings with name plates and set staffs and programs; indeed this *was* the meaning for which we used institution in the first edition. But it is now the very least component of all we mean. For *that* kind of institution we now use "training center." We will particularize our meaning of training resources system, or system for short, again when it first occurs in the text (p. 9), trusting that readers will then settle into our use of it. That system is the immediate partner of the participants' work organization(s) in the pretraining and posttraining phases of the essential cycle of training and of the participants themselves while training is in process.

As our attention shifted from training to the wider and complex contexts of work organization and culture and the powerful influences of both on the possibilities of improvement in action, we have also reexamined the practical distinction we drew originally between education and training and still find it useful. Interest and capacities for change and learning govern both. But while in education students learn *inter alia* what they are interested in and capable of, training goes one step further: to be properly included in training, work organizations and participants must—should—have already opted to be interested in the particular changes training expects to promote and have already assessed that they can learn whatever is necessary to effect and sustain such changes in the work situation.

Inspite of considerable doubts we also decided to leave "training" in the title. We preferred "learning" over "training," and "human resource (or systems) development" would have indicated the broader scope of the book. However, it seemed best to retain the title the book is already known by, which is clearly addressed to trainers and those who make decisions regarding training, i.e., the actors who visualize, fund, design and manage, in other words create—or fail to create—opportunities for significant learning.

Most of the changes made in this new edition are additions; they have crowded out the readings included at the end of chapters in the first edition. A more comprehensive and rounded companion volume of readings is now under way, with the same stress on basics and particular attention to filling the still numerous gaps in what professional literature is readily available in developing countries. We considered adding an annotated bibliography but pared the idea down to a few sentences here. More than this, we fear, might diffuse our focus, which we want to hold steadily on training praxis and on learning more from it, ours and others. Also, especially in this era of copying and all too facile "transfers" of technologies and learning, *our* selection of readings might make it temptingly easy for readers to shortcut their own personal search for readings to illuminate their own experiences.

In the recent literature, Donald A. Schoon's *The Reflective Practitioner: How Professionals Think in Action* (New York: Basic Books, Inc., 1983) catches best what we mean by learning and by helping others learn, i.e., by training. The book is based on recordings of what goes on in professional offices as an experienced, recognized architect, psychotherapist, scientist, town planner, manager—a "master"—works with a "junior" colleague or intern over a design, a review of a session, a case. They "converse" not so much with each other as with the situation made up of quite concrete considerations such as purpose, site characteristics, client preferences and others. In the process they "reframe" the problem, test fresh solutions together and visualize the consequences, firm up some components in order to free up some others. The process is full of stops and starts, some dead ends and much excitement.

Recognizing the givens in a situation, the more or less fixed components, is basic to our practice and comes early each time. They intertwine intricately, together making up what Fritz J. Roethlisberger (of Hawthorne Studies' fame) used to call the "stubborn reality" of things, "to stub your toes on" if they get neglected. He wrote with humor and insight about his wrestling with stubborn realities in his intellectual autobiography, *The Elusive Phenomenon* (George F.F. Lombord, ed,. Boston, Mass.: Division of Research, Harvard Business School, 1977). From mapping and paying healthy respect to stubborn realities it is possible to go on to identify what we call "areas of freedom" in our practice. This is the crucial step to action, for it is in *these* areas that learning can be useful, that is, can lead to improved performance and be supported and sustained by the work organization.

For rigorous conceptualization and analyses of givens and of areas of freedom we continue to draw on writings from the Tavistock Institute and its now many derivatives. Socio-technical system, primary task, relevant environment and other very useful systems terms which now permeate the literature have sprung from this source. Two authors in particular, Eric Trist and Fred Emery, have continued to add seminal writings right through, from the beginnings forty years ago. The recent two-volume *Systems Thinking* (F. E. Emery, ed., Penguin Books, U.K., 1981) presents an important collection inexpensively. The revised edition of Daniel Katz and Robert Kahn, *The Social Psychology of Organizations* (New York: John Wiley and Sons, 1978) includes an extensive discussion of open systems and also a useful synthesis of systems literature. For the development of institutional systems, Seymour B. Saranson in *The Creation of Settings and the Future of Societies* (San Francisco: Jossey-Bass, Inc., 1972) provides much insight: at issue is not something surrounded by walls and with a nameplate at the front gate but institutionalized, i.e., reasonably reliable and permanent arrangements to work with for a while.

Important recent readings are about the environment in which training proceeds. Environments nearly everywhere have become more "turbulent," that is, unpredictable, as technologies change fast, information multiplies and hitherto powerless people become powerful. Pervasive shifts on the macro-scene make fresh positioning of training and trainers imperative. Composition, program content, style, settings, and much else have to change if training is to be relevant and truly aid development. Paul R. Lawrence and Jay W. Lorsch in *Organization and Environment: Managing Differentiation and Integration* (Boston, Mass.: Harvard University Press, 1967) began one important line of literature, leading to useful formulations of "contingency management."

A second stream deals with the empowerment of hitherto neglected groups themselves, for example, David Korten and Felipe B. Alfonso in *Bureaucracy and the Poor: Closing the Gap* (West Hartford, Conn.: Kumarian Press, 1983). Marvin R. Weisbord writes about "third wave" managing and consulting in *Productive Workplaces* (San Francisco and London: Jossey-Bass, Inc., 1987) on analogous lines of empowering workteams and so *Organizing and Managing for Dignity, Meaning, and Community,* his subtitle.

A third line of literature, more radical, starts from the premise that the presently powerful are in no position to help powerless peoples learn what they need to learn in order to be independent and powerful. Paulo

Friere, *Pedagogy of the Oppressed* (New York: The Continuum Publishing Corporation, 1985) argues this clearly. Edgar H. Schein puts rigor into the notion of culture and the development of norms in *Organization Culture and Leadership* (San Francisco and London: Jossey-Bass, Inc., 1987).

New Delhi and Jaipur
India

Rolf P. Lynton
Udai Pareek

Preface to the First Edition

IN A SHORT TWENTY YEARS, training has mushroomed into a large-scale activity. This is so the world over. In industrially developed countries training is a means to reduce obsolescence among people and organizations in the face of relentless technological innovation. The U.S.A. provides our examples for this group throughout the book. In developing countries, far away to the East and not so far away to the South, increased knowledge and skill—and application—are the latent resource that can be mobilized by training without heavy demands on scarce capital and scarcer foreign exchange. For these countries, India is our example. The concept, strategy, and method of training does not differ from the industrialized to the industrializing countries. But India's poverty and tradition, scale and stark need, make the bare bones of the task stick out and clarify the issues.

The immediate question is whether all this training activity, or even the greater part of it, can be justified by its results. Our answer in no, with honorable exceptions. The action question then is how it can be improved. This is what the book is about. Involved in answering the question in action are program directors and trainers now numbered by the thousands, as well as participants in training programs, and their organizations, who are entitled to receive good value for their investment in training.

A few sample figures can indicate the broad dimensions of what we are concerned about. American industry alone spends on the order of three billion dollars on formal training programs each year, that is, a sum about equivalent to all American foreign aid. Investment in skills acquired through systematic training now accounts for over half of the expenditure on all formal education in the country. Six hundred million dollars are spent on management development programs alone. Total annual expenditure on training of all kinds is above ten billion dollars. Professional membership of the American Society for Training and Development now exceeds 5,000. It was 15 in 1943.

India must have about 4,000 industrial training institutions alone and spends seventy-five to one hundred million dollars a year on them. If the wages of participants for the time spent in training are added, as they should be to get at the whole cost of training, the total doubles to 150-200 million dollars. Seventy to eighty percent of Indians who live in villages by farming are served by other training programs and institutions. Reports mention "training camps" each year for over 700,000 village leaders, for instance. Our estimate of expenditure on all kinds of training in India comes to about six billion dollars a year, that is, the equivalent of ten to fifteen percent of the Fourth Plan outlay.

These figures, great as they are, do not upset us. Training is indeed required on a vast scale. But it must yield results more or less commensurate with the expenditure, results in terms of more and better output of goods and services and satisfaction.

Increases in effectiveness and reductions in cost must be achieved, if at all, by individual training programs and training sessions. There can hardly be a training session that costs less than $200, overall, or a training day that costs less than $1,000. A one month's program is a $25,000 product, at least. Here then is the first question that "consumers" of training ought to ask themselves: is *this* $25,000 product what they really want and need? Maybe they ought to get a new machine instead, or spend a similar amount toward reorganization. Do they need *this* training, not any other; for *this* person, not another? We simply cannot assume that this kind of question now gets raised.

If the answer to this question is affirmative, then quite simple costing makes another important point: The trainer's salary is a minor item in the total. The participants' time is the main expense. Table 1 sets out for easy reference the cost of that time for a session for participants earning various amounts, and training in groups of various sizes. Since the trainer's part is the key to the results of training, it is good business to attract top-class people to this profession, to pay them well, and to establish work loads that allow time for adequate preparation of any session. No effort or expense is excessive to help develop their skills further and to ensure an institutional climate favorable to their use. The development of more effective trainers, training programs, and training institutions restates the scope of this book.

Table 1

PARTICIPANTS' WAGES AND SALARIES DURING ONE TRAINING SESSION, ONE OF 100 SESSIONS PER MONTH

	Dollars				
One participant's pay per month	200	400	600	800	1,000
One participant's pay per session	2	4	6	8	10
All participants' pay per session					
10 participants	20	40	60	80	100
20	40	80	120	160	200
30	60	120	180	240	300
40	80	160	240	320	400
50	100	200	300	400	500

The training and development themes overlap and intertwine throughout the book. Both are strongly contrapuntal: they call for new divergent elements to make a change—and also for convergent, unifying strengths to hold the social fabric together; they move people from the comforts of dependence to assertive independence, and must then move them beyond assertion to mature interdependence and collaboration. Big swings like these are difficult to contain within the same program and structure. We see training institutions as having this basic function of demonstrating societies in miniature, like a mirror reflecting development and also initiating and sustaining it. Only trainers who are great as people are suitable staff for such institutions.

Concepts and Words

A word about the basic concept and the terminology we use throughout the book. Training as we see it aims at a lasting improvement "on the job." The kind of education we call training—more of this distinction later—is in truth "not for knowing more but for behaving differently." Training then is concerned with *people-on-jobs-in-organizations*—the whole of this unwieldy amalgam.

All people who plan and run training courses and sessions are designated in this book as trainers. In real life they may be called members of the faculty or of the training or directing staff, or instructors, and so forth. *Participants* describes the people who come for training and is here synonymous with trainee, member, intern, and the like. We use the word *organization* only for the place and program in which participants have jobs, and *institution* only for the place and program that offers training.

Structure of the Book

The book has five parts. (The new edition has three parts—see Table of Contents for details.) Part I differentiates training from other instructional activities and then traces the contribution to the training process of two partners in it: the participants and the organizations in which they work and are to use their training.

In parts II, III, and IV—the core of the book—we look at the training process from the point of view of the third partner, the trainers at work on a program in a training institution. The parts deal in turn with the three major phases in training: pretraining, training and posttraining. It is significant that the pretraining part is by far the longest. For training to be well organized, every major activity has its roots in the pretraining phase, even follow-up services which have to go into operation only much later. In the pretraining phase trainers choose training strategies appropriate to the organization's training needs (chapter 3), prepare the participants and their organizations for a program (chapter 4), choose training methods to attain specified purposes (chapter 5), and build them into a program design (chapter 6).

Part III deals with the training phase; the transactions between trainers and participants, and among participants themselves. The fact that participants are in groups introduces social complexities and possibilities. Chapter 7 examines the trainer's attitudes and activities particularly in relation to the social processes that help or hinder learning. Many different training styles turn out to be effective—for different trainers. The trainer's personality comes into focus in chapter 8 as a very important factor in choosing training methods and activities. Part IV, on the posttraining phase, examines the contact trainers maintain with participants and their organizations after the program is over, through personal support and services of many kinds (chapter 9).

In part V we raise our sights to encompass the training institution as a whole and the development of training as a profession—through research and action. To be effective over the long run, trainers need the support of colleagues and a favorable climate in which to work. The principal plays a key role in promoting both (chapter 10). For training to progress beyond intuitive practice requires systematic review of experiences and planned research, not by experts primarily but by trainers themselves. Research, particularly action-research, can and must become second nature and properly organized as a major part of a trainer's work.

To make the book directly useful to the practicing trainer and principal, we have included many descriptions of experiences, ours and colleagues', in various institutions; research findings in summary; and additional readings. This material is set off from the continuing text in various ways. Descriptions that directly illustrate the main text and can be read as part of it are indented, for easy reference or omission, whichever the reader prefers. Numerical data are set out as "tables," diagrams and graphs as "figures." "Exhibits" contain conceptual material or sample forms and other aids that enable the reader to try out some idea mentioned in the text. Finally, there are two kinds of "readings." One kind consists of summarized research findings on some points. To avoid unbalancing the main text, they are set out in separate "boxes" and are only referred to in the text. The other readings are longer and follow the appropriate chapter. They go into more detail in various matters than we want to include in the text of this book. Some offer a different approach or point of view than ours.

To facilitate reference to these different kinds of data, each chapter has a detailed contents sheet.

The book is the product, most of all, of direct training experience. Before we became colleagues in 1963, one of us had been a trainer and a principal in local and international programs for industrial and community organizations, the other in programs for teachers and for farmers and rural development workers. Two years of wonderfully close collaboration followed at the Small Industry Extension Training Institute, where Pareek became Director of Extension Education, and Lynton was the Ford Foundation Consultant attached to that department and also team leader of the international consultant group attached to the Institute as a whole. Being new, SIET Institute offered unusual opportunities for thinking afresh about many key tasks that in other institutions were enveloped in traditions, and for getting our colleagues to join in. We are full of admiration for the efforts and achievements of many of them. Colleagues in several departments read and commented on parts of this book at various stages.

Colleagues elsewhere whom we have consulted are too numerous to mention individually here. The initial plans for the book went to forty people known to us in various parts of the world. Some have a reference or a reading in the body of the book.

The final readers must have special mention and warm thanks. They are five: Betty Mathews, then Ford Foundation Consultant in Public Health Education in India, now Professor of Public Health Education at the University of North Carolina; Goodwin Watson, Distinguished Service Professor and Director of the Laboratory of Applied Behavioral Science at Newark College, New Jersey; Shib Mitra, Director of the Department of Psychological Foundations of the National Council for Educational Research and Training, Delhi; Warren Bennis, Chairman of the Organization Studies Department at the Massachusetts Institute of Technology; and Harriet Ronken Lynton, one of our already long-suffering wives.

Some parts of the first three chapters of the book were initially used in an inter-institutional faculty program in 1965. The list of secretarial staff involved in typing successive drafts since that time is long: Dhun F. and Maharukh F. Mehta, Sundri Merchandani, Siloo Nakra, Joyce Pearson, H. N. Seethamma, V. Srinivasan, and in the U.S.A., Charlotte Mansfield and Sandra Cameron. Only those who have at one time or another labored to decipher our handwritings and our propensity for using all available space on a sheet of paper for rectifications and insertions can really appreciate the contribution this staff has made to the book.

What has impressed us most throughout the process of consultation with colleagues and collection of data is the near unanimity of concern that training as now practiced needs to shift gear in a major way. The consensus seems to be that there is enough dissatisfaction and also enough competence and endeavor to make significant progress in practice.

Rolf P. Lynton
Udai Pareek

Table of Contents

List of Figures, Boxes, and Exhibits

FIGURES

BOXES

EXHIBITS

PART I

Training: Aims, Contexts, Choices, and Dynamics

Chapter 1

What Is Training?

Seek simplicity and distrust it.

—A. N. WHITEHEAD

Firstly, gradualness. About this most important condition of fruitful scientific work I never can speak without emotion. Gradualness, gradualness and gradualness. From the very beginning of your work, school yourselves to severe gradualness in the accumulation of knowledge.

— *Pavlov's Bequest to the Academic Youth of Soviet Russia*

All "graduations" in human development mean the abandonment of a familiar position,...all growth...must come to terms with the fact.

—ERIK ERIKSON

POVERTY-STRICKEN India spends $45 billion on training each year, wealthy USA nearly twice as much. Expenditures of such magnitudes call for a periodic sharp look. Training in particular needs such scrutiny. For one thing, while training as an activity has been going on ever since couples begot children and growing children started to work, as a distinct field with its own roles, structures, and budgets it is still young. Secondly, this new field is expanding fast, as if it might be an answer to many anxious prayers. Thirdly, controversy seems to envelop every attempt to find benefits commensurate with the escalating costs of training.

No one doubts the contribution that training can make to development of all kinds. Training is essential, obviously so. Doubts arise only over its contribution in practice. Complaints are growing about its ineffectiveness and waste. The training apparatus and its costs have multiplied but not the benefits. Many organizations feel obliged to fill the apparatus with people but do so without enthusiasm. Training like a tax, has been levied on the willing and unwilling alike. In fact, some countries have made it a tax or at least an expenditure strongly encouraged. French law, for example, requires factories in some industries to spend a fixed percentage of their budget on personnel training or forfeit any unspent amount in taxes; the purpose behind this policy is the equitable spread of the costs of upgrading the work force in general.

Dissatisfaction persists and it too is growing, most notably at the working level where the benefits of training should show up most clearly. The growing disillusionment shows in many ways: in reluctance to send the most promising people for training, for instance, and in inadequate use of personnel after training. With disillusionment mounting in the midst of expansion, training has entered a dangerous phase in its development.

Extreme swings of opinion, from loud acclamation to utter disparagement, usually denote only impatience and a lack of skill. This is no less true in the case of training than in other endeavors. An inexperienced operator on a machine uses movements that are too large and tiring. A small child alternately runs or sits before "just" walking. A new teacher speaks too loudly or whispers before settling into an appropriate speaking volume. The extreme views on training are analogous. In sober fact, training is neither a panacea for all ills, nor is it a waste of time. What is required most of all is to use the divine sense of impatience for acquiring insight into what training can or cannot do and skill in designing and carrying out training effectively and economically. In short, to take a good sharp look.

The searchlight of inquiry may make the task and its challenges stand out too starkly, too simply. This risk seems worth taking in order to achieve the greatest possible clarity. The reader's own experience will be the best guard against oversimplification. Using experience with training in India, Indonesia, and other rapidly developing countries has this same advantage, too, at similar risk. The contribution that training can make to development is needed there so acutely and so obviously. At the same time, the limited resources available in these countries make this contribution hard to come by. These lines are sharply drawn: on the one hand, no promise can be ignored; on the other, no waste is permissible.

The point about waste may also help readers who are inclined to fret with impatience when clarification of an issue requires slow, meticulous attention. Why bother? First, of course, because all life is lived minute by minute, and the minutes in succession hold all the potential there is for good and ill. Second, when impatience surfaces, it may also help to remember the high cost of training. Three hundred dollars per training hour is common, even in poverty-stricken Asia. The very best use of that hour is worth meticulous attention, even on this score alone.

ASSUMPTIONS FOR PREVAILING AND ALTERNATIVE CONCEPTS OF TRAINING

The way training is usually set up now is something like this: Pressure to improve performance in some field, say health services or agriculture, builds up. Policy decisions are taken to give existing staff "some" training and to add more staff. The matter is urgent. (In developing countries things are always behind hand by definition and hence urgent.) The first training course has to start without delay. Its length is roughed out. The syllabus is developed quickly at a desk and discussed with other officers down the corridor. It ensures that the subject "gets covered." The "subject" fans out as its application is considered and as more and more people want to contribute to planning the course. Soon the syllabus is overfilled. Trainers are told to follow it strictly; otherwise they could not "get through it."

Agencies are asked to send staff to the first course. The notice may be short, but they feel obliged to send their quota of participants. Qualifications are minimal: a certain academic standard and so many years of experience. The experience qualification is loosened when necessary so that the course is sure to be full.

The course starts. Lecturing seems almost the only way to "get through." Trainers console themselves with the thought that participants will at least be "exposed" to the subject, somewhat "oriented." As soon as the first batch leaves, the next batch arrives. There are so many people to train and time is so short. After the first round or two, the syllabus is standardized. Thus a new training program is established.

The assumptions underlying this kind of process are usually not stated. There is "no time." There is also little inclination to touch matters that look unmanageable and may be unsettling, either to those responsible for the course or to those who will decide about sending people to it, or both. But the underlying assumptions can be stated and checked against experience. And more useful assumptions can be developed. We will therefore start with the assumptions underlying the training process.

Exhibit 1.1 lists four assumptions implied in current training practices and a second list of four parallel assumptions that look more useful. The first two assumptions are about individual learning. They lead to the other two, which concern responsibility for training and action.

1. Knowledge and Action

Much of the training provided today proceeds as if knowledge and action were directly related. This assumption is itself a striking illustration of the wide gulf that separates the two. Often the very same people who organize or countenance the imparting of knowledge under the heading of training on other occasions vociferously claim that knowledge by itself has "no use." They do not recruit new graduates even in agriculture and engineering until they have gained "experience"; yet experience is only gained over many years of hard work and hard knocks. They *know* this, but they do not act on this knowledge when making plans for training.

Exhibit 1.1

ASSUMPTIONS UNDERLYING TWO CONCEPTS OF TRAINING

1. Participants' acquisition of knowledge of the subject leads to action.	1. Motivations and skills lead to action. Skills are acquired through practice.
2. Participants learn what trainers teach. Learning is a simple function of the capacity of participants to learn and the ability of trainers to teach.	2. Learning is a complex function of the motivation and capacity of individual participants, the norms of the training group, the training methods and the behaviour of the trainers, and the general climate of the institution. Participants' motivation and use of training is influenced by the climate and support in the work organization.
3. Individual action leads to improvement on the job.	3. Improvement on the job is a complex function of individual learning, the norms of the working group, and the general climate of the organization. Individual learning unused, leads to frustration.
4. Training is the responsibility of the training establishment. It begins and ends with the specific program.	4. Training is the responsibility of three partners: the participant's organization, the participant, and the training establishment. It encompasses a preparatory, pretraining phase and a subsequent, posttraining phase. All phases are of paramount importance to the success of training.

Many traditions make it difficult to use this distinction between knowledge and action or to accord the distinction the basic importance it deserves. The traditional reverence for the sage, the guru, gets in the way. Trainers would be less than human if they were not tempted to enjoy this tradition for themselves.

A trainer's personal memories of student days may also prevent change. The basic learning processes at school and in training may indeed be similar. But they head for different goals and strike different limits. On a continuum with personal maturation and growth at one end and improvement in performance of predetermined tasks at the other, education lies nearer the former, and training nearer the latter. Education is primarily concerned with unveiling the world to students enabling them to choose their interests and lifestyles, and also their carriers. Training, on the other hand, is primarily concerned with preparing people for certain activities delineated by technology and by the organization and settings in which they work. Education helps students to choose their activities. Training helps participants to improve their performance. Education deals mostly with knowledge and understanding. Training deals mostly with understanding, skill, and action.

It seems urgent to nail down tightly the distinction between knowledge about something, on the one hand, and skill and experience, on the other. What to expect from training, how to design effective programs, and what training methods to use—these depend first and foremost on this distinction. William James and Elton Mayo labored over half a century to clarify this very distinction between cognitive learning on the one hand, and internalization of a skill on the other. It has been dealt with in poetry and philosophy, in the classics as well as in modern scholarship. Now we must use this distinction to achieve more effective training.

Focusing training on skill in action makes the task wide and complex. The "subject" widens so much that other disciplines and broader contexts must be included in order to make sense of action in the world of people, things, and time. Thus training embraces an understanding of the complex processes by which various factors that make up a situation interact. Presently, participants begin to practice new skills in situation resembling the complexities of real life—the pressures, limited resources, choices and uncertainties, and conflicting motives of people, including the participant's own. For many kinds of action, greater self-knowledge, too, is a necessary part of training.

2. Training and Learning: Two Points of View

Learning is a kind of action, and like other kinds of action, depends on many things. What is taught is only one of them. So the connection between what trainers teach and what participants learn is at best indirect and partial. To assume that teaching and learning are related simply, as cause and effect, has inherent defect: it equates trainers' viewpoint from which they teach with the participants' viewpoint from which they learn. As trainers and participants work together, they may understand each other's viewpoints better and take them into account. But to proceed on the assumption that their viewpoints are identical is folly.

What then explains the continuing prevalence of so patently unrealistic an assumption in most training? Very likely, personal more than intellectual difficulties are involved. Indeed, trainers seem to grasp intellectually the principle that training must start from "where the participants are." Yet they take no action to find this starting point, to ascertain what participants already see and understand. Many trainers seem reluctant to establish such a premise. These include trainers who are ready to take the credit for participants learning something intended by the trainer but refuse to accept responsibility for participants learning something different. The former result, according to them, is due to the trainer's skill and devotion; but the latter is due to the participants' lack of capability, low motivation, or contrariness. Many trainers enjoy the idea of molding others in their own image. But what most participants are likely to learn from trainers such as these is, in fact, greater dependence or opposition, neither of which is an attitude found in the objectives of training, nor are they useful on the job.

The implications of placing learning and the points of view of participants in the center of the training process, and of treating the trainer's activity as related to the participant's viewpoints, are far-reaching. They mandate that a trainer's functions include stimulating and motivating participants to acquire certain kinds of knowledge and understanding and to practice certain skills because they recognize they need them. Training would then consist largely of well-organized opportunities for participants to acquire necessary understanding and skill. Trainers appreciate that they are close to only some aspects of the learning process and, in the final analysis, able to control only their own behavior. They are like farmers who prepare the soil, plant good seed suited to the soil, and tend and nurture the new growth. They harbor no illusion that they can make things grow or determine their ultimate size and shape.

3. Learning and Action: Participants and Their Organizations

However well we learn a useful skill, acquisition in itself by no means guarantees action. Bitter experience abounds and ought to have taught us that. Participants returning from training often find their new capabilities ignored, even resented. They look for support and find instead indifference or opposition. Doubts then assail them about the usefulness of the training. Enthusiasm wanes. Soon they accept their colleagues' advice to "forget it." And so another has been trained only to suffer disappointment and frustration. Next time they will know better than to invest so much of themselves in new initiatives and developments.

The simple linking of individual training and effective action ignores the manifold problems of introducing and sustaining change in an organization. Putting an individual's skill to use depends on a number of people and often on additional resources. It calls for the encouragement and support of a receptive organization.

The organizational approach means training should commence with a set of *organizational* questions. Instead of asking what *X* or *Y* needs to learn in order to carry out a new activity, the first training question should be addressed to all involved in the projected change. What do they, given their different functions and different positions in the organization, have to do differently? What things, therefore, do they have to learn anew for which training is needed not only individually but also collectively? These questions concern those who collaborate directly on the job and also those who sanction new developments and provide new services and organizational support. These very different assumptions lead to a systems approach to training.

The systems approach to furthering action often involves training minimum concentrations of staff at several levels of the organization; the provision of supportive follow-up services from the original trainers, consultants and other resources in the training system*—often for a considerable period—and the allocation of resources within the working organization for various stages of the change in process. Instead of thinking in terms of someone's participation in this or that training course, it calls for training strategies that include pretraining and posttraining activities, and sequences of training events related to career plans. Taking a longer view, this approach tries to deal with the entire network of factors that determine an organization's readiness for development. What is required is not an occasional change, but change on a continuing basis, more or less, in interaction with a changing environment. In such an ongoing process the organization is both a recipient and a contributor.

Yet, even with this approach, it is useful to bear in mind that a prickly problem, a real uncertainty, remains. The gap between what trainers teach and what participants learn leads to unintended consequences of training. These consequences may work to the disadvantage of the organization, or to its advantage.

An unintended consequence of training may stagger a manager, for instance, when an engineer decides to leave the organization soon after returning from a training program. The engineer may have come across a more promising opening in another company while taking the course. The course may have stimulated entrepreneurial thoughts and now the engineer wants to become self-employed. For reasons such as these some managers refuse to send staff for outside training. They are afraid of losing them or, alternatively, having them return to insist on unsetting changes for which the superiors are not ready. Timing training in relation to an organization's needs and opportunities, and exercising discretion in the selection of participants, are important ways of balancing individual

* We use the term training system, or system for short, to denote the whole range of training resources available to a work organization, actually or potentially. These resources include trainers; consultants; and other personnel in training departments, centres, or in other formally designated establishments; and also others in less formal associations like professional networks, or working independently. This resource system also includes training materials and media for use in formal programs and also informally. This system also includes self-instruction: opportunities for skill practice, fieldwork, and other settings used deliberately for learning. For our justification of this use of "system," see the Preface to this edition (p. vii).

growth and organizational needs but they do not mesh automatically or necessarily, and it is useless pretending they do.

Often managers take a more positive view of the unintended consequences of training. If a member of their staff has gotten more from training than expected, so much the better. Personal growth is a good thing. These managers may or may not be aware that their generally positive attitude toward people and personal development helps to make the organization a good place in which to work. Their attitude elicits initiative and free application from the staff and provides work satisfaction that staff members might lose through leaving. It makes for the kind of organization which, if some leave, others will join.

The same positive policy can be deliberate. It can be derived from the rapidly changing work to be done, notably in developing countries, and the speed with which new technologies, management methods, markets, and so forth, crowd the organization. Staff cannot realistically be trained for such changes one by one. It is more fruitful for managers to see their task as one of fostering employees who are generally inventive and receptive, aware and thoroughly alive, not just now and then, but habitually. Training, unintended consequences included, will then be seen by managers as a means of achieving this goal.

4. Responsibility for Training

To invest trainers with the full responsibility for training is unrealistic if action in an organization is the aim. This misunderstanding now protects many training systems from the demands for more effective training that participants and their organizations could rightfully make; to further confuse the issue, it also protects the work organizations from demands that trainers and their systems could make for clear training goals, carefully selected participants, and organizational support for the improvements to be achieved through training. It is a kind of collusion.

Participants, work organizations and training system are all partners in the training effort. To be effective, their collaboration should start with the definition of training goals and strategies. After training, collaboration should continue in follow-up services from the system and support for innovations from the organization.

ACTION THROUGH TRAINING OR ACTION THROUGH FORCE

Alongside the quartet of assumptions that inspires much current training we have proposed an alternative quartet (exhibit 1.1). The new quartet takes into account more adequately our experience and seems therefore a better basis on which to proceed. It calls for far more thought and rigor than the first set and requires careful consideration of expectations, needs, relationships, and costs. The initial investment of care and attention is very taxing. Organizations are entitled to ask whether training is worth the effort.

Is training even necessary? Surely similar ends can be attained without training and achieved with greater expedition, certainty, and economy by management "doing its job," parents "doing their duty" by their children, teachers "teaching," and community leaders "leading"? Maybe people in positions of authority merely need to exercise authority; that is, ensure that their views are implemented. They are in a position to know what is necessary. They ought to insist on it—kindly, of course—listen to objections, make adjustments where possible, consult, "take people along," "get them to do" willingly what the authorities have decided while giving the impression that the decision is "really their own."

The many phrases used in singing this familiar tune reveal how out of fashion it is, but also how very much present; unmasked, this is the theme of force. Its antecedents and personal implications deserve a brief closer look. Force, in fact, is the primary moving power of traditional relationships and often comes readily to hand even today. Its success has been monumental. Cathedrals and temples, massive forts, great old roads and water systems, even that timeless monument to a loving relationship, the Taj Mahal—all were built, details aside, by a few who imposed their will on thousands by a personal combination of kindness and cruelty. India at the height of her glory and power centuries ago was characterized by relationships of force. Likewise, other countries. If force, authority, was productive then why should it not serve now? Why not train just a few masters to get work done through force and manipulation exercised on servants by the string of up-to-date phrases for this very phenomenon. Moreover, only a glance across some frontiers reveals that large-scale changes are being accomplished through force also today.

Many people impatiently advocate force and even use it, openly or camouflaged. In truth, resorting to force to achieve better action tempts us all in our heart of hearts. We may call it "authority" or some other nice word. Perhaps right here, embedded deep down, is the actual source from which genuine opposition to training for action flows. And facile approval, excessive expectations, and kind words for training are simply varied manifestations of the selfsame opposition.

Opposition, then, may be deep-rooted and stay with us. But it is founded neither in the relative efficacy of training compared with force as means for securing action, nor in their relative consonance with the requirements of modern developments. At best, force engenders action that is limited to a given occasion, and often limited to the actual presence of a powerful supervisor.

Training, on the other hand, leads to action that can be repeated, to self-motivation, and to further improvement through onward practice. In short, although force may result in action, and repeated force in repeated action, only training can lead to sustained, self-generating development. Training, not force, promises what is essential to modern technologies and economic systems: flexibility in action through understanding and confidence; inventiveness, initiative, and ability to make decisions; and respect for the contributions of others and readiness to collaborate with them.

Training is therefore properly part of the grand march toward greater equality between people, toward more widespread opportunities, participation, involvement, and rising expectations. However stumbling the progress, these are milestones along a clear path in all spheres of new life. The preference for force is understandable. Those who subscribe to it would apply force, not act under it; their real opposition is not to training, but to the kinds of development training seeks to foster. In a training-oriented regime the subscribers to force would have to share power with others or, more likely, lose it, and thus forego their positions in society.

As a consequence of training for development some people therefore stand to lose. They have to reorient themselves toward a new kind of society, one that is developed and maintained through hard work in partnership with many others. Only then will they be able to discard the naive attractions of force. Others are caught in their life history, such as the child who submitted to a parent's authority, only to repeat the pattern of parental authority on the next generation. The new society would cheat such individuals of a prospect in which they have much invested. Still others are willing to pay the price of force as long as it provides order, neatness, and predictability in their world. That they cling to this promise when it starts to fray reveals the depth of their fears—fear of an unknown world ahead, with familiar landmarks gone and experience perhaps irrelevant; fear of being unfettered, without rules or instruments; fear of other people, whose trustworthiness engenders skepticism.

The case for training stands firm. It has deep roots and is broadly based. The present inadequacies of training may be glaring, but they can be examined and removed, and real progress can be made in action.

Chapter 2

Four Fresh Scenarios
Active Engagement with Cultures
Areas of Freedom: Three Phases
Ranges of Influence

Culture and Other Contexts

> To create a real character and to portray him against a mere conventional background of painted canvas and makeshift stage props borrowed from a local customer is to falsify every word and gesture of the character himself; for what is living derives from the continuous interaction of an organism with its environment, or rather, the actual person with his entire world. To neglect the environment is just as bad an error as to forget the organism in which its forces are momentarily concentrated. . . . The temptation to explain specific traits or events by references to large general influences is as often as not a disguise for laziness or psychological incompetence.
>
> —Lewis Mumford

Action—and therefore effective training for action—requires choices: direction, aims, scale, means, pace. At the policy level these choices are traditionally left to a small elite in many countries: chief executives of industry and banks, ministers and senior civil servants, army generals, bishops, heads of social and educational institutions both public and private, and politicians from the same few families. Born and bred into the top drawer of society, these leaders carry this responsibility and its burdens from generation to generation. The image is quaintly colonial Victorian, a local variant of "the white man's burden."

This schema posits that the implementation of training policies, predetermined by this august group, is the only concern of training institutions. The director of an institution has program directors who, in turn, have trainers to carry out the programs; office holders at each level implement the instructions as they filter downward. Trainers are the final link in this chain of command when they take *their* turn to instruct trainees in the understandings, skills, and behaviors they are to follow. The image of this final transaction in the chain comes perilously close to "training" household pets or circus animals. The circus trainer motivates, entertains, persists, threatens, and rewards—in short, does everything within reason to achieve the performance desired by the paymasters and organizers.

This kind of training, limited to the perceptions and wishes of a group in power and carried out by successive layers of followers (by the establishment, in other words), is really the opposite of development, since development involves questioning old orders and changing them. For precisely this reason Paulo Freire and others maintain that training can never lead to significant development. They argue that the establishment will not allow this possibility and, even if it were desired, all attempts to change the old order would be obliterated in the myriad dependencies that have become the followers' way of life. According to these opponents of training, only a new pedagogy of the oppressed can lead to development.

If, in spite of the high risk that "training" as we mean it may be gravely misunderstood and abused, we still retain the term in this book and its title, it is only to make sure that all, up and down the whole system, policymakers and users of training as well as training directors and trainers will feel addressed by it. Training, their accepted label, can serve for the true development of people and of societies just as it can also be abused by its perversion and the resultant confusion.

FOUR FRESH SCENARIOS

Sufficient experience with training that results in true development exists to suggest that in many places, also in developing countries, the traditional arrangements and images of training are eschewed; or they are followed more in the letter than in the spirit simply to allow powerful people of traditional disposition to maintain appearances. In actual practice training bypasses such people. Trainers faced with these situations approach the work with a genuinely different disposition. They stimulate and help participants to involve themselves and to develop understanding and competences that reflect fresh but realistic aspirations and personal styles, rather than slavishly "following instructions" from on high. In terms of their personal needs these trainers have replaced dominance with assistance. With this shift in emphasis, what has become of the traditional chain wherein every level of the system dominated the level immediately below and instructions were simply followed? What has happened to the social contexts and cultural dimensions, supposedly quite fixed or, at least, difficult and slow to alter, e.g., the top group's control of policymaking for the entire system, the narrow selection and promotion only of trainers from "good background," the admission only of well-connected participants, and the development of simple, controllable training strategies and programs and their self-serving evaluations? These and other standard features of the past have given way to wide varieties of arrangements serving the same purposes. But the new arrangements in all their diversity seem to share a common direction: they move people and situations whom the classical dispensation visualized at the periphery of things, the very last circle from the center, toward center stage; in so doing they change not merely the order of the play but the script itself. Consequently, where traditional arrangements persist they are receding into the background; they are noticed and acknowledged, but accorded less and less importance.

The new play has four scenarios in which important developmental learning now characteristically takes place. In the first two the setting is not in training programs as such, and only learners crowd the stage. If policymakers, trainers, and other traditionally important people are present on stage, they, too, are there as learners, no different from anyone else. Everyone is busy learning.

1. In the first scenario all participants are active and take part of their own volition: in Ruskin's words from the title page of this book, they all want to "behave differently," which is his touchstone of education. In focus here are the several major changes in living and working styles, both personal and organizational, in which people have engaged themselves in recent years in large numbers. Among these, on the personal side, are the far-reaching changes that millions of families make on moving from rural to urban locales. Parents manage to cope with the new setting, while their children quickly outgrow old guidelines and relationships and make their own way in giant strides, displaying ranges and rates of learning that are truly amazing. Several degrees less but still impressive (without trainers and traditional systems!) is the phenomenal surge in numbers of people who now habitually run and exercise, control their diets and smoking, plan their families, and practice other kinds of self-care in response to the frightening increase in heart disease and cancer, growing community concern with the environment, and similar sweeping considerations.

Organizations, too, have become radically innovative in places. Through diverse processes more subtle than training, leading work organizations have learned to involve staff in redesigning their immediate work settings and in rebuilding organizational structures, processes, and norms. In the course of doing this tasks change, roles are often augmented, and career paths freshly directed. Higher productivity and lower costs reward managers and owners. Most of the learning required for such changes takes place on the job in its day-to-day course, with people in the organization helping each other irrespective of status. These methods simultaneously reinforce that highly desirable norm—helping.

In sum, cultures formerly characterized by old orders that depended on status have rapidly been modified by multiple new practices and customs.

These have originated from many places in society, not from one source, and certainly not all "from the top down." Trainers and formal training have played little or no part in these changes, at the start or later.

The media and other more subtle social forces have stimulated and now sustain the climate for such widespread learning.

2. The second scenario for important changes in arrangements for developmental learning differs from the first in that many people feel threatened by the changes, fearing for their own self-interest, or view them with ambivalence, or subscribe to them under duress. The traditional elite and their supporters stand to lose by what is developing, at least their exclusiveness by caste, sex, race, age, family, and inherited wealth. One reason they nonetheless take part is that they are caught in developments long ago encouraged by them on idealistic and utilitarian grounds, such as adult literacy and, more recently, the education of women. Changing international standards with reference to poverty, child care, and the inclusion of all adults in the political process have also eroded traditional barriers. Technical and economic advances often override personal considerations; expertise and competence begin to count more than family connections. To safeguard these developments and to expedite their advancement many countries have enacted legislation which proscribes discrimination by sex or race, reserves seats in legislatures and universities, mandates employment for "disadvantaged" groups, and distributes income, wealth, and public services more equitably.

This scenario in the new script reveals powerful technological, social and political movements and how people respond to them, whether they like them or not, creatively or passively. Signs exist that even within one generation even those developments which most obviously undermine elitist power can become quite as fixed as the earlier cultural arrangements they replaced. Considering the conflicts touched off by the new developments, they are in many places already determining action with remarkable consistency.

In the remaining two scenarios trainers and training systems are again evident, even though they only appear onstage in the last.

3. In the third scenario the crowd has thinned out; people are onstage individually or in small groups. Aside from the low hum of group discussions, the general quiet is punctuated only by sounds of individuals practicing—some notes of music, a computer printing, someone hammering a nail or filing metal. Here and there a television or radio is on. All are engrossed in "self-instruction." Occasionally a person studying alone or with a group exits from the stage and returns with someone who explains, corrects, and helps at the participants' requests, and then exits. This person is a trainer. The trainers are mostly young and behave informally, and the participants interact with them without marked deference. Most of the time the trainers are offstage, in the wings, where they prepare, review, and revise the self-instructional programs.

In terms of major cultural shifts, self-instruction is a great leveller. Through meticulously prepared texts, television programs, and other media it already engages millions of people. They bring their own motivation, of liking or more or less dire needs. The texts provide specific guidance step by step, including self-correction, and offer access to instructors for personalized help at points of special difficulty. Mainly offstage, the social standing of the trainer/author of the programs no longer matters. What matters is their thorough grasp of subjects and methodologies, and their ability to respond sensitively and creatively to participants in difficulty. Only the common classification of these new sophisticated learning technologies—"distance learning"—is wistfully reminiscent of the fading old order, with the trainer at the center; for it is actually not the learning and the learners who are distant but the training and the trainers.

4. In the fourth scenario the trainers are once again on stage, but now actively engaged with the participants in diverse and changing manners. Some seem to be instructing or explaining with the use of flip charts, overhead projectors, lab equipment, some machine in operation, or a blueprint. Participants too are active, discussing points with the trainers; from time to time a participant goes to the board and seems to take over instruction. Participants and trainers seem to be studying something together, trying to understand an event in common. Elsewhere face-to-face counselling is going on, or trainers, moving between sets of people, are consulting with whole "systems" and linking up various groups, which then proceed on their own, without further assistance. Other participants are trying out some new activity with some noting the outcomes for discussion, with or without trainer consultants. And in between the active, changing groups of people are individuals quietly busy by themselves—some resting, some reading, some in evident distress, others elated.

The description of these four scenarios has focused attention in particular on the differences from the established hierarchical order of training rooted and projected in prevailing cultures. That well-known order too is still all-too-evident, side by side and intermingled with the new. The overriding purpose of describing these scenarios has been to show that the old order is not universal and hence cannot be determining. In other words *general* characterizations of culture are no guide to determining the extent to which people may learn to behave differently (with or without help from training). To persist in the illusion that general cultural characterizations *can* provide much guidance may be an instance of succumbing to the very "temptation to explain specific traits or events by references to large general influences," which Mumford in the quotation opening this chapter considers "a disguise for laziness or psychological incompetence." At least it is a subterfuge for inaction, reflecting a lack of courage to try and see, a self-serving protection by planners, directors, and trainers of their simpler and privileged, though often narrowly defined, positions, relationships, and activities in the old order.

ACTIVE ENGAGEMENT WITH CULTURES

Step by step, respectfully and thoughtfully, it is possible to explore new ground and to identify important areas in which people can learn to behave differently—developmentally—and to design interventions to help them do so. Training is one kind of intervention that may help, but is *not* the only one, nor one to be adopted mechanically. In proceeding toward development in this active manner, broad cultural generalizations serve an *alerting* function by pointing out accepted relationships of unusual sensitivity and deserving of special care. But they need not rule out exploration of any line of action.

The use of interpersonal training is an example.

On the grounds of a national profile made up of four cultural traits which he found to be significant around the world, Geert Hofstede strongly advised against using interpersonal training in Indonesia.[1] The following string of examples to the contrary come from a project in Indonesia for improving the delivery of official health services through management training and the development of training systems in eight (of twenty-seven) Provinces.

After two years of working together at national and provincial levels on a series of technical and methodological programs, the need for some interpersonal work emerged clearly. A seven-week residential Advanced Program was therefore organized for key trainers of proven motivation and competence. The first two weeks were devoted to a full-time human relations laboratory staffed by Indian and American trainers of international standing. So successful was this first attempt that subsequent Advanced Programs were regularly oversubscribed, and included higher-level officials as full-time participants in only the human relations part of the programs. The exploratory feature also became the base for identifying Indonesians for further development as indigenous "L (for learning) Group" trainers and for organizing a program for their further "personal development." Again, contrary to general cultural traditions, this program and the practical internship and supervised consultancies that followed it included physical touching and other "body work," and this, too, for both men and women working together.

Other developments, too, went counter to prevailing practice. For instance, the selection of participants and their subsequent placements· and allocated responsibilities changed from a mostly personal to a functional basis. Traditionally, supervisors recommended staff for training programs from within a narrow set of occupational grades and academic attainment, and otherwise by personal

[1] "Cultural Dimensions in Management and Planning" in *Organizational Forum* (1985), Vol. 1, No. 1, pp. 12-15

choice; higher officers then approved or disapproved these selections and sometimes substituted other candidates. In this project the provincial organization agreed to base the selection process instead on functional criteria which the consultants helped it derive from the prospective tasks. Assessments were then based on actual evidence that the candidates possessed the potentialities, personal interest, and commitment which these functions called for, and a commitment that organizational units would make these staff members available with sufficient frequency and reliability to select them for new training and consulting assignments. Initially laid down for programs in this project, these norms for selection spread to other programs also without special effort. Furthermore, to make their local "resource system" as strong as possible, provincial health offices agreed to look for candidates for advanced training also in related provincial organizations, both public and private, even though this would also constitute a departure from established practice and involve interministerial arrangements, including payments and other complexities.

Among the innovations included in this project, a few deprived officials of some customary income-generating activities. If they were trainers themselves, they lost income when it became standard practice to devote much more time than available budgets provided to assessment of needs, program design, session preparation, and, later, impact evaluation and follow-up. Other officers lost income when the use of guest lecturers in programs was greatly reduced. Case sessions were substituted for lectures, which also made it possible for younger officers to lead sessions. Whereas lecturers "had to be" at least as senior in rank as participants, this was not necessary for "leaders" and "facilitators" in discussion sessions of cases or other prepared materials.

Finally, an important shift was achieved by the project in the relationship between the national and provincial offices of the health system. In Indonesia, as elsewhere, this relationship is subject to complex considerations, including overriding political ones, and any change in the relationship involves subtle, but significant shifts by each level in its perception of the other. Classically, the center issues what it labels "guidelines" to establish program contents and schedules, staffing patterns and, often, detailed curricular and training materials to be used throughout the country; provincial offices regard such "guidelines" as instructions to be followed. As this project progressed and proved useful, first one, then more provincial offices began to propose to the center new programs they wished to try out which, if successful, they wanted to institute. The provincial offices also suggested specific modifications in the programs and schedules sent by the center. When the center was asked whether such provincial initiatives were acceptable, the national head confirmed that central guidelines were indeed simply intended to describe *minimal* conditions and programs, and that the ministry expected provinces that had participated in this project and gained fresh insights through it to "go on from there and do better."

This set of examples, all from one project, of interventions that deliberately and actively engaged the existing culture and developed some new norms can serve two purposes here. It can help identify and make concrete useful ways of thinking about and working with cultural dimensions in training. It can also set the stage for what the rest of the book offers, namely steps to improve training so that it can meet not just this or that immediate need, e.g., to adopt a new technology or to run a new procedure, but can contribute to more basic development, which necessarily includes developing the culture itself.

AREAS OF FREEDOM: THREE PHASES

Sensitivity to the general culture and respect for it does not go counter to development but rather hand in hand with it. To familiarize oneself with the culture in general and to be alert to likely areas of particular sensitivities and difficulties is therefore useful. But a general acquaintance does not suffice and may stultify if used to discourage exploration of what might be possible within a given context. To use the freedom available, attention should focus on the more particular cultural dimensions that obtain in situations and environments in which specific developmental action is desired. Every culture is a multilayered fabric, and elasticities and possibilities for modification and substitution differ from layer to layer.

Important guidance comes then from the cultural features in particular environments. As attention shifts from general to particular features, a complex composite of several cultures comes into play. Some cultures differ along ethnic-geographic lines and so also between different parts of the country. In rapidly growing cities some of these differences become submerged while others persist, and the new generation is often less attached to them than its parents. Professional cultures, such as those of physicians or public servants or, as in the above set of examples, the two in conjunction, often take precedence over ethnic differences. They also sometimes overrule limitations to what women or young graduates generally may or may not do. In health systems a lead given by doctors counts for more than that same lead given by others.

So, it is useful to particularize culture to the place in which action is desired, i.e., the cultural mix and dynamics important *there*. A line of action possible in one factory or provincial office may not be possible in another, or at least not possible until its "culture" changes. Additionally, within the same unit one department or work group may offer a better start than another.

Recent performances and tendencies, current reputation, leadership, staffing, and other resources can provide information for cultural mapping for developing a particular system and to mark promising places for starting: areas of freedom to be developed, work agendas, methods and, often, people to initiate the effort. Initial steps, if kept small, can quickly confirm, modify, and detail the map and route(s) for developing new norms and incorporating them into the culture. Whether the new norms will replace the old, or only modify them, or coexist with them, usually becomes clear only later. More often this occurs last, and the culture diversifies and grows in the process.

After detailing and carrying out the initial action, the essence of the third phase is to sustain it with interventions that work, to build on and around them, and to so permeate the system and its culture that true developments become institutionalized. As shown in the set of examples from Indonesia, several agendas and diverse methods are useful for this purpose at various times and places. It is the overall movement and sufficient involvement that matter.

The project in Indonesia, scheduled initially for three provinces, expanded to eight; one year's commitment led to a second, then to three more successful training in one province at a time led to national advanced programs for selected trainers, and membership for some of them in a national inter-provincial consultancy service. By the time the project ended, interventions and programming had expanded and were continuing simultaneously at four levels in the national system. Furthermore, additional work spun off from the health sector to local planning and local government in the Ministry for Internal Affairs.

Two points are important to remember when ordering cultural contexts into phases, levels of generality, and other categories. First, while such segmenting is of practical use in mapping, mobilizing, focusing, sequencing, and managing the required efforts and in monitoring their effectiveness, it is merely a *modus operandi* and does not reduce the complex reality of the cultural context. Multilayered and intricately interwoven reality continues, unaffected by such mapping; matching surveillance and action with the patterns that may be important to a particular development must be, and remain, the overall aim. Even institutionalizing development, the third "phase" above, does not "follow" an earlier phase. On the contrary, it begins as soon as multiple constituencies of potential participants (whether individuals, groups, or organizations) likely to be affected by the development form expectations about its implications. Their awareness raised to anticipation, they study the intervenors' first appearances and actions for clues as to how they will proceed and how far they can be trusted.

The second and related point is that cultural contexts at all levels of generality remain important right through, opening fresh opportunities one moment, closing old ones at another. In the late 1980s world interest, publicized and focused by United Nations agencies, favored program initiatives for child survival. Programs—*any* programs—concerned with the upgrading of women's position in society receive even more pervasive support (except in some sharply identified countries which are widely ostracized). By his known interest in computers and high technology, Prime Minister Rajiv Gandhi opened wide opportunities in India for improving work planning, supervision and management through improved local management information systems. But it is also important to remember that in this same generally favorable climate, some local contexts favored such developments, while in others they languished or energies were directed elsewhere.

RANGES OF INFLUENCE

How far and how actively developers interact with the cultural contexts often determines whether an initiative will be still-born or confined to a quite particular situation or, on the contrary, will spread far and permeate the wider culture. Elliot Jaques' mid-century work with the Glacier Metal Company in London focused on the culture of the factory, the title given his seminal book.[2] The culture outside the factory gates and the personnel as go-between received just enough attention to safeguard that boundary. When Glacier established a branch factory in the very different setting of West Scotland, the boundaries drawn along these lines came to contain the culture of the *firm* .

Pilot schemes and intensive area and demonstration projects have been a favorite modality for introducing changes in developing countries. How much of the wider culture their design incorporates, even in embryo, is a better predictor of their effectiveness than their initial scale. Most have belied early promises of wider application because they have failed to incorporate and engage the bureaucratic, political, and, often, economic dimensions of the wider culture. In training itself progress with quite specific changes whose benefits are self-evident often depends for success on changes in reward structures, relationships between people, and other aspects of the culture of a particular institution, and of the training and wider system of which it is a part.

> The introduction of case teaching into management programs, for example, runs into characteristic difficulties. At the personal level are problems with the faculty. Usually from academia and holding professional titles, they are more accustomed to imparting knowledge to students than to joining them in the exploration of data from the field which everyone has received and studied prior to the session. Moreover, case research and writing call for extended periods in the field, a less familiar setting, and for one to act as listener, observer, learner,

[2] *The Changing Culture of a Factory* (London: Routledge, 1951). For a fuller, recent discussion of culture, see Edgar H. Schein, *Organizational Culture and Leadership* (San Francisco: Jossey-Bass, Inc., 1987).

> not as teacher. In the institution, allocations of time, funds, responsibilities, and often physical layouts as well, have to be changed for case teaching. Furthermore, the different culture of case sessions—participatory, active, creative, exploratory, with the instructor shaping and guiding but not imposing views—puts pressure on other faculty members and sessions that operate along traditional lines. Administrators, too, feel pressures to behave collegially and to flatten organizational structures. Grading performance in case programs requires more complex criteria and processes than standard examinations. Beyond the institutions, in the larger training system and often subject to country-wide standard regulations, the writing of teaching cases usually receives no recognition in the upgrading and promotion of faculty.
>
> To provide a reasonable basis for success all these dimensions have therefore to become part of negotiations for helping an institution introduce case methods of instruction. At the very least, the institution has to commit time and resources to the attempt to modify the cultures accordingly, within and without, so that they support the development if possible, or at least tolerate it, and certainly not negate it.

This understanding of development and the cultural context of training, especially the need and manifold opportunities for engaging cultural contexts deliberately and actively, provides a proper setting for the rest of this book. Attention to training strategies, presented in the next chapter, assume that this more basic cultural work has already been well started and is substantially on the way. Strategic thinking subsequently guides contacts with the work organization and the development of programs of intervention. While in actuality there will be many overlaps, in practice (and also in this book) it is nevertheless important to insist on this basic progression, which differs notably from marketing particular training programs, methods, and materials. The marketing approach is seductively simple: it keeps control firmly in trainers' hands and so serves the established order. Development is more basic, also more difficult, but also quite feasible.

Programs of training, and above all institutions engaged full time in training, need to be models of the developments they urge participants to learn and to undertake. This aspect and its requirements are discussed in part III. The chapters preceding that part assume that training program institutions have indeed built cultures which will enable them to creatively engage in guiding participants and their organizations and communities to development in the true sense of the word.

Chapter 3

Training Strategy

> All occupations engaged in converting actual into preferred situations are concerned with design... of policies, institutions and behaviour itself.... The process spirals through appreciation, action and reappreciation,... The principle is that you work simultaneously from the unit and from the total and then go in cycles.
>
> —DONALD SCHOEN

> Everything is more important in time than anything else, of course, which is exactly what happens when people don't exhibit the right amount of fortitude in planning on a broad basis.
>
> —DAVID E. LILIENTHAL

RIGOR IN engaging resources only in lines of action for which training is a significant variable is one of the first professional responsibilities of a trainer and a training system. This includes a judgement of whether adequate conditions exist for the likely success of a training program. In this respect training is like a manufacturing process. Both the ends and the means must be appropriate to the purpose. Relating them demands clear goals, a plausible strategy for attaining them, and precise specifications for each part of the training task, including the resources of time, skill, and facilities required. Contrary to the popular saying, something is often *not* better than nothing, for "something" may convey a mistaken sense of movement and progress toward a goal when in reality no ground has been gained.

FOUR STRATEGIC ISSUES

To avert futile training programs it is necessary to consider four strategic issues separately: the need for a broad action perspective in establishing a training strategy; setting goals; planning the specifications; and programming the resources and their sequences for these requirements. In the prevailing urgency to "get going," these issues rarely receive the attention their basic importance warrants.

1. Action Perspective in Training Strategy

From an action perspective, training is a systematic attempt to develop the human resources—individual, group and organizational competencies required to manage some present tasks and situations as well as those in the future. An effective training strategy therefore focuses on making training an effective instrument of action in the field. In the course of doing this, training may well spin off action projects; as these projects develop they then, in turn, highlight new gaps in competencies to be filled through training. Training and action are therefore closely linked.

When training is closely linked to action, the trainer's role expands from the traditional instructor/organizer of training programs and sessions to include change agent and system consultant to the work organization. The trainer participates in organizational diagnoses, planning change interventions, actually intervening in collaboration with colleagues operating the technologies and services of the organization, and evaluating and replanning the organization's development strategy.

The organization of training is likewise significantly influenced by this perspective on action, both externally and internally. Externally, the positioning and connections of training must support its functions as a direct contributor to the development of production or service systems and of outside linkages. Internally, the design, differentiation, and interrelations of functions (e.g., of training centers or evaluation) need to reflect the close interdependence of training with developing action. Provision for the continuing development of the training system in accordance with the changing needs of the work organization is also part of an adequate training strategy. This may or may not entail growth. It will certainly affect the development of training staff and administrators and the internal structures of training.

In addition to tight links with the immediate work organization, a training system also needs collegial ties with trainers and systems elsewhere in the field. Professional standards are sustained and the entire field developed through such ties and through the sharing of personnel and material resources. Linkages within a sector, such as agriculture, banking or health services, come readily to mind, but intersectoral linkages are also important, especially in locales where training and trainers are still sparse. When specialized training needs arise for small numbers of personnel, sharing scant resources is obviously necessary and also more economical. Participation in networks of trainers and training systems and in their further development is therefore an important aspect of a training strategy. When a training strategy attends to all four aspects properly, even a small training *system* can choose and use training to meet organizational needs with minimal delay.

2. Goal-Setting—with the Work Organization Taking the Lead

The next step after the overall action strategy is clear is setting appropriate goals for training. What are the changes to be effected? Once this question is answered, these follow: What number and types of people require training, and what resources of time, skill, and facilities will be needed for this particular training? In other words, what are the training specifications?

Much training bogs down in failure right here. It is failure from which there is no hope of recovery, despite any subsequent effort mounted to compensate for it.

Failure at the outset is usually not the fault of the training system but of the work organization. The goals of change, for which training is supposedly needed, are not defined with sufficient precision, providing neither the organization with criteria for measuring progress, nor trainers with guidelines within which particular training objectives and specifications can be delineated. In such a situation the consumer of training stands disarmed. At no point later can the organization say to the trainer:. "This is what we asked you to do and what you agreed to do. It has not been done. Why not? You owe us a reckoning." Without precise goals there is no way one can assess whether a given training program, course, or session was in fact worthwhile.

If this situation prevails at the organization's end, it tempts the training system to make its first classic error, namely, to proceed as though the fundamental question of goals did not matter or as if the training system is capable of doing the work organization's homework. The latter is an attractive illusion. It sets the trainers up as knowing best what is required at organizational, even national, levels. But this is an unpromising posture. Even if the trainers did know best, which is doubtful, by assuming the function of deciding and defining what the organization needs, they drastically limit or even eliminate the organization's commitment to the training program. The organization can later turn around and say, "We did not ask you to train our people for this purpose. How could you dare to decide our training goals? We will support you no further." No amount of protest by trainers, for example, that the organization failed to do its proper homework in the first place, will absolve them. The simple truth is that the trainers ought not to have proceeded in this manner. They should have offered consultation, even collaboration, in working out goals, as will be shown below. This is very different from stepping into the organization's sphere of responsibility.

Trainers who have in fact proceeded this far commonly react to the client's opposition and resentment with righteous indignation: "What were we to do? Nothing? Wait forever?" They are threatened by the loss of a client and encountering a possible decline in the number of organizations and candidates applying to them for training. These threats, in a developing society with vast needs for effective training, ought to be sufficient grounds for pause and review, with no holds barred. Instead, trainers characteristically proceed in the same barren direction with renewed determination and greater speed. They go out and beat the bushes for candidates for the same inadequate programs, "selling" training to the "conservative" or "traditionally-minded" organizations. They reduce minimum qualifications and fees until all seats are more or less filled. It is as though they wanted to show the world outside: "See how wrong you are and how much others appreciate us." But this self-assertion has a hollow ring, even to those who stage it. What Dorothy Sayers calls the human trend to randomness[1] reasserts itself. Activity may continue, but on sufferance and to no great purpose. Training of this type has no more meaning than random human activity.

To be worthwhile, training must do better: it has to be a creative action. Let us retrace our steps, therefore, to take a second look at the strategic tasks of establishing training goals and planning specifications.

The training system cannot set the goals of change. It is very important to be quite clear about this point. National and organizational policies set those goals. Trainers may contribute—but as citizens. The task of the training system is to work only on those goals which training can help to attain, and which are adequately backed by organizational contributions.

> For instance, Indonesian legislation identified the Kabupaten (Regency) as the administrative unit on which the national development strategy would be based. But improving performance at national and local levels took precedence in the first three Five-Year Plans. Now, the Fourth Plan (1984-89) policies, budgets, and programs emphasize improving administration in Kabupaten. Trainers do not question whether these policy emphases, past or present, are desirable. They accept the task and work within this prescription.

The first strategic question, then, on which trainers need to satisfy themselves, concerns the nature of the goals already set. Are the goals realistic? Second, is the training input envisaged in their attainment also realistic? Or is training in danger of being misused? In other words, is this a case of too little and too late?

[1] Dorothy L. Sayers, *The Mine of the Maker* (New York: Harcourt, Brace and Company, 1941).

With very few exceptions training systems now concern themselves with these kinds of questions only when they consider the suitability of a particular applicant for a particular course, and that too, by general implication rather than careful consideration. For instance, since Joe Blow is not sufficiently qualified and lacks experience, let him apply again in two years. Bill Smith, on the other hand, has the requisite age, experience, and educational qualifications; therefore, he can be accepted. Tests exist to measure many aspects of an individual's capability for learning; tests for measuring an organization's capacity for further development, though less well worked out or universal, are also available. Systems that regularly use such tests are among the best in every respect.

The main point here is sharper in any case. The capability of an individual applicant to learn what a course has to offer is the second question to ask about the usefulness of training. The first question is whether the training program under consideration is realistic in the light of the needs of a particular organization and in the general context of its development.

Perhaps the most striking example of the dangers of paying inadequate attention to this dimension is the cumulative residue in industrially advanced countries of newly trained managerial and technical personnel from overseas, mostly from developing countries. Over 40,000 foreign engineers have settled in the United States since 1950 after completing their training there; for all kinds of scientific workers the total for U.S.A. and Canada is over 5-million. That they are able to make a living in competition with native Americans confirms their individual competence. Even if many have stayed on because of attractive living standards, others have done so because they were trained "out" of their country in the same way that school in a less developed country such as India seems to educate young people "out of the village." Training has qualified these engineers for settings and conditions that do not (yet) exist at home. This may be good for the individual, i.e., good education. As training per se, that is, achieving development in the engineers' home organizations, such overseas training has obviously been unrealistic and unsuitable.

In fact, not two but three steps back are necessary before a training course can be properly set up. Let us go right back to the beginning and walk through them systematically.

The first step, after a change has been decided upon, is to make sure that training is actually required for implementing the change. What many organizations need is not training, certainly not in the first instance, but plenty of detailed, operational planning and implementation of plans. Training at this stage would be a disservice if it deprived the organization of skilled people currently needed for such preparatory work.

The second step is to define the part that training could play in effecting the change. What new competencies does the organization require and what part of these can be systematically trained? We need not get lost in the abstract argument of whether or not managers and leaders can be trained. This only feeds on fuzzy definitions of amorphous goals. Several key aspects of a manager's or leader's skills can surely be developed through suitable training suitably timed, for suitable individuals suitably placed in organizations. Other aspects cannot be so developed. Training strategy determines which goals can reasonably be attempted by training.

More taxing and worthy of the most careful consideration are questions of quantities and levels of personnel to be trained, and of timing the training. Only rarely is training of a single person enough to achieve a change in an organization. While one person may go for a special program elsewhere, others need to be trained no less systematically. Leaving the organization for this is not necessary. Work with senior staff engaged in working out the change, staff meetings devoted to examining the implications, perhaps a weekend conference, may serve the purpose well. Whatever the methods—these are discussed later—it is important to establish what minimum concentration of trained personnel of all kinds is required to effect the change. If the training program as a whole cannot achieve this minimum, the effort amounts to treading water instead of progressing toward the goal. Or worse, personnel are trained into frustration.

The principle of accurate timing is to have personnel return from training as and when the organization is ready to use their new competence. Other inputs should be scheduled for the same time: changes in technologies and supplies, the fresh climate of readiness for the change, and so on. Newly trained personnel will then be able to proceed with their new jobs without delay. Only when plans for such detailed dovetailing have been worked out has the time arrived for step three—the selection of particular programs and of suitable people for them.

As a major phase in the strategy to develop trainers and system capacity at provincial and central levels, the Education and Training Division of Indonesia's Ministry of Health offers a seven-week program of advanced training for selected trainer consultants. It is designed for groups of trainers, one group from each province, who have already worked together and will form the core of the training system there. Each group comes with a back-home plan that has already been approved for funding. The trainees are expected to put their new learning to use as soon as they return from the program. This advanced training therefore actually extends over four months or more, if preparation for the programs back home, including organizational and financial dimensions, and evaluation and follow-up in the field are included in the time span.

The responsibility for going ahead with each of these steps belongs to the work organization. Trainer consultants may assist if the organization wishes. They may help, for instance, in defining the training inputs required for a contemplated change and in selecting personnel for training. But that is all. They must not assume responsibility for the steps themselves.

3. Planning Training Specifications—with Trainers in the Lead

Responsibility is reversed when the time comes for defining training specifications. The organization has specified the new knowledge, understanding, and skills required for the change it desires. The training system, in turn, has helped to pinpoint those which can be developed through systematic training. How this is to be done, that is, what training designs and methods to use, are strictly the business of the training system. This is the very core of its job.

There are enough analogies to help us understand this division of functions. For instance, nobody would dream of drilling a one-sixteenth-inch hole with a one-half-inch tool, or of expecting delivery in two weeks of a finished product that takes two months to season. In the same way, training has its specifications. They may state, for instance, that half a day does not suffice to develop new attitudes or leadership skills, or that training one person does not suffice to initiate a change for which a company of like-minded people is required. For a work organization to tamper with such specifications (if they have been carefully tested) is not thrift but waste, and throws doubt on its commitment to getting the development accomplished.

Here are two examples of training specifications:

> Learning a mechanical skill usually requires opportunities for supervised practice. Proper supervision calls for a small training group, say, not over twelve to fifteen. Because this requires careful preparation on the part of the supervisor, the work schedule must be so structured that *X* hours are allowed for his preparation. Participants have to master the skill to *Y* extent before they can usefully proceed to the next steps in training.
>
> Or, for managers of cooperative farms: this job requires competence in a variety of farming subjects as well as in organizing and managing groups of farmers, keeping accounts, etc. Candidates may be selected for training who are already competent in some of these aspects of the new job. They need only learn those skills they do not have. Experience has shown that some of these skills can be learned at work, others more efficiently in full-time training, say in short bursts of 2 weeks each.

By matching methods to requirements, the total timetable of training for a change can also be established. The training requirements for the different parts are added together. Allowance is made for some waste along the way.

The sum may show that 14 months of systematic training is required before the manager can assume full responsibility for the farm. Six weeks may be required prior to that for finding candidates and selecting future managers. If most of the candidates can be assumed to hold jobs that call for one month's notice to their present employer, this month likewise needs to be added, perhaps a calendar month if that is the custom. The entire series of activities to provide key managerial resources for this particular development has to start, therefore, at least $16^1/_2$ months before the farms are to go into operation. This assumes that all else goes well. Perhaps it would be wiser to start 18 months before and maintain the detailed schedule. If this advance calculation is correct, it would be useless to start the entire process even 12 months ahead and proceed with the same expectations.

Training specifications have to cover two further aspects. First, they need to state precisely the contributions to training that agencies other than the training system itself may have to make. The provision of opportunities for fieldwork placement is an example during the course, while adequate support after participants return from training and start the new work is an example for later. The participants' organization will certainly be involved in such planning, but also agencies of various other kinds, e.g., hospitals and communities near training institutions. It is the trainers' responsibility to define the various contributions and to ensure that they are made when needed. Second, the training specifications need to take into account the minimum concentrations of trained personnel required to effect the change at any stage. These have been calculated earlier. The training strategy will embrace the plan as a whole.

The training system, then, needs an external strategy for planning training that develops through a sequence of eight steps. Each step brings the system into closer relationship with the work organization. This sequence is shown in exhibit 3.1.

The training specifications worked out by the training system and agreed to by the work organization need to include services and activities following the participants' return from their training. Some services will be carried out by the training system. From time to time the system may provide information and occasions for contact between former participants and the training staff. Other follow-up activities will be carried out by the organization. The organization may arrange staff conferences or develop various other ways of helping the participants relate their new skills to the general process of change. Still other services may draw both the training system and the work organization into further collaboration.

At the follow-up stage, important information can flow back to the training system. The organization feeds back to the system information about the effectiveness of the training in practice, i.e., on the job. For future occasions the training input can then be improved and made more economical on the basis of this practical experience.

Exhibit 3.1

PLANNING STRATEGY: EIGHT STEPS PRIOR TO TRAINING

The Training System		*The Work Organization*
	←	1. Decides on a change. Specifies inputs required, including new knowledge, understanding skills.
2. Responds by specifying what can be acquired through training.	→	3. Studies who exactly is involved—numbers and levels—and when, all this in relation to other inputs, for example, technological, financial, and organizational.
4. Offers help in working out minimum concentrations of trained personnel required for change.	←	
5. Works out and communicates training specifications, for example, kinds and duration of training for different people sequences, follow-up services, and contributions required from the organization and other agencies.	→	6. Decides to go ahead.
7. Collaborates with the work organization in drawing up a training plan for implementation.	↔	
8. Collaborates in selecting individuals for particular kinds of training.	↔	

4. Programming Strategy by the Training System

Let us assume that the overall strategy has been mapped out satisfactorily, the training goals make sense, and the training specifications are met. The fourth specific step then addresses two further considerations. How to organize the various training inputs for maximum effectiveness and economy constitutes programming strategy and is the chief concern of the rest of this chapter. The other consideration, the choice of strategy, can also contribute to the improvement of the training system, but will only be outlined here to complete the picture; part III of the book is devoted to its further study.

The training system's first task is to use advantageously its current training resources, the skills of its trainers, available time and facilities, as well as the training resources and opportunities in the locality. The range of choice is wide, even for the humblest system, and choosing is possible at any stage of the training process. The system can make use of a wide variety of training settings: participants' work organizations, special small group settings, fieldwork, individual learning, and follow-up services, to mention just a few. A wide and expanding variety of methods and materials are also available to the training system; these are studied one by one in chapter 7.

Programming strategy combines various discrete resources into purposeful inputs. It then relates these inputs in proper quantities and sequences so that they constitute training that achieves real impact. For individual participants the program as a whole then provides an integrated learning experience. For work organizations it provides a comprehensive and consistent source of the new skills required for development. In such a comprehensive set the impact of the training process will be highest and also most economical. Careful evaluation at critical stages can ensure continued impact and economy. All this can follow if training starts with a clear and sound strategy.

THREE BASIC PHASES

For sequencing training inputs the conceptual scheme formulated by Kurt Lewin[2] for developmental activity of all kinds seems to us most useful. It describes development as a succession of three phases: "unfreezing," "moving" and "refreezing." In terms of programming strategy these three require, in turn programs for creating readiness, action learning, and support. This sequence is applicable to both individual and organizational learning; in fact, the two ought to be programmed in tandem.

Unfreezing is necessary because participants, and behind them their organizations, families and localities, come to training replete with ingrained habits of feeling, thought, and routinized action, all of which reinforce each other. In short, participants arrive for training with the very opposite of a clean state. To influence them through training, their normal habits have to be questioned and disturbed, or "unfrozen," early. Training can do this by focusing attention on needs that participants cannot satisfy by habitual behavior. Into this disturbed state trainers then introduce other events which allow participants to try new ways of behaving, that is, "moving." If they find new behavior more useful to meet the new needs, participants can then be helped to make it habitual in time. Individuals thus gain new identities and personal continuity, which then, "freezes." Matthew B. Miles conceptualizes this process as a "change-inducing temporary system." Box 3.1 summarizes his formulation.

[2] Kurt Lewin, "Group Decision and Social Change" in T.N. Newcomb and E. Hartley (eds.), *Readings in Social Psychology* (New York: Holt, 1947).

Box 3.1

CHARACTERISTICS OF CHANGE-INDUCING TEMPORARY SYSTEMS

MATTHEW B. MILES

Temporary training systems are set up for inducing changes in the durable aspects of *persons,* changes in relationships, and changes in *action.* The changes result from decisions made by participants during the life of the temporary system. The characteristics of such temporary system are:

INPUT CHARACTERISTICS

Time limits: the system terminates at a point in time.
Initial goal definition: it deals with a sharply focused range of content.
Boundary maintenance: it has clear and nonpermeable boundaries.
Physical and social isolation: it separates participants from their ordinary pursuits. This:
- Removes barriers to change.
- Reduces role conflicts.
- Supplies a strong protective function.
- Creates sense of a system.

Size and territoriality: it is usually small in size and has defined physical territory.

PROCESS CHARACTERISTICS

Time use: awareness of time limits results in:
- Distorted perceptions of elapsed time.
- Pacing effects.
- Goal redefinition.

Procedures are a set of timed, specified activities of persons, aimed at accomplishing system goals.
Role definition as socialization the system provides opportunities for role redefinition and refashioning of identity.
Communication and power structures: it provides new feedback loops.
Sentiments: it induces some salient states of feelings and group climate:
- Defensiveness: initial uncertainty with respect to the goals of others.
- Play: fluid, spontaneous, game-like behavior.
- Interpersonal liking: acceptance of and intimacy with others.
- *Esprit de corps*: a sense of group identity.
- Involvement: engagement in the system's goals.

Norms: the system stimulates the development of regulatory norms which define and govern behavior.
- Equalitarianism: an increased belief in the appropriateness of equal status relationships during the life of the system.

Box 3.1 (Continued)

Authenticity: emphasis on importance of openness and trust among participants.
Inquiry: problem solving with use of available data.
Hypotheticality: valuing of experimental, provisional, tentative-until-the-facts-are-in approaches.
Newism: favoring novelty and innovation.
Effortfulness: valuing hard work, energy, and effort.

SOURCE: Matthew B. Miles, "Temporary Systems" in Matthew B. Miles (ed.), *Innovation in Education* (New York: Teachers' College, Columbia University, 1964), chap. xix.

MODALITIES IN TRAINING

While all programming strategies need to provide for all three phases of individual and organizational learning, they differ according to the training modalities chosen for implementing them. That choice reflects the needs, opportunities, preferences, and constraints which the particular situation for implementation actually offers. For instance, one situation may favor training through a series of brief workshops interspersed with supervised field practice, or twice-weekly case conferences to review actions already taken, or the joint preparation by participants and consultant of simulations for use in "distance learning."

Modality therefore is a broader concept than the training method; several methods can be used for implementing one modality. The chosen modality provides the frame for designing and sequencing training inputs and selecting methods to produce the desired effects.

Training modalities can be usefully distinguished into four types: contact with learner; formalization of training; management of training; and content emphasis, e.g., by the processes or substantive content of the task.

a. Direct Contact and Distance Training

In contact-training programs trainers and learners are face to face. This limits the number of participants in a program. Distance training can respond more readily to the need to train large numbers and, with the introduction of new technologies, is becoming increasingly important. It can reach participants wherever they are and hence spread new information rapidly. It also incorporates the advantages of keeping people on the job, letting them learn at their own pace, and greatly simplifying requirements for different organizations to collaborate in training. The rapid spread of electronic technologies, such as video taping, closed circuit and responsive television, and rapid data processing for virtually instantaneous feedback have made "distance learning" highly attractive. Correspondence courses and reading programs, humble predecessors of advanced technology, are conceptually similar.

Distance training of all kinds starts with combining the training needs of a cohort and preparing relevant curricula for meeting these needs. Later steps include: preparing a series of modules to be used by an individual or small groups of participants as graduated learning experiences; preparing ways of reviewing the progress of participants and giving feedback to them on what they have been able to learn well and where they need to improve further; supplementing cognitive learning with other methods; and reviewing the final learning outcome.

b. Formal and Nonformal Training

As an alternative to training in formal programs at a particular place or in a program set at a distance with a fixed syllabus, training can be planned and conducted through various "nonformal" modalities. Through action-research programs, for instance, participants can learn many things in a planned way if, during or after their participation in the action, tutoring and supervision and also regular evaluation and feedback based on their experiences are provided.

In the nonformal modalities emphasis is on conscious, guided experiences. Many innovative devices are used to convert routine experiences into learning opportunities and also to create new experiences from which participants can learn. Plans are carefully made to ensure graded experiences and guidance. The mix of action and of learning from it can be adjusted to an organization's needs. For instance, if increased staff capacity has been decided upon as a major outcome, the number of participants with little experience in the planned action can be high, and many more opportunities can be included in the program for reviewing experiences and replanning the program to ensure maximum learning.

c. Centralized and Dispersed Organization of Training

Training modalities can also be differentiated along organizational lines. In a simple centralized model, for instance, one institute is formally charged with planning programs, staffing and funding them, ensuring their conformity to standards and, often, selecting participants. This pattern still predominates in developing countries with just sufficient training resources for one or two central institutes but an urgent need to provide training in many places. The central institute in this design initiates, guides, and supports all aspects of training, and the other units, subsidiary to it, carry out its plans.

At the other extreme are networks of largely autonomous training units, each responsible for its own training plans and programs and for linking with other units as needed or desired. What and how participants learn in a chosen field then depends also, in the dispersed model, on which unit they have joined.

In developing countries mixed models are increasingly becoming common, in which a central institute sets frames of training, such as priority emphases for training objectives, general guidelines for methodologies and materials to be used, and quantitative parameters for participants, time, and costs. Subsidiary units do the detailed planning, staffing, and management, and also contribute actively to formulating and revising system-wide frameworks.

d. Content and Process Modalities: Six Orientations

Training strategies vary again depending on the learning outcomes they seek to achieve. At one end is training for new or improved proficiency in carrying out a particular task, such as operating a drill press, treating a skin burn, or providing for amortization of buildings in annual accounts. At the other end are process learnings, such as improved teamwork or leadership, heightened readiness and ability to mobilize organizational support for a planned innovation, better morale, or a more effective consultant-client relationship.

Figure 3.1 locates these distinctions on a two-dimensional paradigm together with the familiar distinction between theory and practice. The vertical axis represents the subject matter that participants are to learn. Along that dimension one extreme points toward learning a specific task or piece of knowledge, such as the pros and cons of using power drills of various makes for a certain job, or the composition of the national income. We have labeled this type of knowledge "content." At the other extreme is a more pervasive understanding of *how* people and things *function.* This we have labeled "process." To continue with the same examples: in process learning participants would learn how drilling machines work and how national income figures are collected, compiled, and calculated, as well as the principles underlying these functions.

The horizontal axis of the paradigm represents the primary use of the training received. Is it to be used for abstraction, for constructing new concepts and theory? If so, it would fall to the left extreme of the horizontal axis, labeled "concept." Or, is it to improve action directly, in the field

Figure 3.1
SIX TRAINING ORIENTATIONS

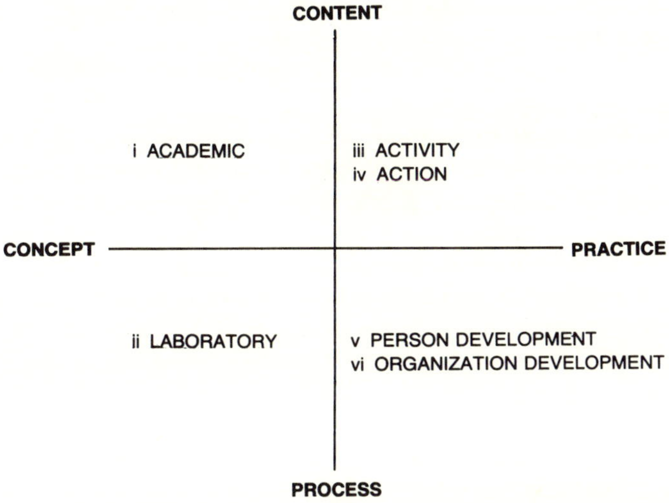

and on the job? We have labeled the right extreme "practice."

Before going on to consider the six orientations in turn, let us pause for a reminder. The diagrammatic clarity of these distinctions is bought at the price of undue sharpness. The distinctions are not as sharp as they seem here, and certainly not so exclusive. That is after all what one must expect from dualistic distinctions. They serve to put some complex and far-reaching affairs of life into pigeonholes in our minds, with each hole containing only as much data as can be managed at one time. The question to ask of these six orientations, therefore, is not whether they occur so neatly in real life, but whether the distinctions we draw between them are useful for our purpose here. This purpose is to throw into sharp relief the different approaches to training. Different approaches result in different strategies and are hence worth distinguishing clearly. We understand that what looks sharp and uncompromising in exposition, actually describes only trends and tendencies in practice which can often be offset or strengthened by extra deliberation and care.

For greater comprehensiveness we will here ignore the distinction we drew in chapter 1 between education and training and encompass both in this exposition. Let us, in fact, start with the most familiar: *the academic orientation.*

(i) The academic orientation gives pride of place to transmitting

content and increasing conceptual understanding. Its characteristic methods are lectures, seminars, and individual reading and preparation. The goals are incorporated first in a syllabus, which will be "covered," and then in examinations which test the students' recall of the content and principles and their ability to "apply" them under simulated conditions.

This type of orientation makes two assumptions. First, content and understanding can be "passed on" effectively by those who know—professors, writers—to those who are ignorant. Second, participants are capable of translating abstract generalizations into improvements in their performance in concrete situations. Universities need not be concerned about the second assumption. But the "academic orientation" is not confined to academic institutions. It is commonly used in many training activities, that is, where specific improvements are expected to take place on the job and in the organization. Many aspects of teachers' training, for instance, offer examples of academic training for action goals. In fact, it would not be an exaggeration to say that the academic strategy tends to be generally preferred in the training world. Program directors have to be argued out of it. It comes naturally, apparently, and is used until something else takes its place. Its attractions include the special status accorded to the "educated" person irrespective of accomplishment, to the neatness and orderliness of the syllabus, and, more basically, to the assured control such orientation gives to the trainer.

(ii) The laboratory orientation is also distant from the job and the organization in real life, hence its name. It has enjoyed prominence and respect for centuries in a variety of disciplines, since it provides an opportunity to gain insight and skill from direct experience and manipulation of a limited number of elements under controlled conditions. It is real to that limited extent, and thus can also provide sufficient distance from real life to permit both freedom to experiment and safety to learn from the consequences of trial. It is through laboratory training that the student of medicine discovers the wonders of human anatomy, the bacteriologist-to-be develops first-hand familiarity with pathogens, and the budding physicist discovers subtle applications of the law of gravity.

The concept of the laboratory has found wider use in recent years, for example in language laboratories. Here we are particularly interested in training laboratories for personal and organizational development. The laboratory strategy can be used for improving skills of social interaction that are essential for managers, supervisors, trainers, community workers, and a host of others who need to influence the quality of human interaction and human relationships in the work environment. For this purpose, laboratory orientation gives weight to considerations of process, not content: how things are done or not done, rather than what is accomplished.

This orientation is used to experience, and then to understand through this experience, how different people (real people—myself, my fellow trainers) think, act, and react; how leadership and other roles are performed in a group; how people become involved in a task or reject involvement. The training laboratory is therefore concerned with human relations and organizational behavior.

Two assumptions underlie the laboratory orientation. The first is that it is useful and possible to help people examine their inner reality, their psychological reality, in order to better understand the sources of their behavior and that of others, and to become aware that these are important factors in actual performance on the job. The second assumption is that people are able to transfer laboratory experience and learning to actual life situations, including other learning and work situations.

This is not a common orientation. It is novel and difficult to handle well. It raises fears of intrusion into people's privacy. As it cannot replace, merely supplement, an orientation that lays stress on content, it seems an expensive extra. The more basic difficulties of giving this orientation the place appropriate to its purpose and its limits include its seeming disorder and unpredictable "coverage," the complexities involved in evaluating its effectiveness, and, above all, the different, nonauthoritarian relationship it calls for between trainers and participants.

(iii) The activity orientation emphasizes practice of a particular skill. Its primary objective is improved individual performance on a specific job. The most elementary version of this orientation is "try, try and try again," until the participant can do the job. Skilled practitioners, particularly if they possess the inclinations and skills of a trainer, can greatly help this unstructured process along. This orientation founded the long and honorable history of apprenticeship, understudy, and internship, and the "counterpart" function of international aid schemes. The advantage of leaving the learning process unaided and unsystematized is the opportunity for exploration it affords participants whereby they can "get the feel of the job," given sufficient time.

Since this orientation puts training "on the job," it avoids the problems of transfer from training back to the job. Finally, it makes lighter demands on the work organization than other orientations.

Two assumptions underlie the activity orientation. The first is that the skill required by the organization is within the ability of the participants to do the particular job, and to "pick up" concomitantly the manner in which the surrounding organization operates. A variant on the first assumption is that participants can conceptualize their activities for themselves sufficiently to deal with any additional needs on the job. The second assumption is that production and training can be combined rather simply.

These are assumptions that may have been generally useful some time ago. Now they are useful for fewer and fewer jobs. Job requirements are, in fact, changing so rapidly and to such an extent that limited job training necessitates repeated retraining. The activity orientation leaves to chance questions of individual motivation and of collaboration between two or more people. The assumption that production and training can be readily combined is also no longer useful. Production goals tend to crowd out training goals, so that often this orientation ends in all work and no training. On jobs requiring very little skill this may not matter. But the number of such unskilled jobs declines sharply as an economy develops. Finally, the activity orientation puts participants in danger of learning outdated or faulty methods of work. In the rapidly increasing number of jobs for which speed, precision, and adaptability are required, the activity orientation is *de facto* of little value and may be detrimental.

> The limitations of the activity orientation have been belabored because it is quite common. Many of the numerous production-cum-training centers in India, for instance, actually institutionalize its confusion. Though apparently logical, the combination of production and training in practice is so difficult as to border on the impossible. When a center concentrates on production, as many do to satisfy their evaluators' itch for concreteness, training becomes very costly. Often it is also ineffective because skilled workers, instead of being allowed to instruct and supervise, are put on direct production to augment the monthly production record. At the same time a center's training function allows organizers to avoid responsibility for inefficiencies in production or other aspects of management.

Institutions that include field placements in their training program often encounter a variant of the activity orientation and its limitations. Training placement often yields nothing beyond sheer activity. The participants are kept busy with a motley assortment of tasks that permanent staff members assign. Or they are ignored, hopefully to "make their own way." Neither method constitutes training.

Updated versions of the activity orientation avoid some of these pitfalls, but never all. As used by an increasing number of systematic training programs, in trade schools for instance, it is based on rigorous detailed analyses of a particular skill. The skill is practiced in parts, often with the use of simple aids. When participants have gained specific standards of accuracy and speed in the parts, they practice the parts together and attain accuracy and speed in the operation as a whole. In this method training time is greatly curtailed and waste, for example of spoiled materials, reduced. However, a "feel for the job" is not acquired even by this procedure, nor is a capacity for further learning should conditions change. These must come on the job, over time, or will not come at all.

(iv) The action orientation is akin to the activity orientation. It does for the organization as a whole—a group, town, or other social system—what the activity strategy does for individuals. The training component of work camps and many other community-action programs is based on this orientation. Its emphasis on action rests on the same assumptions and runs the same dangers for an organization that the activity orientation does for individuals. Its focus, too, is on process, not content. Its emphasis on the "practical" can become so strong that the training purpose gets lost. In the absence of renewal through training, action soon fails in quality, becomes discontinuous, and in many cases ceases. If action is called for above all else, as in disaster relief or in digging a common village well, these limitations need not concern us here. But if an action program is chosen as a training orientation, then action by itself is not enough. It ensures neither sound practice nor the understanding of working procedures required for further development.

The massive Indian program for rural community development has been beset with dilemmas that can be traced to an increasing reliance on an action orientation.With heavy pressure for "concrete results," in terms of seed distributed, wells dug, roads and schools constructed, and the like, the program became all action *by officials;* in this shift the underlying purpose of stimulating participation, initiative, and collaboration by villagers was lost. Thus the officials have been caught in a vicious circle wherein secondary goals have been met only at the cost of primary ones.

With every round it has become more difficult to revert to the original intent. Now, in many places, attention is so relentlessly concentrated on physical results that harassed officials have no time even to think. And without time to think there can be neither training nor learning. Consequently, the basic resources of motivation and skill which the program was to multiply remain minimal, and the few participants are able to achieve only small physical results.

(v) The person-development orientation completes the range of orientations that aim to train an individual. This orientation gives weight to both job requirements and the processes by which these requirements are met. It consists basically of providing participants with alternating opportunities. During part of the program participants work on tasks and problems similar to those faced on the job. In between they analyze and explain the factors underlying the experiences they have undergone, and the points of view with which they approached them. This orientation does not lead merely to improvements limited to a specific job or situation, but to a widening and deepening of the participants' competence in understanding and dealing with many situations. What to think is considered less important than how to think. Action and discussion methods of training are char-

acteristic of this orientation: field training, simulation methods, and the discussion of incidents and cases.

The person-development orientation rests on two sets of assumptions. One set states that participants are already sufficiently familiar with work situations to deal with any new job content or other details expected to be required. They will be able and eager to secure for themselves any additional knowledge they feel they need. They are also already adept at analyzing their experiences and generalizing from them for the future. This assumption suggests that the person-development strategy is most appropriate for training professional personnel, and that it will become widely appropriate for India also, as education spreads and improves and as more and more jobs call for the kind of self-awareness this orientation fosters.

The second set of assumptions is common to all individual orientations. It states that individuals will have the support of their organizations in putting their training to use. To leave the organizational factor to chance leads to many heartaches and much waste. This happens when competent, well-trained individuals cannot use their training because their organizations will not give them sufficient elbowroom to change their behavior. Sometimes individuals may be able to create a little elbowroom and thus do their jobs more effectively and with greater satisfaction than before. But the effect is limited to their immediate surroundings. They are tolerated, no more. The wider organization remains unaffected and, should they quit the organization, their innovations would fade away.

> Given the very high rate of mobility of competent engineers and administrators in India, experienced professional people in this country are increasing their demands and, if denied adequate work satisfaction, simply quit the organization. Attributing such losses to the general economic situation in the country is not convincing. High taxes on personal incomes pare differences in net earnings between similar positions in different organizations to very little, so opportunities for personal satisfaction and development count for more and more. People who refuse to be involved in this question are usually also blind to the expenditure wasted on training from which the organization receives no benefit. The policy of some organizations not to send staff outside for training is at least more logical, and cheaper. But everyone recognizes this for what it is: a temporary expedient.

(vi) The organization-development orientation goes beyond the person-development orientation in just one respect: organizational change is its explicit, central focus and changes in individuals through training is just one means for organizational change. This orientation requires the closest collaboration between the training institution and the work organization. The institution plays a consulting role prior to executing the core parts of

the required training and often again after participants have returned to their jobs.

To begin with, this orientation addresses the question: what does the organization need to learn to achieve a particular change? It next assesses the training needs in detail and relates them to other requirements of change. The organization then uses training to ensure that competent staff is available in those numbers, at those levels, and at such time that the change can be effected. This orientation directly guides the selection of individuals for training and for jobs upon their return. Beyond accomplishing an immediate discrete change, it has the more general and lasting aim of developing the organization's own training function. Basically this is not a matter of setting up (or not setting up) a training department. Rather, it is a matter of fostering an attitude and allocating resources so that staff is developed further through the organization's normal operations. The aim is to achieve in the organization a pervasive sense of continuous development and a heightened receptivity and readiness for change.

The first of two assumptions underlying the organization-development orientation is analogous to the first underlying the person-development orientation, namely, attention to organizational needs and to the processes by which they can be met will induce participants to acquire any additional knowledge needed and to enhance their ability to conceptualize developments for the future. The second assumption also covers parallel ground, but in reverse. The person-development orientation assumes that organizational change will follow individual learning. This is not necessarily so. The organization-development orientation assumes that the individual will change as the organization changes and change, too, in line with organizational requirements. This is the specter of the organization man and is also not likely to be the case.

The organization-development orientation can incorporate two provisions to minimize discrepancies between individual and organizational interests. One is prior involvement of individuals in organizational changes that will affect them and to give them opportunities to contribute toward shaping these changes. The second is to openly acknowledge that such discrepancies may occur and may lead to some shifting of staff within the organization and, if all else fails, to some loss of staff. A training system oriented to organization-development must clarify these issues and insist that the organization resolve them before it embarks upon a training program. To the many rapidly expanding organizations in a developing country such as India, the training system can point out that they are in a favorable position for providing trained staff with opportunities to change to jobs elsewhere in the organization that promise continued personal satisfaction.

The use of an organization-development orientation is so new that a series of six examples in ascending order of complexity may help readers visualize it. The common simple mathematical extrapolations of staff needs at various levels to cope with new or expanding activities are only the bare beginnings of this kind of orientation.

1. Selecting participants in pairs or threes who work side by side or in functional interrelationship in an organization is a simple attempt at an organization-development strategy. The Small Industry Extension Training (SIET) Institute, Hyderabad, has tried to do this in its regular three-month industrial management and area development courses. It is rough-and-ready rule, because two or three trained people from any level in the organization may not in fact be the minimum concentration required. When the basic idea is not understood by the organization, the two or three candidates they nominate for training may not in fact work sufficiently closely together to provide the necessary support on the job.

2. SIET Institute used this type of orientation on a large scale when it recruited sixty potential entrepreneurs from one small town for a succession of four 10-day courses in entrepreneurial motivation. The majority of these participants formed themselves into an entrepreneur's association which showed tangible results within three years in terms of industrial units started and new investments.

3. To stimulate industrial development in a district, a largely rural area with a population of 1.5 million, the Institute decided to concentrate training in two or three district towns and offer them a sequence of training events and services. In the first stage it strove to create a broad base of interest. It proceeded by placing in local factories for in-plant fieldwork groups of participants in one of SIET Institute's regular courses. The faculty supervising the fieldwork were simultaneously able to organize and run weekend courses for sixty or so local entrepreneurs and managers. The second stage consisted of short entrepreneurial motivation courses, again for sixty or so local people, organized locally. Of these sixty people some promising participants were selected for stage three, a succession of regular management training courses at SIET Institute.

4. In its three-tier management programs the Indian Institute of Management, Ahmedabad (IIMA), has attempted to take into account the hierarchical relationships in organizations and the support of changes needed from the chief executive downward. Each program has three stages, and participating organizations have to be represented in all three. The first (six weeks) is for one or two members of middle management; the second (one week) is for a member of senior management; the last (three days) is for the top executive. The stages overlap. The idea is that each participant will be more effective after training by having the support of at least two others at different levels of the organization.

5. A more intensive three-tier program is run by the South India Textile Re-

search Association (SITRA) for individual textile mills. Primarily for supervisory training, the program includes training also for two higher levels (managers and managing agents) and the level immediately below (jobbers). Short special courses and other in-service activities are also arranged for clerical and administrative staff. Training at each level is largely based on feedback about existing practices and suggestions for the next lower level in the organization. Each unit program is limited to twenty participants and lasts four weeks, excluding follow-up services. The Ahmedabad Textile Industry's Research Association (ATIRA) has another "unit program." Financed by four mills and lasting several years, the program aims at training all line supervisors in these mills and ensuring adequate organizational support for them. The program has grown out of collaborative action-research projects designed to elicit training and job requirements.

6. The Institute of Rural Health and Family Planning (IRHFP) at Gandhigram in southern India bases its training on service activities started at least one year in advance of any new training program. These activities, concentrated in six community development blocks, are designed to involve the people themselves in planning and implementing health programs in their communities. Health leaders, elected by the people, form a village health committee that gradually takes responsibility for more and more health activities. The Institute's service staff performs as staff members of the official government health centers at the block level. The Primary Health Center staff participates in the program and evaluates its effectiveness.

In time, official health workers from other areas and other states have come for training in the methods of work developed. Opportunities for developing similar skills are provided through field assignments in the operating blocks. A trainer is assigned as liaison with the staff in each block and assumes responsibility for field activities for the participants.

Each of these examples of an organization-development orientation to training embodies the attempt to take care of the needs that actually arise in carrying out specific changes. This is achieved through planning in advance and flexibility in operation, and is painstaking, hard work. It delays the start of training and demands expensive staff time, not just once, but continuously. Onward work is necessary to keep abreast of developments and to pare to the minimum the numbers of participants and time requirements of training. But, as in construction so in training, this type of investment pays: it is wise to build extra strength into a program initially, then pare down, rather than skimp at the outset. Once the program is under way tighter specifications can greatly reduce the cost of mobilizing, advancing, and sustaining an organization in development.

High cost is not likely to be the main obstacle to the wider application of the organization-development orientation to training. Properly carried out, it is cheaper in terms of results than the present costs of haphazard training for which organizations find money. Two difficulties figure more prominently than costs. One that confronts all careful planning is the reluctance of many executives to commit themselves and their organizations to a definite course of action over a lengthy period. Uncertainties seem to loom too large, and estimates are not worth the paper on which they are written. Much of this hesitation cannot be logically justified. Vagueness clouds the fringes, not the massive core of calculations. Perhaps a more serious difficulty underlies this hesitation, namely, the threat that careful planning and action may unveil the "holy of holies" guarded by senior executives. As a result of detailed studies of operations and requirements, strategic factors of resources become more widely known and discussed. Exclusive guardianship of information has often been an important tool for senior executives in sustaining their power or a company its competitive position. In this connection also attitudes toward training may reveal a responsible person's general orientation.

Selecting the appropriate orientation: The main features of these six orientations are summarised in exhibit 3.2. They are compared in terms of emphases, characteristic methods, assumptions, and action steps.

The selection of an appropriate orientation depends on a number of factors. One is the training goals. Once the organization has clarified its training goals, quite possibly through consultation with a training system, it can settle on the orientation which promises best to gain them.

> For example, the goal of developing individuals with sufficient skills to be able to perform more effectively on their jobs cannot be accomplished by an academic orientation to training. For that goal an activity or person-development orientation is more appropriate. The activity orientation is appropriate when the job calls for limited skill and is not likely to change much in the near future. The person-development orientation is more appropriate if the job is complex and changing. When the main emphasis is on changes in the total organization, it is necessary to use the organization-development orientation.

FASHIONING A COHERENT STRATEGY

A training strategy that sets the stage well for training efforts is thus a composite fashioned from careful considerations of strategic issues, training modalities, and training orientations—step by step and also in combination. The foregoing lists will ensure that major dimensions are taken into account, those for which current information is "soft" as well as those for which available information is more solid. Enough clarity emerges to strike a direction, to examine the map for key features ahead, and to choose an initial route. A map with the route drawn in is a useful image: it is not a blueprint or a precise work plan. In actuality, expected features are often quite different close up; opportunities for better routing open up

Exhibit 3.2

COMPARISON OF SIX TRAINING ORIENTATIONS

Orientation	*Emphases*	*Characteristic Methods*	*Assumptions*	*Action Steps*
1. Academic	Transmitting content and increasing conceptual understanding	Lecture Seminar Individual reading	1. Content and understanding can be passed on from those who know to those who are ignorant 2. Such knowledge and understanding can be translated into practice	Building a syllabus to be covered in the program Examination to test retained knowledge and understanding
2. Laboratory	Process of function and change Process of learning	Isolation Free exploration and discussion Experimentation	1. It is useful and possible to pay attention to psychological factors for separate attention 2. Understanding of own and others' behavior helps in job performance	Unfreezing participants from their usual expectations and norms Helping participants to see and help others to see their own behavior and develop new habits
3. Activity	Practice of specific skill	Work on the job under supervision Detailed job analysis and practice with aids	1. Improvement in particular skill leads to better job performance 2. Production and training can be combined rather simply	Analyzing skill and dividing it into parts Preparing practice tasks, standards, and aids

Exhibit 3.2 (Continued)

Orientation	*Emphases*	*Characteristic Methods*	*Assumptions*	*Action Steps*
4. Action	Sufficient skills to ensure organizational action	Field work, setting and achieving targets	1. Working in the field develops people 2. Individual skills and organizational needs will fit together	Preparation of field programs Participation according to schedule
5. Person-development	Improved individual competence in a wide variety of tasks and situations	Field training, simulation methods, incident and case sessions, and syndicate discussion	1. Training in job requirements with emphasis on process will help participants develop general skills and understanding 2. Organization will support individuals in using understanding and skills acquired	Identifying training needs Preparing simulated data
6. Organization-development	Organizational improvement	Study of organizational needs Work with small groups from the organization	1. Attention to organizational needs as process develops understanding 2. Organizational change will result in individual change	Survey of organizational needs Determining strategic grouping for training Working on organization requirements

while in movement and the pace may also accelerate—or slow down—under actual conditions.

The resources available for training make a difference in the short run. These resources include the faculty of the training system first and foremost, the extent to which the system can draw on additional professional resources and community contacts, and the availability of other facilities necessary for implementing a particular strategy. When available trainers are incompetent to implement a particular strategy, attempting it can only create a frustrating situation likely to lead to failure.

In the Indonesia project with the Ministry of Health, the initial, exploratory consulting visit clarified only that the project would focus on developing training capacities for improving management in three provinces. Which provinces, their relationship to the central department charged with training, and how the development was to be attempted were not specified.

Over the next six months the provinces were so chosen that the Ministry's primary interest in the "Outer Islands" was met, but the set also included one "Inner" province, i.e., on Jawa—to avoid unfavorable discrimination later. Where to start was resolved by the dominant need for service administrators to pay more attention to the actual delivery of services in the field and to improve things there. Since "technical" training was acceptable to key administrators, the intervention strategy began by identifying three technical inputs as vehicles for this: task analysis; case research, writing and teaching; and consultation skills. (Later, after some experience, impact evaluation was added and consultation skills held over for "advanced" training.) In the very first province institutions were included in the training system which were outside the official health system, e.g., medical and teacher training schools and Islamic institutions. Participants were selected from all of these institutions on the basis of locally worked out criteria of performance, commitment, and availability.

Participation of central staff, though provided for at the outset, actually followed successes in the first two provinces. They were given places in all provincial programs and separate programs for central staff thus avoided. Full-time advanced training was instituted two years later. It was designed for trainers who had performed exceedingly well subsequent to "technical" training. These trainers were adjudged by colleagues, superiors, and consultants to possess additional capabilities and were also given organizational support for devoting more time to management training in the health system.

All except one of the major steps in this Indonesia project were foreseen in the strategy developed over the initial six months of technical assistance. The last step, the institution of a national consulting service, went beyond that strategy and was added when the needs of the system and the capabilities of the same trainers to meet it became clear. That happened in the fourth year of the project.

Training strategy, therefore, is not a static blueprint; it is open to clarification, modification, and further development through experience with it. Its initial formulation, testing in practice, and ongoing review and development cost much time and effort, but this is quickly justified by making training effective and also economical. Time and money are often mentioned as factors that rule out otherwise desirable strategies or the efforts required to craft one: programs have to be large, start with minimum delay, and must be cheap. Without gainsaying these requirements, it is nevertheless difficult to be patient with their particular limitations. Too many people have already been "put through" too many courses, with too little benefit in return. What could be more time-wasting and expensive? Time is an acceptable limitation only if brevity can induce heightened intensity and rigor in the program, for example, by working with smaller training groups, more and better faculty, more careful training designs, and fewer gaps in time. But once the limits of substitution have been reached, and they are sooner or later, to go below the minimum specification of time and other resources is both irresponsible and damaging.

Rather similar dangers are incurred when a training system scatters its efforts in attempting to serve a large number of organizations throughout the country, and perhaps abroad as well. This eliminates its use of strategy involving programs for organization development, since the system cannot achieve the concentrations of participants and resources necessary. We doubt the value of scattering "something, whatever is possible." This "something" may well be too little to be effective and hence constitute waste. The proper choice, surely, is to use appropriate strategies in as many places as possible, and not institute training where it cannot be done effectively—yet. This decision, difficult as it often is in the face of untoward pressures, is more realistic and economical. Similar hardheaded choices are made and accepted in other fields. There is nothing strange in recommending them for training.

General conditions in developing countries, in fact, put a premium on just such hardheadedness. Rapid change and the urgent need for greater independence of action and for skills of collaboration on the part of individuals and organizations call for training strategies that emphasize process and organizational dimensions, i.e., strategies involving laboratory, action, person-development, and organization-development orientations. If few training systems are well enough developed as yet to handle these strategies, this mandates renewed emphasis on faculty and on institutional and system development. Increasing these resources, not simply carrying on somehow, should command priority.

Training systems in turn need strategies for their own maintenance, strengthening, and further development, addressing the same set of dimensions as the training strategies they help participants and their organizations to develop: workforce planning and staff development to keep up with new technologies and larger changes of scale; system structures, of units and overall strategic planning and resource management;

and, in the environment, developing close professional and working relationships with other institutions and concerned agencies—in short, everything required to equip a training system to keep on performing its primary roles effectively. In the specific context of this chapter, the system must be able to choose and implement with minimum delay those training strategies which would best meet the needs of the organizations it serves, and which also fit its own character, special capabilities, style, and vision for development. Not every system can meet the training and development requirement of every kind of organization. There is room for several kinds of training units and systems, each with distinct strengths. We shall return to the exploration of the issues involved in choosing organizational and institutional development strategies to suit training systems in part III.

Chapter 4

Overview of the Training Process

We must lead men to the particulars themselves, and their series and order, while men on their side must force themselves for a while to lay their notions by and… familiarize themselves with facts.

—Francis Bacon

Any change in any of the factors, independent of the way in which it is brought about, will, by the aggregate weight of the cumulative effect running back and forth between them all, start the whole system moving… with a speed depending upon the original push and the function of causal interrelation with the system.

—Gunnar Myrdal

For every training strategy, no matter which, the proper focus right from the very outset is on one or more people — on-the-job-in-the-organization—this whole amalgam. Wherever the focus moves during the training process, the starting point becomes the focus again at the end, hopefully with a difference. The difference lies in what-people-have-learned-that-they-now-apply. That difference, in terms of more effective behavior, is the measure of the efficacy of training. It is essential to insist on this starting point and this measure. Much as we may wish to reject the complexities involved, nothing less will do.

We have separated the process into three phases: pretraining, training, and posttraining. "Preparation," "training," and "follow-up" would be more aesthetic, but these words hide the important fact that all three phases have preparatory and follow-up aspects.

THREE PHASES IN THE TRAINING PROCESS

Phase 1: Pretraining. The process starts with an understanding of the situation requiring more effective behavior. What performance is to be improved? The "what" precedes "whose" by two steps. The first basic step is to delineate the task and, concomitantly, the small or not-so-small system of people who perform it—the "primary task group" as it has come to be called. Included here are the people involved in resource–input and product–output functions and in the planning and managerial functions requisite for keeping the effort together and focused. When the task has to be changed, the composition of this group or the division of work among its members may also have to change. Who is to be trained then has to reflect the new arrangement of functions. To provide sound guidance for the training required by individuals, the job description of any function must go beyond technical specifications to include relational requirements. In short, an operational description is needed of each person's job which reflects how it is to be carried out with improved effectiveness. This covers, in addition to technical requirements: (a) the kinds of personal contact the job requires the doer to have with others, for example, colleagues, customers; (b) the pressures on the job, such as quick decisions and heavy responsibilities; (c) any wide variations in the quantity of work and the time required to complete them; and (d) other salient features.

The second key aspect of the situation to be understood is the organization's receptivity to more effective behavior on the part of the people to be trained. Who feels the need for this new behavior? The person involved? The immediate superior? A distant office? These issues raise questions of motivation and relationships. They are personal to the potential participants, to others in the organization, and also to the participants' families. They will affect their ability to learn and thus the effectiveness of the training.

Phase 2: Training. Participants do not leave the above questions behind when they go for training, whether for a session, an evening course, or a residential program (though in a residential situation the back-home questions will tend to fade into the background for a while). This entails disadvantages as well as advantages. In an evening program, these questions will be immediate, since participants are reminded of them by the daily reality of their work situations. Undoubtedly the back-home questions are on their minds when the training starts and new impressions crowd in on them—new subject matter, new people, a new atmosphere.

Participants focus their attention on those new impressions, severally and in combination, that seem useful, stimulating, and engaging. There is no way of knowing (perhaps they themselves do not know) how the participants will weigh personal interest in relation to technical importance or acceptability by colleagues. Is something to be learned because it is needed? Fun? Promising? Promising what? Greater achievement or promotion? Is it acceptable to colleagues but not to the immediate supervisor?

Or vice versa? These are but a few of the questions that move in the participants' minds as they begin their training and select what they want to learn from the program getting under way. There is no guarantee, of course, that the participants will in fact learn what they have chosen. Their selection may be in error. They may lack the necessary capabilities or may be frustrated by inadequate or irrelevant training design, methodology, or relationships. But the main purpose remains: participants explore in a training situation what interests them, and a training institution's basic task is to provide the necessary opportunities.

Having explored, participants try out some new behavior. Subsequently, either of two sequences takes over. If they find the new behavior useful, they try it again, check it for effectiveness and satisfaction, try it repeatedly, and improve it. Finally, they incorporate this new facet into their habitual behavior in the training situation. If they do not find it useful, however, they discard it, try some variant, or discontinue learning in this direction. The intricate process of selection and testing is continuous and more or less conscious. The more accurately participants incorporate the realities of actual work situations at home in their testing and practicing, the better this rehearsal will prepare them. This itself is reason enough for contacts between work organizations and participants during training. It is also important that work organizations meanwhile prepare the conditions for improved performance by their participants upon their return.

Phase 3: Posttraining. When training per se concludes, the situation changes. Participants once again give full attention to work, colleagues, and families. They return prepared with some anticipation of these encounters. Likewise, people at home entertain more or less definite expectations of *them.* If they went away, these expectations may have changed or firmed up in their absence. When they return, a process of adjustment begins for everyone involved. For instance, the newly learned skills undergo modification to fit the work situation. Participants may find their organizations offering encouragement to use the training and also support for continuing contact with the training institution. On the other hand, they may step into a quagmire of negativity. Colleagues, organizations, and family members may have resented the extra burden their absence placed on them. They let participants know their "holiday" is over now, and they had better work harder to make up for lost time. In such a case contact with the training institution may be broken off, or simply wither away, in spite of any help the training system offers.

More effective behavior of people-on-the-job-in-the-organization is the primary objective of the training process as a whole. In the simplest training process, improvement is a dependent variable, and participants and organizations independent variables. A model of training in its simplest form is presented in figure 4.1.

But training is actually a more complex process than figure 4.1 suggests. In the first place, the training system itself needs to be included. It may be a temporary system, such as an occasional program, or a permanent institution, such as a training department. In either case, the trainers-in-the-system also learn through the various opportunities available for checking their effectiveness, i.e., through feedback. Thus the independent and intervening variables also become dependent variables. This elaboration is shown in figure 4.2.

Figure 4.1

SIMPLE MODEL OF THE TRAINING PROCESS

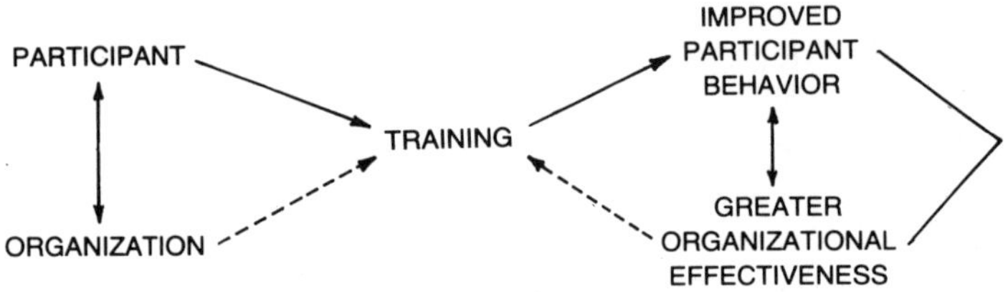

Figure 4.2

ELABORATED MODEL OF THE TRAINING PROCESS

The process as a whole, with its three partners and three stages, is depicted in figure 4.3. It is a spiral model, overlapping the people-on-the-job-in-the-organization. This spiral model is useful in visualizing a training program as an entity, as well as each event and series of events that make up the program. For instance, there is a pre- and a post-phase for each session and, in between, the phase of actual acquisition and development of new knowledge and skills.

The spiral in the model in figure 4.3 shows the phases through which participants pass as they learn, then return (with enhanced capabilities, we hope) to their jobs. At various stages in the process the other two partners contribute "inputs" to assist the participants. These inputs are shown as arrows: arrows originating inside the spiral depict inputs of the work organization; arrows originating outside the spiral, inputs of the training institution. The arrows are merely visual conveniences. The large spiral itself comprises a continuous spiral feedback system.

Figure 4.3

SPIRAL MODEL OF TRAINING PROCESS

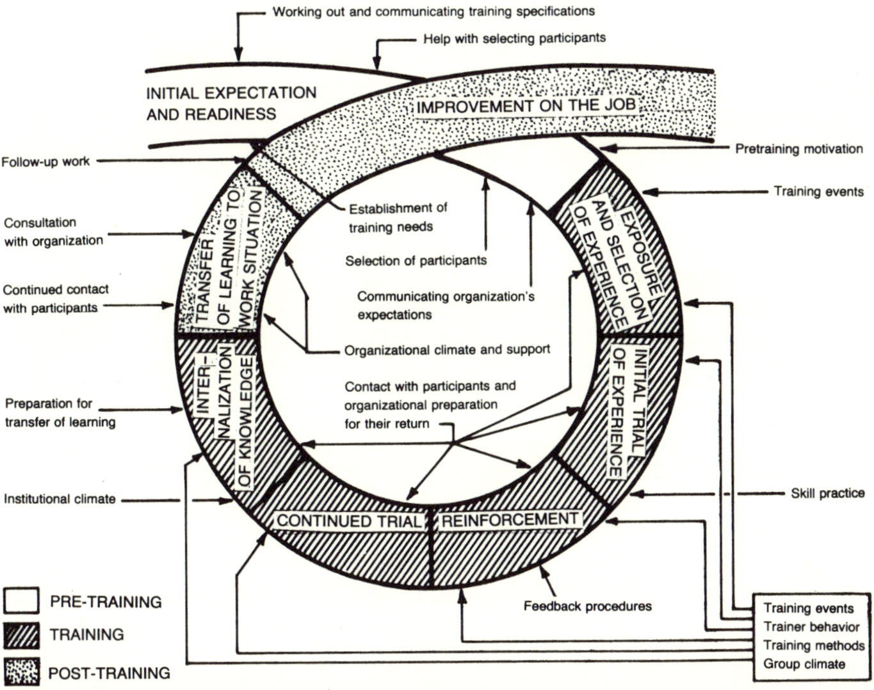

We will use this spiral model to explicate the training process, further focusing in turn on participants, work organizations, and finally, in part III, on training systems.

THE LEARNING SPIRAL FOR PARTICIPANTS

1. Pretraining: Expectations and Motivation

To learn, people need to feel the need for learning. This is true for any kind of learning. The need can be desperate, as for survival, even economic survival. More often, learners need more skill to qualify for a particular job or to feel more effective in it, to understand particular things or events, or to feel that they are continuing to grow. Some people feel this latter need readily and take pride in their ability to learn new habits. Others reject or play it down, because learning for them is akin to an admission that they are not already competent. These two types of people and others face the prospect of training with very different expectations and are right in thinking that they will derive very different experiences from the same training session or course. Here the essential point to grasp is that participants' motivations and viewpoints will determine their focus of attention and learning.

This basic fact holds true not only for the general prospect that training has for participants but for the details of the particular course they are considering. Do they see it as suitable for themselves? Do they feel qualified for it? Do they have the necessary background, neither too little nor too much? Is it suitably timed? If a participant is burdened with sickness in the family, has a wedding to arrange (an Indian domestic crisis), or is expecting a baby (an American one), it is hardly an auspicious time for training, not even nearby. A participant's mind can be preoccupied with domestic events and fantasies, unable to focus on the training course.

Very importantly, participants wonder what their selection for a particular training course tells about them compared to others. What does it say about management's evaluation of them? For what level of employee is the course intended? Does their selection mean they are heading for a promotion or, negatively, that they are the ones most easily spared? Who are the other participants? What do others apparently think they need to learn? The general reputation of the course and the institution running it, the manner in which people are selected for it, and its cost—all these play in the personal calculation each prospective participant makes before even entering training. The Advanced Management Program at the Harvard Business School has come to signify imminent promotion, valuable contacts, and high personal value for those selected to attend. Many other training programs, on the contrary, are considered rather meaningless chores. An organization's main reason for sending participants may be simply to have its name figure in the attendance list. Participants are aware of the positive and negative images of training, and approach participation accordingly—eagerly or reluctantly, inclined or disinclined to learn.

2. Training: Exposure to Opportunities for Learning

Expectations, whatever they may be, are brought by participants to a training programme. Exposure to the learning opportunities training offers will hopefully result in a series of five stages. Each series commences with the selection of an item to learn and concludes with a new behavior becoming habitual. Participants may undergo several series simultaneously and may well interrelate them.

a. *Selection of some items for learning.* Regardless of the motivation or degree of readiness she brings, a participant commences training and is exposed to its opportunities for learning. Out of the numerous new impressions that crowd in on her, she chooses some for particular attention: these constitute the subjects, people, and atmosphere that attract her more than other subjects. They satisfy some of her needs and are, therefore, meaningful to her. Although the training program may be thorough and well planned, because of personal preference participants will learn different things from it. Each participant, and not the trainer, "decides" the focus of her attention and her expectations from it. "Decides" has been placed in quotes to signal that many factors, not all conscious or apparent, go into a participant's choice of focus.

b. *Initial trial of experience.* The participant now explores and uses the item she selected. She thinks about it, and translates her interest into specific behavior. She tries it out. Does it fit into this way of thinking? or that way? Into other people's expectations? Her purpose in this initial trial is to see its effect on her organized system of thinking, including her own self-image.

c. *Feedback from the initial trial.* The participant's experimentation may be rewarding or discouraging, or merely open-ended. This depends on her own reaction to the trial, and the reactions of the other participants and the trainers. If the feedback is positive, and the item tested "fits" her, she is satisfied. This is an important step in the process of learning. The participant then also *feels* she is learning.

d. *Reinforcement and continued practice.* Satisfaction from positive feedback reinforces the participant's new pattern of behavior. This amounts to practice. Repeated practice followed by repeated satisfaction will result in establishing the new pattern of behavior firmly.

e. *Internalizing what she has learned.* Learning based on repetition tends to be mechanical and barren until the participant ceases to be self-conscious of it and uses it routinely as a part of her habitual pattern of behavior. This process of assimilation takes time. The new item, or the modification of an established habit, affects many parts of the participant as a person. It becomes woven into her experiential texture and makes her a somewhat different person. In Erikson's[1] scheme of thinking the most important learning requires a period of "moratorium," a period of withdrawal from everyday pressures and expectations. During this period the participant allows herself and her life to be reshaped. It is like a honeymoon, away from friends and relatives. At a much

[1] Erik H. Erikson, *Childhood and Society* (New York: W. W. Norton and Co., Inc., 1950).

lesser depth, all learning has this essentially reflective, withdrawn stage. It ends when self-consciousness of the new ways has disappeared. The participant has then truly learned something new, has made something new her own.

Some such sequence as this describes the learning process of one participant of any one item. Hopefully, the training program will engender not just the learning of a few discrete items, but will generally induce the courage for, and an orientation toward new experience in which further learning is attractive. If in the overall cycle learning becomes enjoyable as a process, the participant will be more open to learning in the future.

3. Posttraining: Transferring Learning to the Back-Home Situation

The training session or program ends. The participants leave for home with whatever they have learned. If things have gone well, they go back to their organizations with somewhat new patterns of behavior, as somewhat changed people. With motivation and enthusiasm newly heightened by the satisfaction of learning, they are eager to put what they have learned to use on the job. In doing so they behave differently, in fact, from the way they behaved prior to training. Now, back on the job, they have to add one more dimension to their learning, an organizational one.

a. *Organizational support or lack of it.* Once again the participant watches for feedback. How do others react to her new behavior? If her colleagues and superiors approve of it, she is encouraged and inclined to continue to behave in the more effective way. If they ignore her return or any indication of change in her, behaving as though she had never been trained, she will be discouraged from persisting with attempts to use what she has learned. Some anxiety will persist until the reception is reasonably clear.

b. *Improvement on the job.* In the final analysis, training is successful if participants' job effectiveness improves as expected. Verbal support for more effective behavior does not suffice to ensure this result. Other preconditions, such as adequate equipment, basic attitudes of colleagues, and organizational policy, have to line up with the change. Discrepancies on the job lead to participant frustration at the very time that their expectations are highest. This final failure of training is all too well known to young people returning from training overseas. Others fear it to such an extent that they do not return to their home even to try. Alternatively, when conditions are favorable, changes actually take place. More important for the long term is the favorable outlook such success creates for further learning in the work situation itself.

The participants' learning depends on continuity. It must suffer no breaks during any of the several stages. The risk of a break is highest at those stages when the usefulness of an item or its acceptability to others is questioned—at the first trial stage, for example, or on returning home. At these stages the process must be able to carry the accumulated burden of doubt and anxiety, or it will fail. These are the stages when the onward process resembles a spiral staircase. Either each round supports the next, or even a momentary frustration causes morale to plummet and prejudices further opportunities for learning, thus forming a vicious circle. At these crucial stages participants need support and need to feel it.

THE TRAINING PROCESS FOR PARTICIPANTS' ORGANIZATIONS

Learning proceeds along the participants' viewpoints; training does not. In the forefront of training are the purposes of the work organization. The wishes of the participants and the training system come only afterwards. Hence there are three points of view, each one different. Training has to relate all three. It does so by offering learning opportunities of such kinds and qualities, and so timed, that they support the participants' learning those things important to their job performance. The rest of this chapter outlines the contribution to the training process required from participants' work organizations. The rest of the book details the roles of trainers and training systems. The contributions of participants' work organizations to the training process are concentrated in the pretraining and posttraining phases, but they can also be significant while participants are in training. The contributions of the training institution are concentrated in the training phase, but are also significant in the other two phases. We have postponed to later chapters a detailed examination of the required collaboration between work organizations and the training system during each phase: what each needs to do, and what the two should do jointly. Here we have tried to establish the objectives which should concern the participants' organizations at each successive phase in order to ensure effective training.

1. Pretraining: Objectives, Selection, and Motivation

An organization's concerns before training lie mainly in four areas: clarifying the precise objectives of training and the use the organization expects to make of the participants after training; selection of suitable participants; building favorable expectations and motivation in the participants prior to training; and planning for any changes that improved task performance will require in addition to training, such as physical and organizational rearrangements, including, perhaps, some capital expenditure.

a. *Clarifying objectives of training and the use of trained personnel.* This is where the rigor must start—and where it is almost everywhere now lacking. Most organizations so far have developed only quite general job descriptions calling for certain standard qualifications. In reading the job descriptions for salesmen or certain types of extension officers, for example, one could get the impression that contact with customers and other people is a marginal requirement, whereas, in fact, it is primary. If the omission of this salient fact means that those selected for such posts can be assumed to already possess the skills required for dealing with people, this assumption has not been borne out by experience. In order to specify training needs and, further, to choose appropriate training opportunities for a participant, a full operational job description is most important. This means detailing at least job content, relationships, and time. Since prevailing organizational practices fall far short of desirable standards of job analyses, the training institution may have to make a special contribution in this regard. We return, therefore, to this matter again in chapter 5.

Once the job requirements have been ascertained, the next step is to pinpoint those aspects which can be handled through training. Quite often, new material resources or different work assignments are also required. That the need is wider than training can meet is a salutary recognition and will clarify the organizational support required later by the trained personnel. Finally, operational estimates are needed of how many people may require training and for what purpose. Will trainees return to the same field and the same objectives, or will they go into another field that will be affected as the planned change gets underway?

b. *Selecting suitable participants.* This is a complicated matter. It involves the organization's readiness and the individual's convenience at the time. It needs to avoid questions of popularity or reward for past services. Some organizations have clarified their operations sufficiently to pinpoint personnel for definite plans for growth and diversification. The question of who is to be involved in the selection is also important. Ideally, selection becomes a joint responsibility of organization and candidate that carries through to helping participants use their training afterwards. Certainly, candidates' immediate superiors need to be involved. So do immediate colleagues who will be affected by their absence and by their different job performance after training. The people with whom candidates work know better than others their suitability, preferences, and prospects for training. Moreover, if others are not involved in the process at this stage, they may express their resentment later, when their colleagues return from training.

c. *Building favorable expectations and motivation in participants.* It is important that the participants selected leave for training assured that the organization considers the training thoroughly worthwhile and is taking steps to enable them to use their new competence when they return. This requirement is clear. The question is how to meet it.

It is a complex question for the same reason that the relationship between training and learning is complex: two points of view are involved. What influences the participants' expectations and motivations is not organizational action or inaction as such, but the view they take of it. This is determined immediately by the context, relationships, and general atmosphere in the organization, and more particularly by the many personal and historical factors over which the organization has little or no control.

Two examples may help to make the distinction concrete and meaningful. To one participant his organization's check on departure details and smooth handing over of responsibilities may indicate high regard and personal care. Another participant may feel belittled rather than elated, as if he could not be relied upon to look after such things himself. Or, when an organization pays a large fee and goes out of its way to facilitate a participant's going, it clearly attaches importance to the occasion. But the effects of this signal of importance vary according to the participant's preoccupations. At one time she may see the organization attaching great significance to her learning something important, at another time she may conclude that the organization wants her well out of the way to effect a reorganization that she has opposed.

This distinction between what the organization does and what the participant sees in the action is now, hopefully, firmly fixed in the reader's mind. It is very important. We will see similar distinction in our discussion of actions taken by trainers and institutions.

d. *Planning changes in the organization related to the projected improvement in task performance.* Often the changes required are quite minor, such as expediting supplies to keep pace with expected increases in production. Modification of the division of work may be worked out by the work group with little or no special assistance. When training is linked to product changes, major expansion and reorganization, or to new technologies, changes in the work organization on which effective training depends are likely to be major. But whether small or large, it is essential that these changes be planned to dovetail with the participant's return after training. If the required changes are likely to take some time, e.g., modification of buildings, acquisition of new equipment, or protracted negotiations within or outside the organization, either training should be delayed or these realities built into the participants' expectations.

Perhaps the main objective of organizational action is to ensure that participants' expectations are realistic in terms of the training they will receive and its potential application afterwards. Organizations can secure necessary information, put the participants in direct touch with the institution, and encourage contact between them and others in their organization or locality who have participated earlier in similar training. The minimum condition is simply some preparatory time; this is mentioned because participants do sometimes arrive for training having first heard about the training program and their going to it by telegram the previous day. Organizations can also involve participants in preparations for the changes to be facilitated by their training, or at least acquaint them with them.

2. Training: Removing Preoccupations and Communicating Interest

The second phase, the participants' major new experience, is wide open to neglect by organizations. Having sent them for training, they may turn their attention elsewhere. The participants are forgotten until the time of their return approaches. If the training is residential, the participants' physical absence makes this neglect particularly easy. But even when they participate in an evening course or some other series of training events, attention to their progress during training is often negligible. Organizations, it would seem, are interested only in some neat imaginary package labeled 'end result' of training and assume its making as wholly the responsibility of participants and training institutions.

This assumption is totally false. Participants in training will give better attention to the program if assured that their families and personal affairs will be safeguarded during their absence. Organizations should at least ensure that no distracting preoccupations occupy participants during training or bedevil their anticipation of its outcome. Organizational contact during training can go beyond this minimum to even sustain interest and positive anticipation, which help participants to learn. Lack of contact may communicate just the opposite, disinterest or even opposition. "No action" is also an action, that is, it has consequences. The context is very important. Excessive contracts may communicate a mechanical rather than genuine interest, or pressuring participants to verbalize what they have learned as a check on whether they are working hard.

In some way or other, whether the participants like it or not, work organizations contribute something important at various phases of the training process. The only questions are, first, at whom is the contribution aimed and, second, is it effective.

3. Posttraining: Support and Organizational Adjustments

A participant is back from training and needs to be encouraged to use the useful things he has learned. It may help to allow him time to "settle in again." Explicitly so, otherwise he will take the time surreptitiously and feel guilty about it. The opposite, finding a desk overloaded with a backlog of work, for example, is also poor psychology. It signals that he is indispensable, a signal to him, of course, not to the organization. But piled–up work can also be a negative signal, implying that he should jump right back into the same old rut and that people were probably put out by his absence. Facilities for discussing his training experience with colleagues signal that the organization expects him to use his training and also expects others to collaborate with him.

The principle is surely clear. Work organizations sponsor training with definite expectations of what participants are to do upon their return, knowing what they need in order to do it, and aware of the effects of all this on their colleagues. The predictions and related adjustments become more accurate as organizations maintain contact with the trainees during training, assessing their progress and what they anticipate on their return, and make other preparations necessary for instituting changes. Thus all the changes requisite for participants to use their training have been effected.

Thoughtfulness and application to such an extent involve an organization in considerable trouble and cost. It is worth establishing carefully what is worth doing, remembering the investment training represents. Organizations usually find the expenses of training high, both in direct costs and work loss while the trainees are away. Training a young executive earning $2,000 a month in a three-month residential course costing $4,500 plus hotel means a direct expenditure of about $12,000–$14,000 plus travel. Other costs incurred by an organization in making requisite preparations for impending changes may also be substantial. The organization has to decide how to benefit best from this total expenditure. It will usually find that the additional outlay to ensure the returning participant's utilization of training is wholly worthwhile.

PART II

The Training Process in Action

Chapter 5

Establishing Objectives and Preparing the Partners

Men wanted. Low wages. Bitter cold. Long months of darkness. Under constant danger. Safe return doubtful. Honour and recognition if successful.

—This advertisement in a London newspaper for a polar expedition in 1941 brought 5,000 applications.

At any time in history, in order to lose one's identity, one must first have one....Thus, strange as it may seem, it takes a well–established identity to tolerate radical change.

—ERIK ERIKSON

One does not learn anything that one does not love.

—GERMAN PROVERB

THE PRETRAINING stage of training starts in the field, on the job. That is where the needs for new skills arise, where they can be examined in relation to the total change to be achieved, and where detailed training plans can be worked out. These plans then guide the selection of individuals for particular kinds of training. The question of who initiates this sequence requires discussion, but there can be no doubt that very close collaboration between the training system and the work organization is essential.

How does this close collaboration come about? The first answer to this question must be tangential: it usually does not. The effectiveness of training is left largely to chance. Trainers assume they know the training needs of the participants, presumably from past experiences and appreciation of currently required developments. They also assume that work organizations have worked out their particular training needs and may reasonably expect that sending some staff members to the course will effect the changes desired. In turn, organizations assume that the trainers they have chosen understand the needs of the participants and their organizations and that the course indeed will meet these. In short, organizations assume that training systems know their business—an assumption prevalent in most organizations today. Where training is to precede the launching of new activities and programs for which organizations are to be formed or have been newly established, the connection between organizational needs and training is even more tenuous.

No production plan would be launched on a factory floor, no product on the market, based on such unproven assumptions. That training is prepared and offered on this shaky foundation, not just once but repeatedly, suggests that those involved approach training with a mixture of motives. They prefer to carry on somehow, at low levels of effectiveness if need be, rather than examine these motives closely. This is a state of collusion, not collaboration. Collaboration springs, first and foremost, from clearer motives.

ORGANIZATIONAL COLLABORATION THROUGH CLARIFYING NEEDS

Demands for training arise most naturally and obviously when organizations expand rapidly, or when altogether new services are to be introduced.

> For example, Indonesia's National Health Plan provides for a four- to fivefold expansion of health manpower, from about 150,000 in 1983 to above 600,000 in 2000. More than one-tenth of the new positions, i.e., above 60,000 will be supervisory and managerial. Programs to upgrade the cohort of administrators already in service, to induct new recruits, and to provide a minimum of refresher training have been calculated in program weeks and training staff requirements for each year of the fourth plan (1984–89).

> Similarly, in thirty years the State Bank of India increased the number of its branches from 300 in 1950 to over 6,000 in 1983. As the Bank's policy is to recruit branch managers only from inside the organization, the need for preparing an additional 5,700 (plus replacements) was predicted. Training had to bridge the gap between competencies acquired through several years' experience with the Bank and those required for the new role.

Extrapolations of numerical requirements look simple and concrete. Actually, they reveal nothing about training needs except that they are extensive and very urgent. If training is to affect action—and that is what we mean by the word here—then training plans must take into account what improvement or new action should result from training, and the specifications by which these changes can be achieved with reasonable assurance.

This definition of "real" training is often ignored because motives for training differ. Some organizers merely want a certain number of staff "in position" by a certain date, regardless of their effectiveness in those positions. For these organizers training, any training, constitutes action, and action per se safeguards the new program against accusations of delay. "Real" training, they maintain, can come later. Others see training as the means for enhancement of performance through multiplication of personnel. If one person cannot perform at the level desired, let there be two. The training plans for some rural extension personnel in India seem to exemplify this type of orientation, as do programs of weekend training camps for half a million village leaders. Still others visualize training as a massive activity that does not encroach on scarce material resources, or an activity that defies early challenge. Surely, whatever remains to be detailed, training is an absolute good. Moreover, adequate evaluation of it is difficult. Yet others understand training primarily as a means for taming new recruits who are eager for changes and thus threaten to make life difficult for their seniors, or for dealing with "problem" staff in general. Finally, others wish only to have the organization's name appear on the roster of participants for the sake of publicity, as a means of enhancing the organization's status.

The motives for promoting training have certainly not been exhausted in the foregoing paragraph. But we feel that the list suffices to make our point clear: the motives for training are not at all simple and more likely than not are quite mixed. The motives listed above are reactions to external and personal pressures of various kinds which people hope to allay through training.

Besides the expansion and replacement of personnel, needs for training arise from two sources. One is the changing nature of jobs and changes consequently required in the internal functioning of the organization. The other source is imbalances and misunderstandings which lower the organization's standards of operation.

The needs for change, and therefore training, originating in external sources are usually easier to identify and to dramatize than those that arise from internal discrepancies. A faster machine or a more economical manufacturing process, an important restriction or a new tax, a liberalization of credit for purchasing the kinds of products the organization makes, or the launching of a country-wide new extension service—all these obviously demand a response from both the work organization and the training system. The organization may adopt a new process, step up its rate of expansion, or shift to new lines of products and services. The system can publicize such external developments and the various possibilities and implications for taking part in them. Collaboration between them may be particularly useful when significant external developments and needs are foreseen and their magnitude and implications forecast. The communications of such facts and estimates may anticipate pressures on organizations toward change and serve to initiate training in good time.

A study and communication of needs for change that arise from sources within an organization can similarly anticipate pressure in advance of the event. But it is difficult for an organization to do this alone. The difficulty arises partly from people's hesitation to look for such information. Trainers and consultants can help in resolving this difficulty. Box 5.1 summarizes the results of an employee survey to feed back to an organization some facts about itself. The feedback was the beginning of a management development program which focused directly on the problems highlighted by the survey. The results of this study suggest that the creative use of new information for conferences and meetings at all levels of a departmental organization may be one of the best and most dynamic avenues to management development and organizational growth.

Box 5.1

MOTIVATIONAL VALUE OF FEEDBACK TO THE ORGANIZATION

H. BAUMGARTEL

An experimental study was carried out in the accounting division of an electric light and power company. Six departments took part. They employed 60 managerial and supervisory personnel and 640 other personnel. The results of an attitude questionnaire were written up in a brochure. A copy was given to everyone. In the four experimental departments this communication was followed by a program of discussions and meetings. The results were considered and implications for action sorted out. No feedback program was organized for the other departments. The questionnaire was then administered again.

A comparison of the results showed that the experimental departments showed "statistically significant positive changes in the majority of items. To mention only the most important differences...non-supervisory employees expressed more interest in their work, felt their work was more important" and had a better image of their supervisors. They also "felt that their group was better at getting the job done, that they were freer to take job problems to their supervisors, that their supervisors better understood their point of view, that their supervisors got along better with each other, and that they understood better how their supervisors saw things."

The results of this experimental study lend support to the idea that an intensive, group discussion procedure for utilizing the results of an employee questionnaire survey can be an effective tool for introducing change in a business organization. It may be that the effectiveness of this method, in comparison to traditional training courses, is that *it deals with*

Box 5.1 (Continued)

the system of human relationships as a whole (superior and subordinate can change together) and that *it deals with managers, supervisors, and employees in the context of their own jobs, their own problems, and their own work relationships.*

We have speculated that the following conditions are essential for such a feedback program to be effective in any organization. There is reason to believe that the same principles apply in the use of sales and production information as well as with data concerning human factors. This information must be about the organization itself—often research findings from other companies do not convince the present management. The information must be quantitative and objective—personal opinions and impressions are often distorted; there must be some external point of reference. The information must have some stimulating quality by being:

— new information—a good cost accounting system provides new data on departmental costs.

— information contrary to common belief—several studies, for example, have shown that older workers produce more than younger workers.

— information about things not ordinarily discussed—how many times do personal feelings about the boss ever get talked out in staff meetings?

The information must provide direction for, or alternative ways of achieving, positive changes—just knowing that there is high turnover and low "morale" in department *X* isn't enough; one needs to know what factors create the problem.

SOURCE: Howard Baumgartel, "Using Employee Questionnaire Results for Improving Organizations," *Kansas Business Review,* Vol. XXII (1959), pp. 2-6

The first function for trainers in the pretraining phase, therefore, is to highlight the needs for change that arise from both internal and external sources and to let this knowledge impinge on the work organization. They can persist in this function through whatever clarifications and vigor may be needed to galvanize the organization into purposeful action. Certainly they would fail in this alerting function if they soft-pedaled the implications of any failure by organizations to meet actual and predictable training needs.

Four Degrees and Means of Collaboration

Trainers and consultants can proceed in a variety of ways. The choice depends on the likely scale of the training program in an organization, the extent of change an organization is capable of tolerating at any time, and also on the system's resources for the work of clarification. Experience clearly favors very close collaboration between training system and work organization. Clarifying the organization's training needs calls for very skillful and hardheaded work by the system. While providing maximum assistance, it must leave no room for doubt that the responsibility for action or the implications of inaction or inadequate action firmly rest with the organization. If the system can convey this important understanding consistently, through the attitudes of its staff as well as through their approaches and actions, it will save many heartaches later.

Going from the simplest and most distant relationship to the most sophisticated and closest collaboration, we can distinguish four possibilities open to the system for matching its training goals with the needs of the work organization. The time required usually lengthens as the process becomes more thorough and collaboration closer.

1. *Course announcement.* As the barest minimum requirement, just a gesture towards collaboration, the system can publicize its own training goals and the training strategies it prefers and is competent to use. This, at least, puts the deci-sion to apply for training up to "the other," be it an individual or an organization, and is to that extent better than direct "recruitment" of people for training. The next step marks the first real collaboration. This is the system's requirement that the work organization, the system's statement of goals and the organization's commitment, can be reflected in the way the system announces a training program.

a. Statement of the system's training goals. When the system announces a program in this manner, organizations can promote candidates for the program through some understanding of what the program is attempting to achieve. A full statement can indicate some of the implications of the program also, and organizations can take these into account in reaching their decision. Here is an example of such a statement:

> The *X* Institute was founded in 1957 to develop training, research and consulting services which may help industrial organizations to respond effectively to the many new demands of national independence, modern technologies, and economic policies. Represented on the Governing Council of the Institute are (a list)...
>
> The *Y* program is for executives between thirty and forty years old who, because they belong to the owning family, have been promoted to top decision-making positions at a young age. It aims in the first place at acquainting them with modern management techniques in the fields of... so that they can better use data for their decision. More than that, it aims at helping them examine the process by which decisions are reached in the company and to practice more effective ways of contributing to this process.

After a brief description of the training methods to be used, the announcement adds something to the effect that the system's consulting wing can consider requests for posttraining services in the organization.

b. Requiring organizational commitment. Requiring applications to come with the explicit backing of the work organization ensures that the organization is informed, prepared to grant any necessary leave, and is willing to face at least some implications of training. The commitment is greater if the system requires the candidate's organization to pay the training fees and perhaps also the candidate's salary during training.

Thus the best course announcements clarify the choice for the organization and its general implications. They are a definite improvement over simple soliciting. But the procedure they initiate is still one way, a take-it-or-leave-it proposition.

2. *Meetings with senior officers.* Some systems make it a practice, before launching a new program, to meet with senior officers in the organizations they intend to serve. The occasions may range from informal discussions with individuals to formal sessions and seminars with officers from several organizations at one time.

The advancement here, from the first to the second degree of collaboration, is that planning of training has become a two-way process. It also clearly signals the system's interest in working closely with those organizations whose needs it expects to meet. Both these actions of the system serve as eye-openers for an organization's officers. The system raises for their consideration general developments which either already call for organizational attention or are about to do so. It may present estimates of the likely implications of these developments for organizational changes and training needs. To have discussions on this at high levels and to involve executives and policy makers from several work organizations, underscores the important function training serves in facilitating change, and also makes clear that all organizations have training needs, including the best. High-level participation in a formal meeting can also represent a substantial organizational commitment to careful consideration and ensuing action, whereas even a series of informal talks with individuals may leave the extent of organizational commitment in doubt.

Such meetings and seminars hold a temptation that has drawn some training systems into grievous errors. Under the guise of consulting with senior officers and working out, together with them, the kind of training program to be attempted with their subordinates or colleagues, some systems have tried surreptitiously to convert the occasion into a training program for senior officers. This temptation is greatest when the training needs appear both obvious and urgent to the training system. Its assessment may or may not be correct. That is not the issue. Either way, the conversion of a meeting from joint exploration of needs to another purpose is not lost on senior officers. However well intended it induces resentment and destroys trust just when needed most. If the program goes ahead at all, memories of this deception by the system may hold the organization back from closer collaboration for a long time to come.

In one new system, which started as a quasi-staff college for an official extension service, repeated confusion of this kind led to a marked estrangement between the organization and the system. The resentment became so great that the organization rejected every institutional proposal irrespective of merit, "just to put the institute in its place."

If senior officers are to be trained, then this should be the topic of discussion and sanctioned. Failures here do not signify that senior officers have nothing to learn or that they are not prepared to learn after a genuine discussion of needs. It merely means that they refuse to be belittled, a response that surely commands respect.

3. *Homework for the work organization.* As the next step toward closer collaboration the training system can require detailed information about changes in jobs for which the organization wishes to prepare itself through training. If the requirements are general and call for a series of programs, the system can help the organization work out a comprehensive training plan spread out in time.

> a. Detailed analysis of current and new job requirements. Most job analyses now in use are inadequate even as descriptions of current activities. They specify a series of required qualifications in subject matter knowledge and technical skill, and that is all. To serve as a basis for training designs, job analyses must go beyond these simple lists and describe how a job is to be actually performed, under what physical conditions and time pressures, and with what access to colleagues, superiors, and additional resources. In short, job analyses should be operational. This is true for both new jobs and existing ones. For new jobs an operational analysis is based on detailed forecasts, that is the only difference; the projected analysis can be revised later in the light of actual experience.
>
> The most useful and economical analyses focus on the crucial requirements of the job, that is, requirements that make the difference between effective and ineffective performance. For existing jobs, comparing in detail the behavior of an effective and an ineffective performer can pinpoint these crucial requirements. Critical incident techniques provide for descriptions of both effective and ineffective behavior on the job, usually in checklist form.
>
> The checklist of determining training needs used by the U.S. Government for the job of administrative officer in the federal service is given in exhibit 5.1. The next higher officer, who supervises administrative officers, is asked to record his or her observations on this form and to add whatever explanatory notes are necessary. The instructions are to:

Isolate and list each individual duty of position.

Group related duties into a classified list.

Establish the nature of responsibility for each duty.

Estimate frequency, importance, and difficulty of each.

Evaluate the employee's performance on each.

Check as training needs any deficiencies that are significant and which can be corrected by training.[1]

An operational job description covers at least four kinds of specifications: knowledge and skill content, relationships involved, time spans, and settings and roles. Exhibit 5.2 shows a list of questions designed to elicit the necessary information for the job of manager of a cooperative farm. This job was new and for an organization yet to be developed.

When technological or other developments call for changes in existing jobs and for possible retraining, it can be very useful to compare what various people expect an incumbent of a job to accomplish. Perceptions of an immediate superior, of colleagues, and of subordinates are commonly at variance, and all may differ again from the way an incumbent sees the job. Such discrepancies make for difficulties in the organization. Moreover, an adequate training design can hardly be worked out till the perceptions of those involved are congruent in all important respects. Residual differences can be earmarked for checking later against experience. Awareness of residual differences may, meanwhile, enhance motivation for training and action.

Exhibit 5.1

CHECKLIST FOR DETERMINING TRAINING NEEDS

Nature of Responsibility	*Duty*	*Frequency Importance Difficulty F* I* D**	*Performance*	*Check if Training Needed*
	Personnel Management-Actions			
PSCA	Preparing job specifications			
PSCA	Interviewing applicants			
PSCA	Arranging appointments of personnel			
PSCA	Etc.			
	Fixed Management—General			
PSCA	Preparing payrolls and vouchers			
PSCA	Issuing travel orders			
PSCA	Awarding contracts			
PSCA	Etc.			
	Office Management—Space			
PSCA	Negotiating space lease or rental			
PSCA	Assigning office space			
PSCA	Planning equipment installation			
PSCA	Etc			

[1] *Assessing and Reporting Training Needs and Progress,* U.S. Civil Service Commission, Personnel Methods Series No. 3 (1956), p. 25.

Exhibit 5.1 (Continued)

Nature of Res-ponsi-bility	*Duty*	*Frequency Importance Difficulty F* I* D**	*Perfor-mance°*	*Check if Training Needed*
	Policy			
PSCA	Composing policy statements			
PSCA	Interpreting policies			
PSCA	Etc.			

No./Circle P,S,C, or A:
P = Perform (by self)
S = Supervise (immediate)
C = Control (through others)
A = Advice

* Use 1,2, or 3
1 = High degree
2 = Average
3 = Low

°Use+,/, —, or NA:
\+ = Outstanding
/ = Adequate
— = Weak
NA = Not applicable

SOURCE: *Assessing and Reporting Training Needs and Progress,* U.S. Civil Service Commission, Personnel Methods Series No. 3 (1956) p. 25

b. Meshing organizational plans for change with training strategies and methods. New job requirements are addressed by the training strategies and methods the system selects and the latter, in turn, must fit into the organization's plans and ways of working. The second requirement needs to be checked and ensured no less than the first. Exhibit 5.3 sets out a five-step model for checking the readiness of an organization for one kind of training strategy and method, laboratory training in this instance.

A similar procedure can establish in advance of training what preparations the work organization proposes to make for the return of newly trained participants and for using their new competence. If participants' colleagues are involved in the change, how are they to be prepared? Through what kind of training? How are their superiors to be prepared, and service staff involved in their activities?

Exhibit 5.2

COOPERATIVE FARM MANAGER: SOME QUESTIONS ABOUT THE JOB AND TRAINING

1. *Technical Knowledge.* How much does the manager have to know about:
   a) Poultry
      Dairy
      Crops
      Soils
      Other farm subjects

   b) The overall functions of:
      Personnel hiring
      Incentive payments
      Job planning and supervision

c) Finance:
    Budgeting by major items
    Costing by major items to guide production choices
    Accounting

d) Purchasing supplies

e) Marketing:
    Finding customers
    Packing and dispatch
    Collecting payments

f) Equipment repair:
    Pumps
    Electrical
    Vehicles
    Buildings

2. *Relationships*. What are they? With whom? How often? How close? For example:

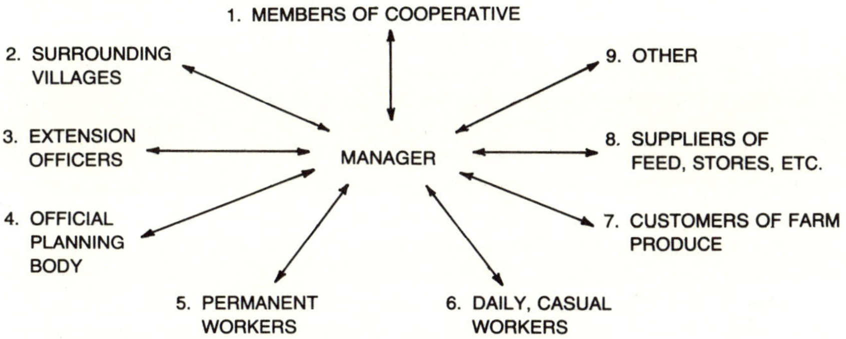

3. *Time*. To what extent is the manager responsible for:
   a) Maintenance of buildings and equipment
      Soil—compost, systematic soil improvement
      Livestock—upgrading, etc.

   b) Making farm plan, for example:
      Cropping patterns
      Market and cost estimates
      Investment
      Staff—for example, training

   c) Own career—a life's job? a step toward?

4. *Settings* in which different aspects of the work is done and roles, for example:
      Meets people in groups—villages, Board?
      Attendant meetings away from farm? Leads meetings?
      How many other people live on the farm?

Through hardheadedly following this line of considerations, the organization may find that it needs a series of different training events for various staff. From this core of recognition plus basic information a training plan can be developed.

> Some organizations collaborating with the National Training Laboratories have worked out a three-step strategy of laboratory training whereby key officers develop required skills in human relations, collegiate collaboration, and organization. The first laboratory is only for top officials from various organizations, and is therefore labeled "stranger laboratory." The second laboratory is for key officials from several units within the same organization, and has been named "cousin laboratory." Finally, the "family laboratory" brings together personnel who normally work together.

4. *Full collaboration*. There is a final advanced relationship in which the training system and the work organization are in full collaboration, as full-fledged, played-in partners in an enterprise of importance to both of them. Questions of initiative and responsibility are no longer topical; they have been sorted out long ago. Close collaboration like this is characterized by general sureness of method and fruitfulness of outcome. As new questions arise, they are considered and dealt with smoothly and efficiently.

It is useful to distinguish collaboration between a training system and fully operating work organizations from collaboration between a system and a new organization that it is helping to develop.

> a. Collaboration with fully operating organizations. It is useful to distinguish further large organizations that only rarely need specialized outside help to round off their internal programs from organizations whose needs are broader and less well-defined.

> Large work organizations generally work out their own training needs and plans. They have full-time staff development and training departments for this purpose. These departments also carry out routine training programs within the organization. Large organizations use outside training systems for two purposes: specialized training for numbers too small to warrant an internal program; and

Exhibit 5.3

FIVE-STEP MODEL FOR DIAGNOSING STATE OF TARGET SYSTEM

1. Are laboratory training change goals appropriate to the target system?	If not, stop and reconsider appropriateness of laboratory training.
If yes, then:	
2. Is the cultural state of the target system prepared for the laboratory?	If not, stop and examine areas where more preparation is needed or where value conflicts should be reduced.

a) Degree and type of value conflict?

b) Legitimacy of interpersonal phenomena?

c) Degree, range, intensity, resolution of conflict?

d) Concepts of control, authority?

e) Interdependence of target system?

f) Relationship of trust and confidence between change agent and target system?

If yes, then:

3. Are key people involved and committed?	If not, stop and examine ways to develop more commitment to program.
4. Are members of the target adequately prepared and oriented to laboratory training?	If not, stop and examine ways to develop more commitment to program.
If yes, then:	
5. Is voluntarism (regarding participation) insured?	If not, stop and examine attitudes toward laboratory training: Why people go or do not want to go to laboratories. After diagnosis, attempt to accurately indicate the place of laboratory training in career development.

SOURCE: Edgar Schein and Warren Bennis, *Personal and Organizational Development through Group Methods* (New York: John Wiley & Sons, Inc., 1965) p. 216.

personal development for middle and senior executives, in which contact with executives from other organizations holds major advantages. But large organizations are also increasingly drawing on outside consultants to ensure freshness of view and to subject internal programs to periodic intensive review.

Medium and small organizations need far more assistance from outside resources. They may ask for help in working out adequate job analyses and overall training plans; in designing adequate procedures for selecting and preparing candidates for particular training programs and for receiving them back into the organization can range from provision by the system of simple devices for use by the organization, for example, survey questionnaires and selection tests, to training as a wholly joint project that pervades the entire organization. Joint work on a specific training program can become the starting point and means of readying the organization as a whole for widespread and far reaching development.

The supervisory training project launched in 1964 by ATIRA and four textile mills is an Indian example of this closest kind of collaboration. It involved intensive studies of the job supervisor, experimental job designs, new recruitment and selection procedures, and reviews of the management structure impinging on the supervisor's job. The mills financed the three-year project. ATIRA provided the research and training staff and undertook to train and retrain all supervisors working in these mills.

b. To establish new services. In rapidly developing countries, training often has to precede the development of a new service and the establishment of an operating organization. But contrary to prevailing practice, this does not mean the absence of collaboration; quite the reverse, in fact. This situation offers the system an opportunity to work closely with policy makers and headquarter officials from the outset. Later, when the required activities are studied in the field in order to design specific jobs, additional people and organizations can be involved in the new service: consumers, suppliers, local leaders, and others whose interested help will be needed. What the training system must guard against in helping to start a new activity is the reductive lure of dreaming up the job and the training needs at desks or at meetings of its own staff.

The Institute of Rural Health and Family Planning at Gandhigram, Madurai District, offers an example of close collaboration in establishing a new service. To prepare itself for training various kinds of family-planning workers, the Institute first prepared a preliminary set of job functions based on the outline of the National Family Planning Program. It then placed its own staff members at block and village levels to perform these job functions. While developing this work they recorded their activities in detail, including time spent, contacts made, and problems encountered in the course of performing the various functions. On the basis of regular analyses of these diaries and discussions among the staff, the job functions and methods of work were modified. This process continued until the job designs were confirmed in practice. The operational job description then became the basis for a training design for family-planning workers. The blocks in which the job designs had been established were the field in which participants in the training programs practiced their new skills.

The four degrees and means of collaboration between the training system and the work organization are summarized in exhibit 5.4.

The primary aim of the training system in all its dealings with the work organization during the pretraining stage is to ensure that the organization develops realistic training goals and that these goals match reasonably closely with those the training institution can offer. The goals become realistic since they take two sets of factors into account. On the one hand, changing job requirements and the implications these change will have for the rest of the organization are considered. On the other hand are the time and other training specifications assessed by the system as necessary to meet the training needs, and within the limits of its own resources. As these mesh, a realistic program is established.

Exhibit 5.4

COLLABORATION FOR ESTABLISHING TRAINING NEEDS

		The System	*In order to*	*By means of*	*Limits*
1.	(a)	States training course	Clarify issues for organization's decisions	Brochure/course announcement	One-way; no modification through organization's response
	(b)	Requires applications to come through organization; organization to pay fees/salary	Increase organization's commitment to training goals	Brochure/course announcement	One-way; no modification through organization's response
2.		Discussions with senior officers	Signal interest in collaboration and respect for senior staff	Meetings and seminars	Relation to needs indirect and uncertain
3.	(a)	Requires detailed job analyses	Focus organization on operational needs	Course announcement	Organization's ability and inclination
	(b)	Requires organization's plans for change	Focus organization on complete program of change	Course announcement	Organization's ability and inclinations
4.	(a)	Collaborates with existing organization.	Ensure matching training goals and motivation for change	Extended face-to-face contact	Organization's ability and inclination plus resources
	(b)	Collaborates to establish new services	Involve related organizations	Extended field work	Organization's ability and inclination

TWO DILEMMAS OF DEVELOPMENT

Two final points: First, the question of who in the organization should be involved in the exploration of training needs and the ramifications of meeting them can be very important to the effectiveness of training. Logic does not resolve it. A policy decision by the board of directors to set up training opportunities for young professional staff, for instance, may have sound logic to commend it: younger staff need not break through a crust of outdated experience and they have the longest careers in which to use this training. Conflicts such as these are particularly common during periods of rapid development. Rapid development means that senior over the years is really superior to that of their younger colleagues. Their knowledge of technical subjects, for instance, may be outdated and their experience of years ago no longer relevant. Administrative power may be all they have left. Now even this last bastion of superiority is threatened by a policy decision to provide training for junior staff. The threat is greater if the decision is taken without genuine concurrence from the senior staff. "Genuine" concurrence is not easily surmised since, after all, how can they openly object to training for the promising younger staff? Training for themselves would also pose a threat. Purportedly, they are already proficient. Thus, a real dilemma develops.

The second point is this: such dilemmas, common to the process of development, are not resolved by pretending they do not exist, or presuming that they are unimportant to the people caught in them. Neither does recognition eliminate them; however, it does ensure that the dilemmas will at least be taken into account in any decision made, which appeases somewhat the people affected by them. Otherwise, another problem tops the original dilemma—people feel belittled and brushed aside.

> The multiplication of branches of the State Bank of India may serve to illustrate the inevitable dilemmas and problems arising from them. One implication in recruiting 1,000 branch managers from within the Bank is that most new managers are much younger than other managers. On the operative side this runs counter to the popular image of the banker as "guide, philosopher, and friend"—for which a few gray hairs might be more appropriate. Internally, problems are bound to arise from the wide range of ages represented in posts of equal grade. Are older colleagues or superiors willing to trust the decisions of managers who are far less experienced than they? Will they provide them easier access to wise counsel to offset their inexperience? Or will the seniors decide instead to rein in younger colleagues by taking decisions higher up? If the latter should happen, how can young managers carry authority with their own staffs, many also older than they, knowing that their actions are tightly circumscribed? To what extent does the Bank wish to encourage branch managers to show initiative and experiment?

Openly facing the dilemmas and implications of development is not only necessary for smoothing the paths of change, but for arriving at job designs which not only exist on paper but can be carried out in practice.

Job designs that allow for prevailing dilemmas can offer an excellent basis for training and for the institution's internal preparation for it. This approach must be stressed over and over again. There is no other. Training is a service function. If a young bank manager needs to learn decision making, training can help her acquire this competence. If, on the other hand, she has to refer matters to superiors, or cannot be sure of support from that quarter, training will show her how to stall more gracefully. Which is to be the objective of training is a work organization's decision; likewise, the resolution of other dilemmas organizations face in development. Their resolution cannot be left to the training institution. Lack of clarity about the job is bound to lead to lack of training. The obverse, that clarity about the job leads to appropriate training, is not, unfortunately, automatically true. Otherwise, this book could stop right here. Job clarity, in all its implications, is just a prerequisite to sound training.

CLARIFYING INDIVIDUAL MOTIVATION FOR TRAINING

Training needs are, first and foremost, organizational needs. As pressures for change impinge on an organization, from outside or inside, it responds—through expansion, adoption of new technologies, development of new functions and reorganization of existing ones, and through several other options. Many of these organizational responses call for training. So far we have not concerned ourselves with the question of "who" in particular, i.e., which people need to be trained, how they are selected, and how they are prepared for training. This is the second dimension, the personal one.

The training needs that an organization has hammered out in response to various pressures for change become in turn the pressures on individuals to change. To deal effectively with impending new jobs and situations, individuals find that they need new knowledge, understanding, and skills. What they do not already possess they need to acquire, through training.

Individuals respond to the demand for change usually in one of three ways: they may decide to change, if necessary with the help of training. Or they may decide not to change themselves, but take up another job by requesting a transfer within the organization or by going elsewhere. And finally, they may decide to change neither themselves nor their job in the hope that the need for change will pass them by, either fortuitously or by their active resistance to it. So much for individual options. The fact remains that organizational change depends for cost, speed, and smoothness on people who decide to change themselves, that is, to learn, and where required, to undergo training.

For those people directly engaged in hammering out training needs, the personal aspect of change is vividly clear by the time they have completed that initial task. Somehow—working out training needs may be the most effective and economical way—all those affected by the proposed change need to gain this personal awareness because their motivation toward training is primarily shaped by the meaning they attach to it. If they are aware that the need for training arises out of changing jobs and situations, training will at least seem reasonable. They may see the opportunity for it as recognition by the organization that they have further capabilities to develop. They may feel elated at being chosen—their interpretation—to join the core of people qualified to spearhead new developments. They may see it as a signal that they are heading for promotion. On the contrary, if they see no need for training for themselves, or at least for this particular training, they may view the training opportunity as a veiled criticism of their current performance, that the organization is saying, "Improve, or else! This is your last chance!" Or they may see it as an indication that the organization considers them easiest "to spare," or wants them out of the way while changes are made in their department, or as a kind of vacation as reward for years of devoted work. Personal motives, too, come into the picture. Applicants may volunteer simply to have their name associated with a prestigious institution, to have a break, to escape a conflict-ridden situation, or for a variety of other reasons not directly related to a training course.

Motives of unpredictable direction and strength will tend to recede as the changes actually required in jobs and organizations become clear and insistent. Just as a training system would be remiss if it shielded a work organization from the full impact of required changes, so an organization would be culpable if it shielded individual staff members from the personal implications of impending changes. In both cases, the limit is only the tolerance of the recipient for a given challenge. With normal, healthy people, that limit is not readily overstepped. In our opinion, the question of how a potential participant in a training course perceives the opportunity is far more important than whether the participant or the organization takes the initiative in requesting it.

SEVEN SYSTEM FUNCTIONS WITH CANDIDATES FOR TRAINING

The system has a series of seven functions to perform for matching applicants and training requirements and for preparing the candidates accepted for the program.

1. Announcing the Program

The initial formal announcement of a training program ought to contain sufficient information to prompt candidates to apply. Typically, the announcement contains a general statement of the needs to which the training addresses itself (for example, export marketing), followed by more detailed training objectives: the categories of people for whom this particular program is meant (for example, age, experience, position); the training and principal methods to be used (for example, active participation, field-work); the duration, dates, location, and cost of the program; and the admission requirements and procedure. Some systems introduce the course faculty in their announcement.

2. Selecting Participants

If the organization's training needs are clear, and also the minimum qualification participants must have for a particular program, then motivation of an applicant is the most important unknown left. Understanding this is both the most important and the most difficult function of the selection procedure.

Does what an applicant needs accord with the needs this program sets out to meet? In part this is a specific question. If the applicant desires greater competence in certain mechanical and mathematical skills, a course in management just now appears unsuitable even though his organization is certain that managerial skill is what he needs and could use in furthering his career. At least some steps need to be taken by the organization to align the applicant's expectations with what the training course can offer.

Nothing mechanical or absolute is intended—or indeed possible—in suggesting careful procedures to align what participants want from training with what an institution can offer. The unforeseen consequences of training are often the most fruitful. What we want to stress here is the importance of two factors in a candidate's motivation.

The selection procedure—application forms, written tests, interviews, individual or group tasks—can be designed to elicit particular data on these two aspects of a candidate's motivation. In individual interviews, and in observing and listening to candidates working on a joint task, such as a case discussion, it is possible to note the nature and strength of feelings different candidates express, and to build a picture of what seems to concern each most. It is important that questions in written tests and applications elicit personal rather than generalized data. The general question so commonly used, what the candidate intends to use this training for, only yields stereotyped, safe answers. Asking a candidate to pinpoint a situation in her recent experience in which she thinks this particular training would have been useful, solicits a personalized answer.

The following series of three questions can yield data useful for selecting a candidate for training.

i. Describe a recent situation in which you were involved in which you would have liked to use the training offered in this program. What happened? What did you do? What left you dissatisfied?

ii. List the new technical and other skills you would like to command for dealing with a similar situation in the future.

iii. Would you be free to use these skills in the situation you have described or would other changes also be required, including changes beyond your direct responsibility in your organization? If other changes were required, list the people who would have to make them. What additional competencies would you need to influence them to this purpose?

3. Guarding against Distracting Preoccupations

Let us assume that the selection procedure has shown a candidate to be suitable for the course. He has the necessary minimum qualifications, experience, and also sufficient motivation. The next step is to offer him the opportunity. At this stage it is necessary to ensure that no foreseeable circumstances will disturb the applicant's training.

Particularly if the program is away from home and family and of several month's duration, experience has shown that many applicants need protection from distracting preoccupations. They need assurances, for example, that their families can manage without them for that length of time and that they have access to any funds and help they may need.

In Indonesia it is common for civil servants in professional positions to supplement their limited salaries with regular earnings from private practice and other work; supplementing any stipends during training and their reliable payment to participants' families therefore assume great importance. In India family holidays and other traditional events are often more difficult to handle. Participants' absence from home on these occasions may represent a major break with the past and one that seems, especially to the older generation, out of proportion to the value of a few days' training.

The training institution should be quite explicit in advance about the standards it will enforce on these occasions. It is up to selected applicants and their organizations to decide then whether they can join the course on these conditions or whether, even at this early stage, they had better postpone participation to another time. It is also worth an organization's while to free participants from worries such as these.

4. Aligning Expectations

Once selections have been made, and the candidates have agreed, additional information can usefully flow both ways. The system can send out the list of participants. More important for aligning expectations may be the provision of lists of people who participated in similar training programs earlier and can answer questions regarding it, the institution and its staff, and such pedestrian concerns as what to pack. This sort of preliminary exploration may help keep candidates minds open both with respect to the particular problems the program can help them resolve and the kinds of experiences they may anticipate. One expectation to communicate about training is that expectations, too, may change during the course of it.

Communications from the training institution aim to prepare candidates for an experience of real relevance and give them assurance of the system's intention to ensure this. For example, during the six weeks between the selection of candidates and the beginning of a program, SIET Institute sent out three batches of information and questions.

The first batch: The brief acceptance letter included three information sheets: one pertained to administrative matters such as details of hotel bookings, procedure for paying hotel bills, what to bring in the way of clothes, bedding, etc., travel plans and arrival times, and the procedure for paying fees. The second sheet described the first part of the program and outlined the second half. The third sheet was a questionnaire asked three questions:

a. In which training areas have you chosen concentrate your attention at the workshop and in your preparation for it?

b. What kinds of information do you have available about the areas in which you want to concentrate? For example, immediate experience and current training information, other experiences elsewhere, reports.

c. What additional information would you like other participants to bring if possible?

The second batch, twelve days later: A cover letter contained a list of topics and suggestions received to this date for the second part of the program and promised a further list one week later. It also included a provisional list of participants.

The third batch, eight days later: This consisted of an additional list of topics and the confirmed list of participants.

5. Requiring Candidates to do Homework

To think that the training period can be enhanced by requiring participants to do some systematic preparation before they arrive is pleasant but unrealistic. Experience suggests that it is worth asking only for a little and that, too, of a particular type, such as assembling some data for use during training or deciding on project proposals which, after approval by the trainers, participants, can immediately implement upon return from training. Such requests are in line with the practical and personal orientation the institution wants training to have and the close association it desires to maintain with participants' work organizations.

The Indian Institute of Management, Ahmedabad, has used participant projects successfully in its programs for young executives. Its project proposal form, which is part of the procedure to be completed for selection, is presented as exhibit 5.5. Participants are asked to choose a project that they can complete in two months and has the approval of their organizations. The time span is determined by a second training event for the same group, scheduled about three months after completing the main four-week program. This one-week event consists of discussions of the completed projects with faculty.

Exhibit 5.5

PROPOSAL FOR MANAGERIAL PROJECT

Name:	Designation:
Organization:	Contact address:
Telephone No:	Telegram address:

Title of Project:
Background of Project:
Specific issues/problems involved:
Objectives in undertaking project:
Nature and sources of data to be collected:
Approaches to be used in collecting data:
Please check (X) against the following:
The above project can be completed in two months ☐
The above project has been approved by my sponsor ☐

SOURCE: Indian Institute of Management, Ahmedabad, Program for Young Executives, 1966.

To ask for more homework than this seems to be asking for trouble. First, it is not likely to be done. If the institution lets this pass without comment, doubts about the need for doing subsequent assignments arise. If the institution comments, it is likely to appear punitive. Second, participants heading for full-time training and a long absence will surely be preoccupied with handing over responsibilities and arranging their personal affairs. Pressed for time, they are likely to regard any request for homework in advance as an indication that the training institution is out of touch with the realities of their situation, and their expectations would suffer accordingly.

6. Increasing Individual Motivation for Training

The system can take two further interrelated steps to build up the applicants' readiness for training. One enhances their motivation beyond the minimum. The other involves them in planning the program. Any gain on these scores is likely to be reflected in their quick progress immediately after the program starts. A quick start becomes doubly valuable if it sets the pace and tone for the whole program. These additional steps, therefore, deserve the institution's careful attention, though they are less familiar. They can be organized separately in advance or at the very start of the training program itself.

To enhance individual motivation for training, the training system has three methods at its disposal. The first is part and parcel of what it communicates to applicants through all its contacts with them. If, as a result of these contacts, applicants feel confident that training foci are clear, that the system commands the resources to realize them, and moreover, shows perceptive concern for the people taking part in the program, they will surely look forward to the experience with increased interest. They will expect to work hard and to profit from the training program. Even the puniest procedural detail contributes to the process whereby applicants build up this important advance picture.

The other two methods aim specifically at increasing the applicants' motivation for training. One consists in collecting data about their present effectiveness on the job and sharing it with them. We have already discussed the feedback procedure for an organization as a whole (box 5.1). The personal purpose is similar and the procedure for it simpler.

> In the case of teachers, for instance, Ned Flanders[2] found that systematic observations by a colleague of a candidate's behavior in a session and sharing indications of his effectiveness with him subsequently greatly enhanced the candidate's motivation for training. By careful paring of colleagues and avoidance of evaluative comments, initial uncertainty and awkwardness with the procedure were greatly reduced. Only the collection and sharing of actual happenings were required. As a result the candidates saw weaknesses and possibilities for improvement, which they then decided to explore in training.

[2] "Teacher Influence: Pupil Attitude and Achievements" (mimeographed; Minneapolis: University of Minnesota, 1961).

The third method for enhancing motivation for training in advance of the program is more elaborate. It consists of organizing a short special program for this very purpose. Courses based on David McClelland's work on achievement motivation and short training laboratories are examples. In box 5.2 we have summarized McClelland's approach and presented his set of twelve propositions for enhancing people's motivation and the scheme through which he relates them.

Chapter 7 discusses training laboratories as a training method. Special courses for enhancing individual motivation for learning essentially nudge participants into a conscious scrutiny of their viewpoints, feelings, attitudes, and relationships with others and the world in which they live and work. While pondering this picture participants usually find aspects not to their liking. They look forward to improving them in the forthcoming training program.

7. Involving Participants in Planning the Program

The principles behind this step is familiar. The main problem is how to

Box 5.2

PROGRAM FOR INCREASING INDIVIDUAL MOTIVATION

David C. McClelland

Pilot attempts to develop Achievement (Motivation) have gradually led to the formulation of some theoretical notions of what motive acquisition involves and how it can be effectively promoted in adults. These notions have been summarized in the form of twelve propositions which are subject to research. The propositions are anchored in experiences with pilot courses, in supporting research findings from other studies, and in theory.

Proposition 1. The more reasons an individual has in advance to believe that he can, will, or should develop a motive, the more educational attempts designed to develop that motive are likely to succeed.

Proposition 2. The more an individual perceives that developing a motive is consistent with the demands of reality (and reason), the more educational attempts designed to develop that motive are likely to succeed.

Proposition 3. The more thoroughly an individual develops and clearly conceptualizes the associative network defining the motive, the more likely he is to develop the motive.

Proposition 4. The more an individual can link the newly developed network to related actions, the more the change in both thought and action is likely to occur and endure.

Proposition 5. The more an individual can link the newly conceptualized association-action complex (or motive) to events in his everyday life, the

Box 5.2 (Continued)

more likely the motive complex is to influence his thoughts and actions in situations outside the training experience.

Proposition 6. The more an individual can perceive and experience the newly conceptualized motive as an improvement in the self-image, the more the motive is likely to influence his future thoughts and actions.

Proposition 7. The more an individual can perceive and experience the newly conceptualized motive as an improvement on prevailing cultural values, the more the motive is likely to influence his future thoughts and actions.

Proposition 8. The more an individual commits himself to achieving concrete goals in life related to the newly-formed motive, the more the motive is likely to influence his future thoughts and actions.

Proposition 9. The more an individual keeps a record of his progress toward achieving goals to which he is committed, the more the newly-formed motive is likely to influence his future thoughts and actions.

Proposition 10. Changes in motives are more likely to occur in an interpersonal atmosphere in which the individual feels warmly but honestly supported and respected by others as a person capable of guiding and directing his own future behaviour.

Proposition 11. Changes in motives are more likely to occur the more the setting dramatizes the importance of self-study and lifts it out of the routine of everyday life.

Proposition 12. Changes in motives are more likely to occur and persist if the new motive is a sign of membership in a new reference group.

VARIABLES CONCEIVED AS ENTERING INTO THE MOTIVE CHANGE PROCESS

A *Input or independent variables*	*B* *Intervening variables*	*C* *Output or dependent variables*
1. Goal setting for person (PI, PII)	Arousal of associative network (salience)	Duration and/or extensiveness of changes in:
2. Acquisition of Achievement (Motivation) associative network (P2, P3, P4, P5)	Experiencing and labeling the associative network	1. Achievement (Motivation) associative network
3. Relating new network to superordinate networks Reality (P2) The self (P6) Cultural values (P7)	Variety of cues to which network is linked Interfering associations assimilated or bypassed by reproductive interference.	2. Related actions: use of feedback, moderate risk taking, etc. 3. Innovations (job improvements)
4. Personal goal setting (P8)		4. Use of time and money
5. Knowledge of progress (P3, P4, P9)		5. Entrepreneurial success as defined by nature of job held and its rewards
6. Personal warmth and support (P 10)	Positive effect associated with network	
7. Support of reference group (P11, P12)		

NOTE: PI, PII, etc., refer to the numbered propositions in the text.

Source: David C. McClelland, "Toward a Theory of Motive Acquisition" *American Psychologist,* Vol XX (1965), pp. 319-33.

put it to work. The aspect that usually makes for difficulties is the unspoken fear and distrust trainers and consultants have of participants: Will they ask for training they cannot provide? And will they lose control of the process and other system resources for which they are responsible? If consultation takes place at all, the system often restricts it to a participant's organization and to very general questions. If organizers consult with individual participants at all, quite often this is mere adherence to principle and constitutes an empty gesture better left unmade. If they are not ready to listen to answers, they ought not to ask questions. A useful principle is to involve participants in planning the program—or event—only to the extent that the training system is truly willing to take their views into account. Experience has shown us that even a small start in this direction will widen the area of willingness in time. It is a more promising starting point than the other extreme: running the entire gamut dictated by principle, with fear clutching one's heart. Ironically, the fears may become justified in the latter case.

Involving participants in analysing their jobs and the requirements of impending changes offers a useful start.

> The first days of SIET Institute's regular three-month courses consist of program consultations on the basis of job analyses and prospects. Much of the work is done in small groups composed of participants from similar organizations. They pinpoint the training needs they share. These groups are then brought together to report these needs to each other and to the faculty. The program also provides for detailed individual study of field reports from earlier courses. The reports indicate the directions and standards of training. By studying these reports, participants ascertain what needs particular study and practice in similar work to be done by them, and recommend these areas for inclusion in the program.

Participants may initially view these steps as gimmicks rather than genuine attempts at joint planning. Past experiences usually tell them that the organizers will not actually change the program, no matter what the outcome of these sessions, and that the sessions are at best an occasion for exercising courtesy. Their assessment may indeed be right, even when the system is genuinely interested in having such sessions. If they repeatedly run them for similar groups, organizer may well begin to assume that they and their colleagues in the system already know the participants training needs well enough from prior experience. This assumption gains support when participant training needs sound like a broken record. If they do, the program design probably needs review. For instance, instead of offering open questions, organizers could present system understanding of training needs for comment and proceed from there. They can also review the task given to the discussion groups and make it more specific and demanding. Possibly, too, this early in the program the groups require more faculty help in acknowledging and sorting differences between participants, in order to reach generally meaningful specifications of needs. Initial doubts usually last until participants see their views actually reflected in the program.

Another possibility open to organizers is to ask participants to take responsibility for designing specified blocks of time in the program. This can be an alternative or an addition to their involvement to a limited extent in planning the entire program.

At the Sloan School of Management, Massachussetts Institute of Technology, experimental groups of students are left to design nine-hours work per week for themselves within broad faculty specifications. They decide what work to tackle and how, and which faculty members or outsiders to draw into the program. Initial results have been very encouraging. Programs designed by students are at least as heavy as the faculty's and motivation is very high. The results accord with industrial experience wherein small work groups are mandated to fix their own targets.

SUMMARY

In the pretraining phase the three partners in training—the work organizations, the participants, and the training system—build a picture for themselves of the training to come. They do this inevitably but it is best when done from knowledge and understanding. Otherwise it will be a concoction born of ignorance, imagination, and emotions. This chapter has tried to show that it is in the training system's direct interest, and also within its means, to influence the expectations with which participants come to training. The picture they bring of training is more realistic and useful when they have had the institutions help in making it. Through systematic efforts more information can be collected, expectations reformed, and new stereotypes developed. All this is part of the total training process in which the next phase is the actual training.

Underlying this process are questions of motivation, both for the work organization and for individual participants. They are best clarified if the demands of technological and other changes press hard and directly on organizations and individuals. The system endeavors to make sure that this happens and that high motivation for training will emerge from the impact. If the demands are yet to come, and training has the important function of preparing for change, then the system can help in forecasting changes and their implications. On no account is its function one of shielding the organization or the individual from the demands of change. Just the opposite is its duty.

The pretraining stage is one of forging links. First, the three partners in training are linked. Second, linkage of the three main phases of the training process is initiated. As in the well-worn adage, training, too, is no stronger than its weakest link. Not only does the preparation for training, which the system has the responsibility to undertake (the subject of the next chapter), depend on this first linkage, but the training program also. This same "pretraining" link must also bear the weight of the posttraining phase of follow up services and of generally helping participants and organizations to integrate the training received into normal operations. As in construction, the foundations underpinning training may be hidden from view, but they had better be sound.

Chapter 6

Designing the Program

> The accent must be on auto-regulation, on active assimilation—the accent must be on the activity of the subject. Failing this there is no possible didactic or pedagogy which significantly transforms the subject.
>
> —Jean Piaget

The work organization is now clear about the contribution training can make to the changes to be effected. It has both an overall picture of its training needs and an understanding of the specific training needs of the different kinds and levels of staff to be involved in these changes. This clarification of training needs has been hard, painstaking, and often slow work. But clear definitions of needs now mean clear training objectives. And clear training objectives, in turn, make for clear evaluation of the effectiveness of training. So if skimping had to intrude, the pretraining phase was not the place for it.

The work organization and the training system have also discussed major issues and the most promising modalities and orientation for the coming program and have worked out an overall training strategy to address these needs. Such a strategy takes into account the organization's particular mix of opportunities and constraints, and also the resources practicably available in the training system, including the trainers—their particular competencies first of all, but also facilities, such as access to field stations and technologies. The organization has gone further and distributed the work of meeting its training needs among the various training resources available—senior personnel, its own training department, and one or more outside training agencies and programs. Its options included sending a work team to a professional conference and two or three promising supervisors simultaneously to an established management course or a technical program, perhaps even abroad. These various training resources make up the training system available to the organization and it is important that all the components interlink and can be orchestrated together. These and other dimensions of the training system are the particular concern of part III.

For each component unit of the training system, its particular contribution in meeting the overall training needs are its training objectives. The rest is important context.

For instance, the training objective of a branch manager has been defined by the organization: groom at least two department managers for promotion within twelve months. One objective of the training department during that same year is to make twenty cashiers proficient in operating new accounting equipment and another twenty in general sales work, all forty ready prior to the installation of the new equipment. Meanwhile, an outside training institute has been given the objective of developing fifteen departmental managers for promotion throughout the organization; the latter expects these to gain an understanding of the entire range of general management functions at the branch level, and additional skill in staff management without day-to-day supervision.

On the training objectives, however adequately defined, each partner now brings its resources to bear on designing a program that holds the greatest promise.

DESIGNING THROUGH SUCCESSIVE APPROXIMATIONS

A circumspect procedure is required for starting the design process. It is similar to that required for developing the overall strategy, but within narrower confines, and must include all the key components and successively finer approximations. Only here more of the context is preset and each training agency proceeds substantially on its own.

This departure from working jointly with a work organization that is clear about its needs and insistent on having them met through an adequate training strategy to taking full responsibility for developing a program design is fraught with risks. Trainers, left to themselves, tend to become so bogged down with accommodating professional and individual interests in the design that the training objectives are relegated to becoming vague background. A common alternative is that, to save time, trainers proffer a standard, ready-made "package" that actually addresses the particular objectives crudely or only partly. Understandably, trainers also look for opportunities to use the tools—methods and materials—in which they excel or want to practice and explore, with the result that design discussions often start with the eager championing of particular skills and training methods and the allocation of responsibilities along these lines. A second risk in design development by trainers on their own is that important underlying assumptions may remain unexamined. One concerns the kinds and qualities of relationship to be developed between trainers and participants, another the supporting services, material and emotional, that the agency needs to provide as part of a program design.

All the key components—training objectives, resources available, participant motivation, to mention only a few—belong quite properly in a program design but cannot be introduced serially, unlike items on a meeting agenda which can be taken up one matter at a time and decided before moving on to the next. Training designers, as they clarify an overall design through several stages, have to keep all these components firmly in view at each stage: the training objectives, the proper inclusion of all components, and the proper relationships and linkages between them. Each major component requires choices and detailing—but more of this later.

This chapter, too, therefore concentrates on the program design as a whole. Inevitably, training methods, climate, and other components of program design are mentioned which will be examined in detail only in the next two chapters.

FIVE STEPS IN PROGRAM DESIGN

Five steps are involved in designing a training program. The orderly step-by-step description of them makes them appear mechanical, like mathematical extrapolations. We shall stress orderliness here while fully aware that, in fact, a high level of creative and tentative work is involved.

1. The first step is to use the training strategy (or, usually, a combination of strategies) that the organization and system have settled on together for "roughing out" an overall design. The process for this is akin to an architect producing alternative initial drawing and possible positionings of a proposed building on a given site.

> For example, an outside agency has been charged with helping fifteen departmental managers gain (1) an understanding of general management functions at the branch level, and (2) increased skills in independent staff management. The first objective suggests giving weight to activities with an organization-development orientation, that is, priority attention to job content and organizational processes (see chapter 3). The second objective, to gain skill in independent staff management, suggests combining laboratory and person-development orientations, since these methods pay the greatest attention to the processes of accomplishing things on the job and to a conceptual understanding of these processes.

The training methods generally favored for strategies for these purposes are simulation and case programs. Field training may be added for working on organization development, and also laboratory methods.

2. The second step is to break the general training objectives into constituent parts. The first rough breakdown is into component knowledge, understanding and skill.

The first objective, understanding general management functions, relies heavily on knowledge and understanding, and less on skill. The second objective, better staff management, relies more on skill, and less on understanding; the department managers who come for training already possess, or have access to knowledge about staff management.

The initial breakdown of training objectives into knowledge, understanding, and skill is not difficult. What is more challenging is the matching of these components with appropriate training methods, arriving at an estimate of the number of sessions and other events required, and clarifying for each event the particular part of the objective it is to meet. The task is taxing because the component training objectives are only rarely discrete and usually overlap, and because it is difficult to estimate just how much practice needs to be scheduled to ensure a given level of proficiency by participants..

The first objective, understanding general management functions, may be attempted by a series of six case sessions. All may deal with situations calling for understanding by someone in the position of a branch manager in some organization, but four may present problems in different functional areas and two present problems of coordinating different functions. The second objective, enhancing skills, requires a more elaborate training design. Most appropriate may be a training laboratory (including a series of skill sessions, for example, in interviewing), a series of cases that focus on different staff problems to be resolved by the branch manager, and perhaps some simulation sessions.

The end product of breaking the general training objectives into constituent parts and matching the components with appropriate training events and methods is a list of events with purposes and specifications stated for each. The data for each event or block should cover eight items: general and specific objectives, content, training methods, time, evaluation methods, review time, and person(s) responsible for the event.

Exhibit 6.1 shows a section taken from the curriculum used at the Institute for Rural Health and Family Planning, Gandhigram, for Family-Planning Health Assistants deployed at the village level. The three-month residential course has a number of such blocks or events. Data on each block is typed and given to participants. Additional details, for example, of time for review and reflection and methods of evaluation, are also provided to both trainers and participants. The value of this method of organizing a curriculum is that training tasks and objectives are specifically linked for every block, whether a block of sessions or a block of field practice.

3. The third step is to use the specifications of different training methods in order to arrive at the total time and facilities required for meeting an objective. This yields subtotals, which can be added together to arrive at a rough grand total of time and facilities required by the program as a whole.

Exhibit 6.1

SECTION OF CURRICULUM FOR VILLAGE LEVEL FAMILY-PLANNING HEALTH ASSISTANTS*

Session Number	*Contents*	*Objectives*	*Job Function*	*Job Tasks*	*Teaching Method*	*Time Required*	*Faculty Member*
	Section 4 *Village Community and Power Structure*	To enable students to have an understanding of/skill in:					
1. 2. 3. 4.	Definition of "Community." Need for the study of community, rural and urban. Social institutions—caste—religion—education, etc. What is power structure and leadership? Methods of identification of leaders. How is this leadership useful in implementation of Health and Family-Planning Programs (source credibility, group acceptance, etc.) What is a sociogram? How it is useful in finding out interaction between communities?	1. The word "community" and its meaning 2. Characteristics of a community. 3. Social institutions in a village. 4. Sources of village leadership. 5. Methods of identification of village leaders. 6. Customs, attitudes, and beliefs of people as related to health.	1. To make a general survey of village including preparation of map, study of social structures and their relationship, etc.	1. Collection of general information. 2. Preparation of sociogram of a community. 3. Identification of leadership.	1. Lecture-demonstration and exercise. 2. Field visit to study the community structure and social institutions in a village. Lecture-discussion.	2 hours 1/2 day	Rao De
			2. Identification of leadership in every community.	4. To help the ANM identify female leaders.	Lecture-discussion.	1 hour	De
			3. Helping the ANM in selecting female leaders in the village.	5. Collection of information on personal attitudes and beliefs of people toward family planning.	1. Lecture. 2. Field practice for leadership identification and preparation of sociogram.	2 hours 2 hours 1 day	Rao Rao De
5.	Customs, beliefs, etc., of the communities and why the Health Assistant (Family Planning) should know and how to use them.		4. Meeting individually resistant couples and identifying their barriers.	6. Meeting of dropouts and resistant couples individually with leaders; identifying difficulties and helping them to overcome them.	1. Lecture-discussion. 2. Gathering of information on attitudes and beliefs of people on family planning by survey.	2 hours	Rao De

* SOURCE: Institute of Rural Health and Family Planning, Gandhigram, India

Exhibit 6.2 shows this calculation for the training of departmental managers for these objectives and by the methods indicated earlier. Most striking are the different amounts of time required for attaining different training objectives. For a series of case sessions to foster understanding of management functions, the total time required is 27 hours for participants and 18 hours for trainers. For improving staff management the corresponding totals are 63 hours and 97 $^1/_2$ hours.

Exhibit 6.2
TRAINING 15 MANAGERS FOR TWO OBJECTIVES:
TIME AND FACILITIES REQUIRED

Objective	*Training Method*	*Time (Hours)* *Participants'*		*Trainer's*		*Facilities*
		Prep.	*Training*	*Prep.*	*Training*	
1. Understanding general management at branch level	Cases (6)	18	9	9	9	6 cases; discussion room with blackboard for 9 hours
Total		27		18		
2. Better independent staff management	Laboratory		30	$7^1/_2$	60	Discussion room with tape recorder for 30 hours;
	Cases (6)	18	9	9	9	6 cases; discussion room with blackboard for 9 hours
	Simulation sessions (4)		6	6	6	Materials; discussion room with blackboard for 6 hours
Total		63		$97^1/_2$		
Total for whole program		90		$115^1/_2$		12 cases (4 functional, 2 coordinating, 6 staff management; discussion room 54 hours (with tape recorder 30 hours; with blackboard 24 hours)

4. The fourth step is to decide on the different packages in which this program could be offered and to ask the organization to select one.

Package 1: Two-week, full-time residential program:

This would be ideal because laboratory training requires the isolation and intensity best achieved in a continuous program. The greater the attitudinal component in the increased staff management skill required, the more important the intensity of training experience becomes.

In most Asian countries the budget for this package would be of this order (in US$):

Residence and facilities for 15 participants x

12 days x $ 25/day	$4,500
Two trainers, cases, and overheads	$3,600–4,800
Total	$8,100–9,300

Any travel expenditures for participants and trainers would be additional. Complete costing would also add the fifteen participants' salaries. If they each earn $330 per month, the cost of the training program would go up by about $2,475.

Package 2: Two-week, full-time nonresidential program:

This program would be located close to the work and residence of participants. This would not only mean the end of more or less undivided attention on the program, but would involve the return of participants every evening to families and friends whose routine expectations based on past experience make changing more difficult for them. Inevitably, training by this package will be less intensive. Studies have shown that this reduction in intensity may not affect the effectiveness of training that aims at increased knowledge and information, but definitely affects training directed toward new attitudes and human relations skills.

The greatest advantage of this package over the first is a marked reduction in cost $4,500. If the trainers come from outside, their travel and residence (2 x 17 x 25 = $850) would have to be added.

Package 3 : Six-day full-time training laboratory followed by 16 sessions of 1 $^1/_2$hours each during or after working hours.

This package, and any others that avoid a full-time program, can only be offered if the trainers reside in the same locale or at least have other work and payments that keep them there. If so, then it may combine to great advantage the features of packages 1 and 2.

Its budget would look like this:
Residence and facilities for 15 participants x 6 day x $25/day $2,250
Two trainers, cases, and overheads..$3,600–4,800.

Total $5,850-7,050

If the second part of the program, case and simulation sessions, can be held outside working hours, the total salary cost of the program will be halved. But the program may then have to be limited to two sessions a week (plus two long evenings of preparation). This schedule would stretch the program over two months. If this period is too long, it may be worth the extra cost of conducting at least a part of the program, for example, preparation, during work hours, or to double the number of sessions per week in order to finish the entire program in a month.

Package 4 : Daily sessions during work or after working hours:

This is the cheapest package and might be a useful design for teaching training objectives that require frequent contact with jobs in their work settings. It is not a promising package for the training objectives we have used as an example here. The cost for trainers, cases, and overheads would be unchanged: $3,600–4,800. Participants' attention however, would be divided. There would be a predictable heavy loss of training time as participants change gear every day from operating to training and have to warm up for each session. If the results achieved through the other three packages are to be realized in this one, total training time—and the cost of training—would have to be substantially increased.

Other packages are possible, notably full-time weekend programs with part-time programs in between.

The choices of training packages and budgets that the institution can offer the work organization are summarized in exhibit 6.3. As noted above, the fourth package, training outside working hours, is not at all the bargain it appears at first glance.

Exhibit 6.3

FOUR TRAINING PACKAGES AND BUDGET ESTIMATES (US$)

Package	*Participants' Salaries*	*Residence Meals*	*Trainers and Overheads*	*Total Cost Excluding Travel*
1. Two-week, full-time residential program	2,475	4,500	3,600–4,800	10,575–11,775
2. Two-week, full-time nonresidential	2,475	540*	3,600–4,800	6,615–7,815
3. Six-day, full-time residential plus sixteen				

sessions outside working hours (total eight weeks)	1,240	2,250	3,600–4,800	7,090–8,290
4. Thirty-one sessions outside working hours (sixteen weeks at two sessions per week)			3,600–4,800	3,600–4,800

* $3 per day for lunch and refreshments

5. The fifth step in designing a training program is to dovetail detailed training events into training sequences and, finally, into the shape of the total program package. Both objectives are given special attention here.

OUTLINING PROGRAM SEQUENCES AND THEMES

It is very tempting—and very damaging—to approach the fifth step in designing the program primarily as an administrative matter. A description based on this approach would sound something like this: "There are, let us say, forty $1^1/_2$ hour sessions. If we work a six-hour, four-session training day, the entire program will require ten days. No faculty member ought to take more than one session per day. Therefore, we will offer four different subjects per day." The neatness enchants. So, too, does the possible avoidance of the heavy work which, following on so much detailed work already, certainly must go into approaching the task primarily as a training matter. The proper approach would relate the training objectives, as translated by now into discrete training events, to what is known of the learning process and its various aspects.

There are a number of relevant considerations. We will concentrate here on five: (1) phasing the program to accord with the learning process, (2) relating the program to prevailing expectations, (3) building the training group, (4) incorporating the grand themes of training for development, and (5) striving for consistency in training.

1. Phasing the Program to Accord with the Learning Process

Kurt Lewin's three-stage formulation of the learning process—unfreezing, moving, refreezing—is relevant here. It was referred to earlier (chapter 3) and is relevant again here for work on the grand design of the program and on each of its major parts. In the first place unfreezing, or questioning established ways of looking at situations and habits of action, belongs early in the program and early in every constituent part. Before unfreezing, participants do not attach sufficient importance to the problem to desire new behavior and, therefore, to learn. The training methods which belong early in the program, therefore, are those that offer maximum stimulation and involvement: laboratory, simulation, and some types of training in the field. Through them participants are sufficiently challenged, unsettled, and motivated to deal, somehow, with the disturbing discrepancies, dissonances, and inadequacies that emerge. Unfreezing is for training what ploughing is for agriculture.

Seeding and planting stages follow next: exploration, new knowledge, experiments with new behavior, trial and error, and all the substantive events necessary for moving, for learning. Cases, individual learning, practicing new techniques in the field—these are very appropriate here.

Finally, the stage arrives of fitting new knowledge, understanding, and skills that have proved useful and acceptable in the training situation into personal and organizational patterns of routine day-to-day work and living, i.e., the refreezing stage. Promoting convergent, integrative tendencies toward the end of a program parallels the opposite purpose of fostering divergent, dissonant elements at its beginning. Churning at this final stage, raising more dust than can settle, would be inappropriate, irresponsible, and perhaps detrimental. The opposite is required now: settling down and consolidation. The appropriate events would stress cases, role playing, individual assignments, and reflection.

> At SIET Institute a full-time training laboratory immediately follows the two-and-a-half to three days set aside for opening the course. This laboratory continues for four to five days. It is followed by two or three weeks of sessions that focus on providing new knowledge and practice in area development subjects and techniques. Interviewing is an example of the skills practiced at this stage. The bulk of the program consists of group and individual sessions. A short (two-day) field trip follows which provides a major exercise in collaboration and an opportunity to practice some techniques. Review sessions follow, then more work sessions focused on new knowledge. In the sixth week, just before participants leave for a three-week, in-district study, another laboratory is held full-time for two days. Its immediate objective is to sort out relationship problems in the field teams before the teams leave for their major collaborative tasks.
>
> The district study offers a methodology that participants can put to use on returning to their organization. The subsequent program, which occupies the last three weeks of the twelve-week course, is concerned with writing and presenting joint reports and clarifying any questions that remain.

2. Relating the Program to Prevailing Expectations

This need is foremost at the very beginning and the very end of the program. At the beginning the expectations that need attention are the ones participants and trainers have of each other and of the training program itself. To the extent that these expectations can be linked to reality, and uncertainties reduced or removed at this initial stage, participants and trainers, both, can move more freely to the very limits of the program.

An opening speech might be the first step in that process, conveying to the participants general sanction and approval for the training they are about to begin. It is a kind of initiation ceremony; to call it a ritual is not to decry it, but to describe its primary function. A secondary function of the opening session is to orient participants firmly away from their usual day-to-day preoccupations, toward the training program. Another positive value of this orientation is a reduction of guilt that active people often feel when removed from the scene of action, their urge to get back to "doing something." This secondary function of the opening address is commonly confused with the symmetrical function of the final session—but in the reverse direction. At the end of the program participants need to be oriented away from training, toward the outside world of work and public concern. The initiation ceremony aims to orient them toward stepping back, to review and learning.

The formal opening session is best followed by a series of events in which participants and trainers talk together, get to know one another, and share expectations of each other and of the program. General discussions, group assignments, individual tasks shared in a group, and time for informal contact can serve this purpose well. An example of this has already been described (page 93).

The expectations to be aligned as the program draws to a close are of a different kind and place the trainers in a different role. They concern the work and home situations which each participant will face afresh, usually alone, and in which not the trainers but the participant's work organization, family, and friends are parties. Role playing, incidents and cases, and individual assignments and consultation are appropriate kinds of events for this back-home stage of the program. The roles appropriate for a trainer at this stage are resource person and helper.

> At SIET Institute ten sessions are blocked out for discussions of back-home problems. An individual written assignment earlier in the course has elicited some of them: an actual problem, how it came up, and who the people involved were. Discussion now is mainly in triads. One participant practices helping two others consider the problem one of them has reported. Participants take turns in the different roles—reporting and preparing for action, listening, clarifying, advising, and helping two people toward a useful discussion. A case session is inserted from time to time. The case presents a problem faced by someone else. It reminds participants that back-home problems are common and serves to brush up their analytical and diagnostic skills. Additional sessions focus on a helping relationship, both in concept and practice.

3. Building the Training Group

The program must also reflect the social dimensions of learning. Studies have shown that individuals learn, or at least learn better and faster, when they feel the approval of other participants as well as the trainer's, and when others openly commit themselves to similar improvement. They need to be able to check their ideas and progress as they join in developing norms of acceptable behavior for meeting needs and sort out the various functions in the group which facilitate learning.

For participants to know one another and to develop norms and roles in a training group takes time and opportunity. The program must allow for both, if trainers want participants' attention in learning other things. Training laboratories are particularly well suited for expediting and deepening the social processes in learning. In a general program, laboratories are best scheduled at the outset, with additional sessions included periodically later, when relationships between participants and trainers seem to warrant attention. If the program has encouraged the group to form a renewed closely knit alliance, it has to provide opportunities toward the end for the group to dissolve again in preparation for parting. Otherwise, the last weeks will be increasingly overshadowed by the participants' regrets and fears at parting, at the cost of attention to how can use their training back on the job and to the support that they need and can also organize for.

4. Incorporating the Grand Themes of Training for Development

A fourth consideration concerns the response of the program to the urgent themes underlying training needs in developing countries. Two such themes have already been mentioned: One, the need to introduce divergence and creativity into situations that lean heavily toward convergence and repetition; and second, the need to move away from dependent relationships to independence and interdependence.

A training program is a particularly effective means of addressing these enduring needs just because, in Matthew Miles' phrase, it is a temporary system. It can provide an environment that meets personal needs, reduce defensiveness, and unveils the potential for creativity and innovation. It can be precisely fashioned by its designers as a temporary utopia, with a flexibility that can evoke the best possible contribution from its participants. Everett Hagen's analysis[1] of the innovative personality in developing countries pinpoints the direction for particularly salient personal devel-

[1] *On the Theory of Social Change: How Economic Growth Begins* (Homewood, Ill.: The Dorsey Press, Inc., 1962).

opment through training. He describes an effective innovator as someone who sees a coherent world about him that will respond dependably to his efforts to change it; trusts his own evaluation of his experience; sees the surrounding world as valuing him if he achieves his goals; has high needs for autonomy, achievement, order, giving succor to others, and also for receiving nurture from them. The innovator operates among people with whom the opposite feelings are very common: powerlessness, failure, meaninglessness, alienation, and interpersonal distance. He has to learn to deal with, and live with, these feelings, yet continue to work skillfully.[2]

Well-designed training can provide experiences in all these dimensions. Events and methods have been rated for their resonance to these two basic themes in exhibit 6.4. Simulation, laboratory, and case methods resound to both. Consistent preference for events and methods which are one or two steps forward in the desirable direction will add significance to the entire training program.

5. Striving for Consistency in Training

Another general consideration concerns the trainers' readiness to think of the program in terms of the total time participants spend in it, and not just of the time occupied by scheduled training events. The difference between these partial and comprehensive ways of thinking about the program shows up most, of course, in residential training. There the entire day can be made meaningful to attaining training objectives. The residential and food arrangements, library procedures, games and other leisure-time activities, and contacts with the administrative staff of the institution—all have training components. All communicate something which participants will match and compare with the training they receive in the

Exhibit 6.4

TRAINING METHODS AND EVENTS FAVORING DIVERGENCE AND INDEPENDENCE

Training Methods	*Divergence and Newness*	*Independence and Interdependence*
Field training	Medium	High
Simulation	High	High
Laboratory	High	High
Incidents and cases	High	High
Individual instruction	Medium	Medium
General discussion	Low	Low
Lecture	Low	Low

[2] Ibid, pp. 86-98.

formal program. There is no neutral ground. If the communication from these settings is consistent with what the training program is striving to develop, it enhances and supports training. If the communication is inconsistent, it detracts and raises doubts about the program.

> At the Aloka International Training Center it was a principle "that arrangements should allow, even demand, a multitude of choices to be made by individual members and small groups of members....[This] principle ran right through the training course. There were spare beds and ....members chose the cottages in which to live and might also choose to change. House staff, however, was so restricted that the members had to clean their own cottages, lay tables and wash dishes as a matter of routine. They also devoted an average of six hours per week to manual work on the farm. For the manual work there was a reasonable assortment of tools but not enough to provide a complete set for each member. This ensured that the work program they designed had to take account of problems of coordination and many other limitations.[3]

Exhibit 6.5 gives extracts from a document participants in SIET Institute courses received about their responsibilities outside the formal program.

In question is whether the numerous aspects of the training situation are used to strengthen the program, or whether they are simply left to chance or even unwittingly so arranged that they run counter to the objectives of the program. The question goes beyond formal events to the innumerable opportunities for contact between participants, and between participants with trainers individually, in groups, and in a body. All enhance the consistency and therefore impact on the training program or detract from it. Even the physical facilities are no exception. They also "speak." Just as a horse-shoe seating arrangement makes for contact and discussion, so sharing rooms makes a difference—are the rooms allocated to participants or chosen by them?— and chairs in long rows or grouped at small tables during meals. The great advantage residential programs have over others is therefore twofold: not only do they cut the participant off from the impact of the workaday world, they focus many events on the training objectives and thereby can achieve a consistency and intensity that is most conducive to learning. This is particularly important, and also economical, if changes in attitudes and relationships rate high among the training objectives.

Nonresidential programs offer fewer opportunities to achieve consistency and intensity. But the principle is the same: every available opportunity, in and out of session, should be used to promote the training objectives.

[3] R. P. Lynton, *The Tide of Learning: The Aloka Experience* (London: Routledge and Kegan Paul, 1960), p. 28.

Exhibit 6.5

GROUP RESPONSIBILITIES FOR LIVING ARRANGEMENTS

To allow the widest scope for meeting personal preference and also for practice in effective decision making, the members will be involved in deciding and organizing many things: within the formal program, the most suitable subjects for discussions; facilities—for recreation, and use of games equipment; for leisure time—excursions and other social functions, for the routine of living—questions of accommodation and food.

That effective decisions in these areas will be circumscribed by all sorts of limitations at the institute is certainly true—indeed a truism; all life, all *effective* decisions, are full of limitations—of facilities, funds, and time of other people and of ourselves. The decisions are effective to the degree that they exhaust the freedom of choice within such limits.

The role of the faculty in this connection will be limited, both informally and at "open air meetings." Faculty members can clarify the limits of the specific situation. For instance, although the members will be asked to give suggestions for subjects for a seminar, these shall be related to the work of the area officers, the objectives of the seminar, and the experiences gathered in the seminar. On the other hand, once the limits are clear, the participants will be free to reach any decision within them and it will be similarly up to them to change it again in the light of their experience.

Many a question raised by an individual member concerns him only, immediately at least, and the responsible faculty members will settle it directly or ask him to deal with it himself. Questions that concern more participants or the group as a whole will be referred to all, and the group will need to reach decisions on them as a body, taking responsibility for their enforcement and living with their implications.

Faculty Assignments

To facilitate and speed up administration and decision making in which the members are involved, different faculty members have assumed responsibility for the following aspects and should be contacted in these connections:

1. The course program (Name)
2. Use and care of Institute equipment and facilities, e.g., games (Name)
3. Social events e.g., excursion (Name)
   (The faculty will organize some social events; these will be announced in the weekly timetable)
4. Improvement of buildings and grounds by participants, e.g. through decoration, gardening, etc. (Name)
5. Accommodation, sanitation, and services in hostel and first aid. (Name)*
6. Food (Name)*

*On detailed questions from individual participants, and other matters open to immediate routine action, participants can contact (name), the hostel warden. Only in case of doubt, if differences remain, or if the matter affects several or all participants, will the faculty member get involved, on the invitation of either the group or (name of hostel warden).

Organization of this Group

The members can organize themselves for their responsibilities in these connections in any way they choose. They will have charge of any meetings and conduct them and reach decisions on any outstanding questions in any manner they wish. Faculty members will be present only on request, to furnish information about the areas for which they are responsible. Beyond that, if the participants are unable to reach effective decisions, they can at any time, as a group, ask for a faculty member to work with them as a consultant in decision making. In that role the faculty member would still leave the group to take any decision within the limits set. His function would be to help the group pinpoint the problems that stand in the way of agreement and the steps required to remove them.

SOURCE: SIET Institute, Document for Participants, 1963. Abbreviated.

COMPOSING THE DETAILED SYLLABUS

When program sequences and themes have been established, not once and for all but sufficiently to indicate the main emphasis and rhythms of the programs, the detailed composition of the syllabus can be undertaken. Again, this is not an administrative act, and certainly not a jigsaw puzzle comprising a set number of pieces that can only be combined in one way. Composing the syllabus, too, is a creative task.

The considerations requisite for composing a detailed syllabus can be seen as four pairs of alternates. "Alternates" is the important word. It is indeed important to alternate, not to flounder in middle ground. In physical exercises it is important to stretch/relax, stretch/relax, alternately. Compromising, settling for a half-stretched, half-relaxed posture, would not be exercise . Similarly, in training it is not the average, the lukewarm, that is important—too many of us spend much of our time in that state already! What is vital to a syllabus is the training equivalent of the parental admonition: "When you work, work! When you play, play!"—and do each with gusto!

1. Alternating Stimulation and Reflection

We have talked earlier of the essential of reflection in converting external events into personal experiences, i.e., into learning. Periods of externally designed and paced training events must alternate with reflective time, a period in which participants discern the meaning of happenings for themselves and digest it.

Alternating may be too deliberate and definitive a word to describe the subtle process that is required. A certain amount of time has to pass for an experience to "sink in." How participants spend that time will vary widely. What is important here is that the program provide the time. To avoid the impression that such periods are idle, waiting to be filled, it may be best to label these periods "personal study" or, as in one program, "alone time." Whatever the label, reflective time has to be planned, not left as a residual or chance item at the end of a long day. If unincluded, the days may become jammed with activity, and the participants may return to their jobs feeling they have "had a ball," but wondering what large parts of the training were all about. Such an experience is particularly common in short programs. Irrespective of program duration, continuous activity must not be made a value.

If the program is longer than a few hours or days, participants will inevitably "tune out" of training events from time to time, whenever they feel the need to reflect. They may be physically present but mentally and emotionally are removed. Such is the wisdom and economy of the human organism that it insists on satisfying the need for reflection in much the same way that the body of an overtaxed, indispensable executive succumbs to a cold or worse. Such unplanned "absence" can throw a training program out of gear and, moreover, even vitiate the benefits a properly planned and sanctioned period of quiet would have ensured.

We have emphasized the need for reflective time in the syllabus because it is commonly omitted under the pressures "to cover the syllabus." One US governmental agency runs twelve-week programs for several thousand participants every year, consisting of eleven scheduled hours per day, six-and-a-half days per week. Such an intensive program allows little room for reflection. Another error may also creep in: offering data for plentiful reflection that has little bearing on the training objectives. The ideal syllabus would provide appropriate new data whenever reflection begins to veer from the training objectives for lack of stimulation, and then provide another opportunity to reflect on the additional input.

2. Alternating Personal Involvement and Safe Distance

No involvement means no learning. The starting point is personal experience, that is, events which take on personal meaning. But deep, acute involvement does not favor some important types of learning, for example, analysis of data or understanding and generalizing for future action. Therefore, intensive training using personal experiences ought to alternate these events with sessions which offer analytical and conceptual understanding of such experiences. The one is stimulating, personal, disturbing. Members may suddenly freeze inside, stare instead of look, overthink, become preoccupied with the din of rampant emotions. The other is calm: "Now let's look back." Members can shed their preoccupations, look at what happened, understand it, and listen to other people's reactions.

The ideal syllabus would move participants in the direction of involvement until they froze and stared, then backtrack to a study of other people's experiences for unfreezing, clarification and understanding.

3. Alternating Talking about Something and Practicing It

No skill is acquired without practice, and practice engenders new questions and experiences to talk about the study. It is an alternating process, not the one-day process on which many training designs are presently based: first the theory, all of it, and then the practice—as if practice were "applied" theory, rather than theory generalizations from practice.

When practicing a new skill in an actual situation is dangerous or too expensive, a simulation method can be provided. A practice game in sports and a mock flight cabin for a pilot in training are examples. All kinds of training aids can be developed to make practice feasible, even early in a program. Early practice yields an understanding of theory, and also raises many theoretical questions. How often one hears a participant exclaim at practice, "Oh, now I understand"—and what an accusation this harbors against the trainers! For how much participants have not understood, how much they cannot check if practice comes late in the program the trainers will never know. Practice provides not only an understanding of theory, but the motivation to learn it.

Continuous practice, on the other hand, runs dry. It tends to become mechanical, a valuable quality in only certain jobs. Some research findings on this are summarized in box 6.1.

The ideal syllabus would provide opportunities for practice and improvement in performance tapers off or threatens to fall short of the training objective. Then opportunities to think and talk about those aspects that are still problematic would be provided before practice is resumed.

4. Alternating Individual Events and Group Events

Participants provide stimulation for one another through their different experiences and ideas and through group interaction. The group also provides individuals with opportunities to test and check their ideas and effectiveness as they move toward changing in certain directions, that is,

Box 6.1

CONTINUOUS OR DISTRIBUTED PRACTICE

BERNARD M. BASS AND JAMES A. VAUGHAN

Experimental studies have shown, in general, that over a wide range of situations some form of distributed practice will be superior to massed practice. We must be cautious, however, in specific applications of these results. For example, studies involving motor skills have consistently shown a defi-

Box 6.1 (Continued)

nite superiority for distributed practice, but the findings from verbal learning and other complex learning studies are not so clear-cut. In fact, the results of the latter are exceptionally complicated and depend upon a number of variables such as the response measure, the similarity of the terms used in the material to be learned, and the amount of prior experience the subjects have had on similar tasks. For instance, when the material to be learned is rather brief and not unusually difficult, massed practice has the advantage in that inter-trial forgetting is minimized and learning will probably be accomplished before much work decrement has developed. (The primary reason advanced for the superiority of distributed practice in most instances is that rest periods allow for the dissipation of the work inhibition which normally builds up and interferes with learning in long or massed practice sessions.)

With some kinds of very difficult and complex tasks there may be an advantage to a varied attack such as a few massed with more frequent rest intervals followed by briefer practice sessions with more frequent rest intervals. In some situations massing may be more effective than spacing when rest periods are not of the appropriate length and frequency. A number of studies have found that, with the same amount of study time, trainees who moderately massed practice of complex materials out-performed other trainees who distributed their practice in the extreme with long rest periods between each practice session.

Summarizing earlier literature, Bass lists the following as guidelines for establishing an efficient training regimen:

1. Generally, greater learning will occur when the rest intervals are shorter early in training and longer late in training. This is preferable to holding the rest interval constant throughout the course of training.

2. The less meaningful the material to be learned, the greater its difficulty and amount, the more with the distributed practice be superior to massed practice. Conversely, if what is to be learned is very simple, short, and meaningful, massing will yield superior performance.

3. The less capable and less experienced the trainee, the more he will benefit from distributed practice. Conversely, the talented, experienced trainee may find moderate massing preferable.

4. Material learned by some form of distributed practice will be retained longer than material learned by massed practice.

(Consider how rapidly you forget the subject matter of a course for which you crammed the night before the final examinations, in comparison to courses in which you studied regularly during the semester.) This principle is of major significance in increasing the effectiveness of study.

SOURCE: Bernard M. Bass and James A. Vaughan, *Psychology of Learning for Managers* (Pittsburgh, Pa.: University of Pittsburgh, 1963), pp. 88–89.

learning. Studies show that this kind of test and check, followed by early confirmation, are key elements in committing oneself to change.

But studies also show that group solutions to problems are apt to be inferior to the best individual solutions, that in a group setting individual learning tends to be average in quality and to slow to a pace most participants find comfortable. In short, the pacesetters or otherwise more capable participants (so very much needed in developing countries) may find their new endeavors stifled in group situations.

The syllabus, therefore, needs to provide both individual and group tasks. The types of objectives best attained through group activities include setting goals, developing work styles, diagnosing difficulties, and learning certain social skills essential for testing the social consequences of an individual's knowledge. Other objectives, best achieved through individual work activities, include writing skills, investigating and organizing specific information relevant to an individual task, and testing one's own ability and knowledge. In individual tasks participants can take their learning to the limit of their personal capabilities. Individualized programmed instruction offers possibilities along this line, but only for training with standardized objectives and methods. Individual written and practice assignments offer other and often simpler possibilities. Opportunities for individual consultation with a trainer and individual counseling provide other settings.

Another syllabus would provide participants with group events for stimulation, then individual tasks on which to push themselves as far as they can go, then another group event to affirm their efforts in the new direction, thereby motivating further learning.

A syllabus that alternates stimulation and reflection, involvement and distance, study and practice, and individual and group events, seems to come closer to providing the kind of variety that promotes learning than do frequent changes in subject matter which have variety per se as the main objective. In fact, frequent changes in subject matter may be both unnecessary and wasteful.

MODULAR APPROACH TO PROGRAM DESIGN

An increasing number of institutions are experimenting with composing the syllabus in subject "blocks" or "modules" so that participants in any week or month concentrate on two or three subjects only, and those often interrelated. Continuity of subject matter reinforces learning and ensures better than the stop-start-stop type of syllabus that a meaningful and memorable chunk of a subject will have been learned by the time a block is completed. Also, practice components of ascending degrees of complexity can be interspersed systematically with conceptual work, discussion of individual problems, and other methods. Experience shows that this arrangement economizes time. It is not clear to what extent this economy is due to the arrangement itself, or due to the painstaking preparation by trainers that resulted in such an arrangement.

In the modular approach to curriculum development all the capabilities required to perform closely interrelated sets of tasks are grouped together, e.g., capabilities required to manage institutional finances, including generation of finances, allocation, accounting, and monitoring. All these can be grouped into a program called Financial Management, with self-contained modules developed for each task.

> From a survey of learning needs among health services administrators in the Regencies of one of Indonesia's twenty-seven provinces, the team planning a two-week program for Regency directors identified the topics that the directors and their staff had mentioned most frequently, and then prepared a "training module" for each. Materials and methods most promising for improving practice in the given component were designed into each module. The program as a whole consisted then of a sequence of eleven modules, each self-contained and varying from six to nine hours in length. Whenever possible, a module was introduced in an afternoon or evening session so that participants could read, write, think, and talk about it overnight.

To be maximally effective, modules require great care in preparation. Field data about actual situations and problems encountered by participants in the program are essential, and modules should be prepared and then revised in the light of experience with them in several programs before issuing them for more general use. The long work put into a module becomes worthwhile and even economical since the same module, modified only in detail, can serve in many programs later. On arrival for a program, participants may be asked to take an active part in the sequencing of modules, i.e., building modules into the program as a whole, which leads to intense early involvement.

BUILDING IN FLEXIBILITY

Composing a flexible syllabus calls for many complicated projections. What is the minimum block for a subject, or the minimum time for one kind of event before switching to another? Even more subtle are questions about composing one syllabus for individual participants who differ in experiences and needs, and in methods and speeds of learning, and then making this syllabus standard for successive groups. Such matters are even more difficult to gauge midstream in a program. The difficulty increases when projections have to be made prior to starting a program and prior to close contact with participants. During the program's implementation, too, the temptation to forsake flexibility is strong.

Lest anyone be so tempted and revert to composing the training syllabus in the classical administrative manner, let us emphasize here that projections—ahead of "hard" information—are inherent in the task, regardless of the approach. Summary dismissal does not dissolve them. The task is made easier if it is engaged piecemeal, initially at least, in terms of achieving specific training objectives. The operative principle that minimizes discouragement is not to let the impossible perfect obstruct the possible good; in other words, use rough magnitudes and reasonable approximations. After all, a step in the right direction, even one, is progress. And further insight will come with experience.

The first step is to clarify what in the syllabus really must and also can be decided prior to the program and what can wait. Minimum blocks of subjects and sequences of training events for a given subject can usually be planned well in advance on the basis of the subject's inherent nature and trainers' past experiences.

> One course has repeatedly offered a series of six case sessions or organizational questions in small enterprises as a core component. This block was fixed after two trials, with minor adjustments and one substitution. Its timing, too, was fixed: one case per day for one week prior to a major in-plant study.
>
> Another course offers a package on interviewing: a case, then role playing, a double session of practice interviews, and a review session. This is placed in the syllabus just before the first district visit which entails considerable interviewing. Two follow-up sessions after the visit review interviewing in practice.

What becomes fixed with diligent care can be called the core of the syllabus. It is important for all parties to develop such a core. Solidity in the right places leaves both trainers and participants free to explore and experiment with the remaining parts of the syllabus.

Many other details cannot be fixed in the syllabus and need not be. For instance, if the most effective sequence and times of alternation are difficult to establish in advance, the syllabus can block out the total time required, and announce these details piece by piece as the participants progress through that particular part of the program.

> The syllabus of one training center is subdivided no further than half days. Many variations are possible within a half-day span. Another institution, requiring in its program expensive equipment that has to be shared between several groups, deals with the problem in just the opposite manner, it subdivides the day into twenty-minute blocks. Trainers compose and form the syllabus for just a few days at a time.

Some parts of the syllabus can be planned with greater precision than others. At the juncture of major parts, when the program shifts emphasis, it is very important to ensure that the objectives of the program thus far have, in fact, been met. A detailed syllabus for the entire course would be suspect since concreteness far in advance is surely deceptive. To avoid dangerous rigidity at such junctures, one institution had detailed syllabi ready for each major part of the program, but delayed scheduling the next part until trainers were certain that participants had mastered the prerequisites. When it first developed its courses, this institution did not even go this far, deciding the syllabus only week by week on Saturday afternoons. The main point is to detail the syllabus only when available data permits, and never push ahead of this limit for the sake of neatness.

What flexibility to allow in the syllabus for variations between participants of one group, and between successive groups coming for the same training, must necessarily rest on very rough and arbitrary projections. Experience over the years provides some guidance as to the normal range of variations. But relying on normal, usually impressionistic, standards can become a deadening habit and reduce the composition of a syllabus to mere routine. This must not happen. Systematic evaluation safeguards against syllabus automation. To attain the training objectives a detailed syllabus must address the particular individuals and groups in the particular program.

Finally, the syllabus ought to leave scope for the unforeseen (perhaps unforeseeable). The deliberate provision of some flexibility in the syllabus to meet such contingencies should occasion no surprise. Flexibility performs the same function in training as the limits of tolerance perform in an engineer's drawing. In training, as in machining, the aim is not perfection but performance within certain acceptable limits. Occasional scrap must be expected, also in training. Some sessions simply fail to produce the expected results, or have to be cancelled due to an administrative breakdown or for some other reason. New, previously untried programs, deserve an extra allowance for failure. The same applies when inexperienced trainers are used. Both conditions prevail in developing countries.

Demands for extra program time may arise from unexpected windfalls. An event in the work organization or society at large, or a development in the training group, may occasion a shared preoccupation so great that it would be quite unwise to proceed with the program as if nothing extraordinary had happened. It is also possible that the strong emotions engendered by such an event can be channelled toward a training objective.

> A fire broke out in an institution. Naturally, the participants in a training session ran to help put out the fire. After it was extinguished, the trainer gave an individual written assignment. "What did you see? What cues did you use in deciding what to do? How did you choose with whom to work?" This occasion

revealed that the one participant who had previously "learned" fire-fighting was, in fact, too spellbound to act. His reaction provided very useful food for thought.

The need for flexibility arises, therefore, not merely from lose projections of training time and rates of progress. It also arises from unpredicted and unpredictable events which may be usable for training or act as deterrents to learning. Such deterrents must be removed before participants can resume progress in the desired direction. Nothing will etch in the participants' minds so vividly the trainers' concern with attaining training objectives as the trainers' responses to such situations.

In a forty-hour training week, a five percent tolerance would yield an unscheduled two hours. This does not seem too much flexibility to allow in the syllabus for catching up and otherwise adjusting the program.

MONITORING AND IMPROVING TRAINING DURING THE PROGRAM

To alter a syllabus in light of experiences during the program trainers need indicators to guide them. They can then decide with fair accuracy when to add a session here, to try a different teaching method there, revise a sequence, provide extra practice for lagging participants, or insert an opportunity for reviewing relationships. This points to the importance of building into the program some procedures for concurrent monitoring of participants' progress toward specific training objectives, and for adjusting the program where possible. The aim is more skillful navigation right now, not a review of the program with an eye to improvement next time. Evaluation for that purpose comes later, as does reviewing the relevance of the program's objectives to the needs of the work organization and the job; both evaluations belong in the posttraining phase. Concurrent monitoring accepts as fixed the training objectives of particular events and blocks in the program, and measures to what extent they are being achieved. One way to do this is to measure participants' progress at specific times during the program. The second is to provide regular program review sessions in the syllabus, and use data from progress indicators in the discussion.

In approach and methodologies (though not in timing) monitoring during, and evaluation after, the program are closely related; hence they are considered together in a later chapter (chapter 11). Concurrent monitoring and post-program evaluation are both necessary; it is a serious mistake to regard them as alternatives.

TRAINING SCHEDULES AND TIMETABLES

The trainers have now taken many steps to design a program appropriate to the needs of the participants and their work organization. These steps form four sequences:

1. Long ago they chose an overall training strategy in the light of general training objectives and available resources.

2. They then converted these objectives into a program design, breaking them down, where necessary, into constituent parts, and choosing training methods and materials with appropriate specifications for each. The detailed steps involved in just this sequence are set out in figure 6.1.

Figure 6.1

CONVERTING TRAINING OBJECTIVES INTO A PROGRAM

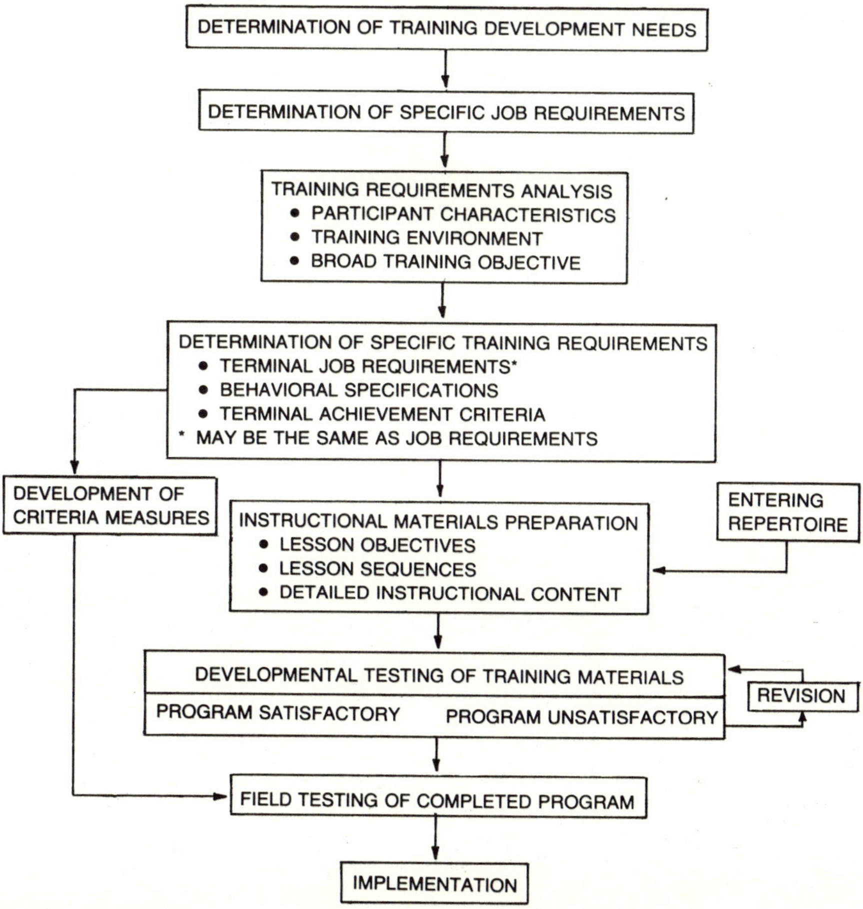

3. Next, the institution correlated the program to the organization's requirements. In doing so, the trainers ensured that the program reflected the different phases of the learning process; allowed time for dealing with expectations—those immediate to both trainers and participants and those arising from the underlying needs of developing societies; and helped the training group to develop well. The trainers then made the training program consistent with the training situation.

4. Using the general program in its approved package as a guide, the trainers then composed a detailed syllabus. They ensured, first of all, that every part of the program was accommodated and all effectively tied together. They built in sufficient flexibility to allow for normal variations between groups and also for evaluating and reviewing the participants' progress so that adjustments could be made in the program.

Weekly and daily training schedules are the visible outcome of this long series of activities. They are usually worked out by the trainers and announced at the beginning of the program in the form of timetables. Some institutions prefer to involve participants in the process of converting schedules into precise timetables. Within the limits set by the methods, specifications, and the trainers, participants are asked to decide the timings for sessions, breaks, and other program events. This opportunity is more readily offered in residential programs, particularly in those institutions that provide faculty and staff housing in their compound.

In one residential program for training young community leaders, the weekly schedule early in the course was specified as follows:

	Hours
Manual work (3 x 2 hours)	6
Discussion of manual work and incidents in living together (3 x $1^1/_2$)	$4^1/_2$
Case sessions	
Small groups (4 x 1)	4
Whole group (4 x $1^1/_2$)	6
Review and discussion of program	$2^1/_2$
Village demonstration	$2^1/_2$
Field visit	6
Case preparation (estimated 4 x $1^1/_2$)	6
Individual written assignment	2
Evening discussions (2 x 2)	4
TOTAL	$43^1/_2$

Manual work and case sessions were concentrated in three days, with this program:

	Hours
Manual work	2
Discussion of manual work	$1\frac{1}{2}$
Case session	
Small group	1
Whole group	$1\frac{1}{2}$
TOTAL	6

Participants were then asked to work these events into a timetable. A weekly review and planning session provided the occasion for revising the timetable. Substantial variations occurred from course to course, and often within the course, as the participants experienced successive versions and explored new ones.

The engineering concept of tolerances and working to limits has a basic significance for training. It can help reduce wild, erratic swings of opinions about training and shift concerns from all or nothing, attack or defense, endlessly detailed syllabus or no syllabus at all, to the moderate range of action and improvement.

Not all programs and not all training groups are equally successful, and often the causes for such variations remain unclear even after valiant efforts to ascertain them. Furthermore, even when the causes are clear the course of events producing them cannot always be altered. That is the human condition. Trainers should give their very best. This is all. But nothing less will do.

Chapter 7

Training Methods

> To put away one's own original thoughts in order to take up a book is a sin against the Holy Ghost.
>
> —Schopenhauer

> I never teach my pupils. I only attempt to provide the conditions in which they can learn.
>
> —Albert Einstein

The Training needs of the work organization determine the resources which the training system can use. The system then has the task of designing a program that can best meet these needs. Notice that this definition of the training system's task is correct both when an agency takes the initiative in offering a program and when it designs one in response to a particular request. The only difference is that the one design is based on training needs that the organizers deem important, the other on needs seen as important by an organization and then worked out by the resource system and jointly agreed.

When training needs are presented to the system's representative(s) for action they meet prejudice. This is merely a sharp way of saying that the training system is not blank or an empty vessel. As in other human enterprises, training administrators and trainers hold views and preferences, and have characteristic ways of looking at and approaching a task and then carrying it out—a distinctive culture, in short. This culture also gives a resource system particular character; and the work organization and its potential participants expect particular advantages from choosing to work with one training system over another. The same applies to particular training units, agencies, and institutions that comprise the training system of an organization. Certain institutions are known for special interests. The Indian Institute of Management, Calcutta, for example, is noted for operational research and managerial mathematics. Other institutions have made a name for certain training methods such as case teaching or in-plant training, or through the strength of certain faculty groups or services.

By the time a system comes to detail the program it intends to offer, its prejudice—preference, tendency, or point of view might be more agreeable terms—has already influenced its participation in the choice of a training strategy, its collaboration with the organization and participants, and, internally, the kind of trainers it has assembled and its approach to the training design. These initial choices influence, in turn, the selection of training methods and faculty roles, not only because they are dictated by the same preferences but also because the earlier choices of strategy necessarily embody preferences for certain designs, methods, roles and relationships. These, in turn, favor the use of particular training facilities. For example, laboratory methods of training call for most work in small groups—and therefore small rooms. That program (or part of one) is best isolated somewhat from other parts of the system's activities—and therefore needs a block of time rather than occasional sessions sandwiched between others. It calls for highly experienced trainers—otherwise, it is better not attempted. These trainers should be the kind of people who do not develop relationships with participants on traditional authoritarian lines. And so forth. Within wider or lesser limits, a system's preference, training strategy, design, methods, and facilities are causally related and support one another. As we examine below various training methods and their specifications, and how trainers build them into a program, it is important to remember this starting point. Not every possibility is open to every system, and that not merely for lack of suitable trainers and facilities; neither is the choice mechanical, matching needs by strict logical extrapolation. No system will consider every possibility logically open to it. It is no use pretending otherwise. Prior general preferences influence a system's choice of training methods and its approach to developing the training group(s) and climate, trainers and their styles, to the many other components of training in action. The next three chapters will focus on the major components in turn.

Here we will briefly examine seven kinds of training methods. There are other methods, of course, but these cover the known range. We have limited description to a minimum and have concentrated instead on the assumptions, dilemmas, the choices posed by each method and by the specifications it demands in terms of time, faculty, and facilities effective for its use.

TWO FAULTY JUXTAPOSITIONS

The sequence we have chosen for presenting these methods starts with training in the course of action—on the factory floor, "in the field"—and ends with generalization—the lecture. The choice is not merely a matter of convenience or good order. In our study of various training methods we also want to challenge two common formulations about training and to substitute others that seem more suitable. These formulations pertain to the juxtapositioning of matters that ought to be related.

The first is the juxtaposition of training and experience. Learning from experience is often used as a foil to systematic training, as though the two were at opposite ends of some scale, or even glared at one another like combatants in an arena. All learning comes through experience but, as we shall see, the connection is neither direct nor simple. All that effective training can hope to do is ensure maximum opportunities for *relevant* experiences and to so organize them into useful sequences and intensities that the elements of chance and waste in learning are reduced. With technologies and organizations rapidly changing and expanding, this is a sufficiently formidable task, in extent, complexity, and value. Far from juxtaposing experience and training, relating one to the other is the first valid formulation, and the major task.

A second favorite gambit in the game of opposites is the juxtaposition of theory and practice. Training is often with theory, and practice with experience. "Practical" people decry theory—and training—as useless. Yet A. N. Whitehead, a mathematician and philosopher, saw "nothing so practical as a good theory." We suspect that the two contestants in theory versus practice want to rate their own interests and competencies higher than the others'. One concentrates on specific, individual experiences—on action; the other on the development of useful generalizations from repeated experience—theory. For training, the task is to find ways of relating theory and practice effectively, to ensure competence in the individual, unique situations that make up life, and the development of useful general guides and ways of thinking, i.e., a conceptual framework for new situations in the future.

EVENTS—REFLECTION—EXPERIENCE

One important distinction to make and to cling to is between an event (say, a session in marketing) and the participants' experience of it. This distinction embodies two points of view that trainers must keep separate. The event is one kind of thing. The participants' experience of it, from which they learn, is another. The event is objective, external, what trainers can arrange and include in the training timetable. The experience, on the other hand, is subjective, internal, what a particular participant derives from an event, the meaning she attaches to it, and therefore what she "internalizes". To be very precise, participants' experience of an event consists of their awareness and receptivity during the time span of its happening. They may daydream, not "tune in" the marketing problem at all, and recall the session later as a period of pleasant memories. The "blue Monday" phenomenon is well known to trainers the world over: many a participant's mind and heart are still preoccupied by yesterday's holiday pursuits. Or they may be so stimulated by just one aspect of the subject, that they are fully occupied exploring it, and pay no attention to what else goes on. The point is that trainers can only control events, and these, at best, are an indirect avenue to ensuring participant experiences and intended learnings. This tenuous connection between external event and internal experience, between training and learning, account for the major problems of evaluating effectiveness in training or, for that matter, in any communication. The trainer organizes events, but realistic evaluation of those events has to be in terms of participants' experiences. No easy matter, this. In order to make reasonably sure participants are "with them," trainers must insert frequent checks. Their scenario reads something like this: "X is what we had in mind to help the participants learn. What, in fact, has A or B or C learned? All of X? Some of X? Something else? Which? The opposite—for example, to hate the subject or be frightened of it? To hate us for keeping on with it? Or are they now ready to take the next step?"

One more general thought before we scan some major kinds of training events and examine their uses in a training program. Learning takes time, reflective time. The number of events is no guide to how much will be learned. Continuous activity, continuous company, may, on the contrary, militate against learning, may deflect participants from the demanding business of changing their minds and expanding their capabilities, i.e., from what we call learning. A training system, so to speak, is not a circus. It does not exist to entertain, to help people forget their daily preoccupations. On the contrary, it exists to help people understand and do something with their preoccupations. All that participants may learn from a very "heavy" program is what it feels like to be under heavy pressure for a long time. If this is the learning the trainers intend to foster, fine. There are jobs and positions in which pressure abounds, and participants can be helped to experience this. But even that experience, to be fruitful, needs reflective time.

Some people reflect best by talking, by putting a colleague in a comfortable chair and making her listen to their efforts to discover what they really think. Others reflect best by sitting still and pondering in apparent idleness, still others by walking alone in the open air. There are people, too, who formulate a problem to themselves, and then attend to various unrelated matters; they know from experience that an unconscious inner mulling will take place, and may awaken in the middle of the night with the answer ready. Participants will have their own methods, or will have yet to find them if their environment so far has not led to this discovery. And at different times, they may find different methods best for reflection. We have already discussed in the preceding chapter the difficulties involved in putting a training program together, its sequence, how to think about the training mix. Here it is necessary to stress again that the training program needs both to stimulate and to allow participants opportunities to think and to internalize events in their various ways. These opportunities, too, are training events and should be deliberately planned. The program needs elbowroom, space for things "to grow" on participants. Experience, learning, deepens and widens. It cannot be forced. It is more likely to be hindered than helped by too tight a program.

LEARNING ON THE JOB—NINE TRAINING REQUIREMENTS

Generalizations about learning on the job, the traditional, common-sense way of acquiring a skill, are rather useless. An initial familiarization with working life takes place, an acculturation. Over time, less for some people, more for others, experiences are gained in practical contexts. A wise, caring, sensitive supervisor or senior colleague may create settings whereby someone of lesser experience is led to fuller competence. In some trades and professions the major steps in the progression have been formalized into time frames, pay schedules, and career ladders. But beyond these general comments, learning on the job leaves essential features of learning dependent on *particular technologies, situations and people.* Often it is not known whether what has been learned by this method, or how much of it, is in fact a useful stepping stone or will presently become a stumbling block. What learning is called for, and for what job and setting, are the practical questions. In some circumstances there may or may not be time to think, and help and stimulation of new ideas are limited to whoever happens into the course of working closely together with someone. Just how chancy on-the-job training can be, has been aptly caught by popular expressions like, "trial and error," "sink or swim," "learning the hard way," "knocking off rough corners." An open examination of the persistent appeal of learning on the job may, superficially, look like flogging a horse that ought to be retired. But it may prove helpful in delineating sharply the criteria by which training methods should be judged.

First of all, there is a basic reasonableness about learning by trial and error. Everything to be learned in a given situation is covered and, too, in whatever order it occurs. Moreover, all of us learn many things through trial and error, for example, walking. And to let one's capabilities develop over time also makes sense. Rarely is it reasonable to let a twenty-year-old do a wise old man's job. Furthermore, many a father learned his job in this manner, so why not his son? It is probably not chance that the time-worn expressions for describing this method are defiant in tone, as though to keep the sons in their place.

The question is: when and where is this method of learning appropriate today? A statement of the assumptions on which it rests will clarify the answer. There are at least three. The first is that the job and the work situation can be apprehended as a totality; it is merely a matter of putting one's senses and mind to work. The second is that the job will remain the same for a long time (like walking), so speed of learning is not a major consideration. The third assumption is that risks of error during learning are small for both the learner and the organization.

It is immediately clear that these assumptions are no longer generally useful, certainly not for jobs characteristic of our time. Most modern jobs are complex and can neither be grasped nor practiced all at once. Moreover, interdependent production makes unscheduled time for reflection or for asking or giving advice difficult to come by. Furthermore, how long it takes to acquire a skill is very important these days. Machinery and organization need to be maximally used to be economical. Moreover, technological advances and all the shifts in an environment associated with development—social, economic, political—make the life span of many skills short; hence they must be learned fast and used soon.

The same speed of change puts a premium on knowing how to learn repeatedly. That is a trait which the subtle processes of growing into a skill over a long period of time do not develop well. People who have learned on the job may become very good at it, but introduce a new machine or a new condition in their work, and they flounder, often finding themselves, as the saying goes, not with ten or twenty years of experience, but with a half-year's experience repeated twenty or forty times. And even that half-year's experience has now become outmoded. Examples of this problem are all around us—in traditional crafts, farming, management, administration, and training itself. Finally, with higher investment and tighter schedules, errors on the job are more costly and therefore should not usually be left to chance.

From this analysis the first four requirements of a systematic training program can be extracted.

1. Provide successive glimpses of the job in such dimensions that the skill required for each can be grasped, practiced separately if necessary, and then put together with other parts when the time is ripe. In other words, what a program puts forward for the attention of participants at any given time must be realistic.

2. Provide time and other resources, such as the trainer's knowledge and experience, in such measure that participants can convert the training event into an experience for themselves.

3. Protect participants and work organizations against personal harm and expensive error arising from lack of knowledge and skill.

4. Make the learning process itself conscious for participants so that they then know how to deal with new situations as they arise and can continue learning.

In many cases these four requirements, or at least the first three, can be provided on the job and many organizations do so. They constitute, in fact, a more or less systematic process, which is what most people have in mind who favor learning on the job. They see participants as apprentices or interns. Participants are attached to seniors selected for their empathy and ability to nurture new talent. They are given work that involves increasingly complex decisions and actions in line with their growing skills. Time is scheduled for reviewing the work. Attendance of trainees to observe departmental and board meetings; consultation to elicit thought, comment, and recommendations; occasional meetings away from work to review and plan—these are becoming increasingly common in large organizations.

Perhaps the most elaborate provision of opportunities for training on the job is a junior board, or its equivalent at departmental levels in industrial organizations. This board is composed of a group of people in line for promotion. It proposes to the senior board fully responsible actions on current and policy issues. It may from time to time and within agreed-upon limits act on behalf of the senior board. All this is regarded as part of staff development and is quite systematic. The additional burden of time and other resources are considered proper investment in staff.

But many organizations do not find this enough. During times of rapid expansion they cannot train the number of people required using this approach. Furthermore, many modern jobs cannot be broken down into parts for separate practice during the course of day-to-day work. Our list of the four basic requirements a systematic training program must meet, has, therefore, to be expanded by five more:

5. Expose participants to ideas and methods beyond those now available within the work organization.

6. Provide opportunities for experimentation beyond the tolerance of an operating organization and for feedback of results.

7. Give participants the experience of belonging to groups outside the organization, especially professional and occupational groups, which can foster a continual exchange of ideas and the development and maintenance of high professional standards.

8. Provide opportunities to step back from day-to-day tasks to think about the

job as a whole, analyze priorities and division of time, and how the job fits into the participants' pattern of life.

9. Provide opportunities for a very intensive experience for participants through a specialized program with highly skilled trainers.

Looking at these nine requirements as a whole leaves the impression that learning on the job has most to offer during the later stages of acquiring a skill. These are the stages when new skills have to be used under normal working conditions. In our tripartite division of systematic training, these stages fall in the posttraining phase—one of crucial importance. It harbors particular difficulties for developing countries where trained but inexperienced staff are often sent to work in scattered locations under little supervision. Much of their onward training takes place on the job without benefit of guidance, support, or time for reflection.

> Librarians for village libraries in India, for instance, are given basic training, then sent on the job where each is totally on his or her own. However, one training scheme provides detailed "apprenticeship" and supervision for one difficult aspect of the work: book ordering. During the first year a senior officer does all the ordering. During the next year the librarian does twenty percent of it, during the third forty percent, and so on. During the first year the new librarian can, therefore, concentrate on the rest of the work in hand. As that becomes familiar, he or she devotes more and more attention to the difficult job of book ordering. More or less systematic schemes along these lines in many subjects provide for occasional senior assistance to scattered staff and to entire institutions.

On the other hand, training on the job has less and less to offer at the earlier stages of acquiring new skills. This is the period in which participants need various opportunities which the operating organization cannot offer. They need less ambiguous roles and tasks than insider/outsider, training/producing that learning on the job demands. In short, participants must definitely be trainees, even when they are members of an organization's own training unit. Their task at this phase is to learn. Only later, and not while in training, should they apply their skills to production.

METHODS

1. Training in the Field

Training in the field is the first step back from learning on the job. Its purpose is twofold: to provide participants with opportunities to test specific ideas and techniques they wish to learn in a daily life situation; and secondly, to offer them opportunities for assessing what, in fact, an organization needs for its development. These are two quite different objectives. The focus of the first is on participants' needs to become more proficient in the use of a particular technique. They are given scope to practice it, and to handle themselves in real-life situations. Important as field practice is for these purposes, that is all participants can reliably gain from it. The trainers' task includes ensuring that the organization's normal working is not unduly disrupted by the participants' practice. The focus of the second objective is the needs of the organization. Participants practice diagnostic skills and the building of closer relationships. To state the purpose of this training method as "applying" knowledge and skill in the field leads to confusion. Whether any particular technique can be usefully "applied" in the present context is quite a different question.

In fact, it may be useful to separate these two purposes of field training.

> SIET Institute offers for both purposes in its regular twelve-week course in industrial management, but offers them at different times and in different places. Technique practice, for example, of work sampling or time study, occupies three days in the fourth week and is carried out in a large factory. Practice in diagnosing needs and visualizing ways of acting on them is the starting point of a three-week study of a small factory that begins in the sixth or seventh week. This study leads to recommendations for action which are communicated to responsible executives. Specific techniques may or may not be used in the field study. That depends on the needs of the factory and the participants' modes of clarifying them.

The participants' role in the field training is basically that of interested outsider. They are present in normal work settings but not part of them. The work would be substantially the same without them; they are supernumeraries. Superficially, this description might not seem applicable to people like management trainees. They are hired in the expectation that they will permanently join the organization, and their training program is an integral part of the operation. But in terms of their experience they, too, are outsiders as they come newly into a department and, having become acquainted with its working, leave to join another. Their role and their experience will be significantly different when, say, a year later, they actually start to work in one or the other departments visited earlier. The difference lies in the nature and degree of their involvement and the share of responsibility they will then carry for the department's activities. Training in the field gives a bird's-eye view that encompasses everything. The perceptive and diligent participant can learn much about any given part but, nevertheless, only from a distance.

The outsider's role carries several advantages in terms of training. It is easier to be dispassionately analytical in that role. Outsiders have no personal stake in what is going on or in the outcome. The role allows great flexibility. Outsiders can move about in an organization, follow up cues, take time to reflect and analyze. No one depends on them to be in a particular spot in certain time or to complete a specified task. They can spend some time in one organization, then move on to another.

From the institution's point of view, training in the field is a very demanding method, calling for extensive and difficult preparation. Four areas for thought and action can be listed: the detailed roles of participants and of the trainers in the field, selection of an organization for field training, and special preparation of participants.

1. *Clarification of participant's role* . The aim in field training is to combine most promisingly the freedom and other advantages of the outsider with access to sufficient, and sufficiently important, data. This combination, and not the type of work participants do at home, is the main criterion for selecting a field and clarifying the participant's role. Since industrial units associate consultants with useful recommendations for action on real problems, the purposes of training and the factory's operations may well be combined in the consultant's role. This is the role SIET Institute assigns to participants during its three-week in-plant and in-district training. In other settings, different roles might be more appropriate. The intern in a hospital and the research worker or training fellow in an academic setting exemplify such roles.

A number of things follow from the choice of role. Each role implies a prior agreement between the institution and "the field." If the agreement can be defined and stated explicitly, so much the better. The consultant role implies that, in exchange for accepting this training opportunity for the participant, the institution has committed them to offering something of value to the organization. Whatever the role, it must allow for two different points of view. The trainers specify the training opportunity; the organization plays no part in this since it cannot decide what the participants are to learn or how. On the other hand, the organization assesses the value of the participants' recommendations. The trainers cannot declare a recommendation, however valid, to be of value if the organization will not accept it. These implicit and differing points of view must be underscored because training in the field is difficult to organize well and the common shortcomings in this type of training can usually be traced to inadequate preparation.

The following examples illustrate the kind of difficulties that inadequate preparation can lead to.

For field *visits* no attempt is actually made to strike a bargain. The organization expects nothing in return and is also unlikely to give beyond what good public relations require. It is doubtful that many such visits really give the exposure that would justify and warrant the time, trouble, and expense incurred. Different from visits are *field placements.* In the United States they are often called "internships." Many offer very little training to participants, while giving an organization the free use of an eager mind and pair of hands. This is liable to happen, for instance, if trainees are placed in a social work agency so short of staff that newcomers are allocated any piece of work "they are able to do." Such "pieces" are usually fairly simple tasks and they may be kept doing them for long periods, no matter what, if anything, they have already learned about them in the first few days.

Or an organization may, halfway through the field training, deny participants access to certain kinds of data important to the completion of their task. This kind of refusal sometimes occurs in industrial units when cost data is needed. It amounts to the organization not keeping its side of the bargain. In contrast to this, for example, are the villages surrounding many training centers which are sometimes labeled "wasteland." They have repeatedly received training groups for fieldwork. Each group has established the "needs" and program required until now the villages need nothing so much as to be left alone. At issue here is neither the trainers' nor the participants' goodwill or intent, but what can be usefully attempted in a village during field training and what cannot.

2. *Clarification of trainer's role.* The trainer's role in the field calls for clarification both vis-à-vis the participants and vis-à-vis the work organization. Both abound with dilemmas. How far can trainers leave participants to their own devices? Allowing them to make up their own minds can be good training, but consequent errors may deprive the organisation of the benefits it expected. Just when do the trainers step in? And how do they step in without belittling the participants' independence and learning? If their schedule permits, how much time should the trainers spend with the participants? The more they are present, the greater their temptation to lend a hand.

A useful rule of thumb for trainers faced with these dilemmas may be active training and correction during technique practice, but a much more withdrawn role when field training focuses on diagnosis and relationships. Many trainers find the latter role much easier if they have a task of their own to mind while present in the field. They are there, accessible for consultation, but need not hang around meanwhile. The role of the trainer in the field vis-à-vis the participant reflects the role assumed in the rest of the training program.

3. *Choosing the organization for field training.* The choice of organization and the agreement reached with it are largely a function of the chosen roles. The training system ought to avoid selecting either the most advanced or the most backward organization. Placing participants in a unit that rates among the best, of course, is easiest but would soon leave them discouraged over finding a problem that would permit a useful contribution to the organization's personnel. In short, the best of operations may not be the best for training. The worst unit, on the other hand, may have too many and more difficult needs than the participants can help resolve given their limited time and skills. Initially very excited at the prospects, the trainee ends up frustrated. This is a common problem when the organization suffers from complicated problems of relationships between key people or when field training is organized in too large a unit. The

institution may end up with unfinished business on its hands, which then raises further problems.

Choosing an organization for field training, therefore, involves a series of difficult and time-consuming steps. Many organizations may have to be studied briefly to find the few appropriate for the training needs of participants in terms of coverage and complexity and to ascertain the organization's needs and likely response.

A checklist can be developed for selecting field sites for participant teams. It may involve much time and care, but the values of good field placements are sufficiently high to warrant both.

4. *Preparing participants for field training.* Clearly the greater the skill with which participants go into the field (because of tested experience of specific preparation during earlier stages of the program), the more confident the trainers can be when leaving them free to explore and make their own way. Working through some of the emotional factors in advance can make participants readier to use the skills they have, and reduce preoccupations over unsettling uncertainties, for example, about collaboration in the group, accommodation, and food. In the Area Development Course at SIET Institute participants divide themselves into the small groups required for field study, then undergo a two-day training laboratory for working anticipated problems in the relationships they have chosen. Trainers can also help participants think concretely about various aspects of the task ahead and design simple aids for use in the field.

Happily, trainers can depend with some certainty on the emergence of two very favorable forces as training in the field gets under way. Most participants are highly stimulated by it and respond to the opportunity with high initiative and devotion. Some exaggerate their role. For its part, the organization usually responds warmly to the participants' earnestness and goodwill, and values their thoughtful questions and comments even before recommendations are focused and embodied in a formal report. Trainers can, therefore, be of good cheer in organizing training in the field. They can feel assured that it is useful and that they are moving with the stream, in the direction of everyone's inclinations.

Exhibit 7.1 summarizes the specifications of training in the field.

Exhibit 7.1

TRAINING IN THE FIELD: OUTLINE SPECIFICATIONS

	a) Specific technique training	*b) Diagnostic and relationship training*
Participant's role	Outsider/learner	Outsider/helper
Data	Situational	Situational
Trainer's role	Active guide	Resource person/consultant

Exhibit 7.1 (Continued)

Time required	Half days or whole days	Regular and frequent, or block of time, e.g., 2–3 weeks minimally
Trainer requirements:		
Ratio	1 to 12–15	1 to 5
Time for preparation	Little	Very heavy
Follow-up	None	Varies widely, can be heavy
Facilities required	Work setting in which technique normally used	1 work setting for 1 to 4 participants, long-term relationship with organization
Special points	None	Long lead time for making arrangements in the field.

2. Simulating Real Life: Role Playing, Games, and In-Basket Exercises

Training in the field is a major venture, and effective roles for participants take time to establish and to perform. To reduce these costs and to provide practice in a variety of situations and roles, it is possible to design training opportunities which are just one step removed from real life. Instead of taking participants into the field, at the cost of extra time and limited responsibilities and roles, the field can be simulated in the training session itself.

Simulations can range from the simple (creating roles and situational dynamics to help participants briefly "experience" and practice different ways of dealing with situations and consequences) to the more elaborate (organized and planned, but simplified causal chains of situations extending over several days). They are "games" inasmuch as the consequences of success or failure are not "for real." However, the experience of *personal* success, failure, competence, satisfaction, and self-doubt, often under intense pressure, can be real enough to be memorable. In all simulations some dimensions are controlled to allow selected aspects to be highlighted. Simulation methods are therefore also called "controlled experience" methods.

The three most common simulation methods are: role playing, games, and in-basket exercises.

Role Playing: The purpose of role playing is to help participants experience what something "sounds" or "feels like," the difference between talking *about* people and talking *with* them, or talking about an action and actually starting. Role playing can be very real in these situations.

Role playing is a very flexible training method. It may be elaborately pre-planned, with the actors carefully primed and session time specifically earmarked for the play and its subsequent discussion. Or the trainer can encourage participants to role play spontaneously during some session. Careful management of time is important for the first version; otherwise discussion time or repeat performances will be neglected. A good rule of thumb is to allow not less than ten minutes for each play, twice as much time for discussion as for the play, and time for at least two plays of the same situation in the session period. That adds up to one hour, with no allowance yet for an introduction or closure. Informal, spur-of-the-moment role playing requires no specific advance preparation or setting. But it does call for additional time and a high level of training skill. Rather than have participants prolong an unprofitable argument, for instance, the trainer can ask them to assume opposite roles. The results of such a degree of reality in the session may be far reaching. One possibility is that neither time nor disposition may be left for anything else in that particular session! We assume that the trainer is able to handle the outcomes of the confrontation.

Role playing is mainly useful for training in behavioral dimensions. Careful designs to highlight trouble spots in participants' lives, role briefing of players, and allowing sufficient time after each play for its discussion are very important. "Role-play kits" can be developed for widespread use through repeated trials, evaluations, and revisions.

Behavior Simulation Games: These focus primarily on the processes of interpersonal relations, on *how* decisions are made, and with what consequences, rather than on the substance of the decisions.

Some trainers use "structured exercises" to denote all types of simulations, but it might be better to distinguish between games and exercises. Games have set rules and predictable results. Often their design is hidden in order to highlight a behavioral process and to dramatize its effects. When the "secret" is out, repeating that game with the same group would be senseless. Exercises, on the other hand, simulate a process and can be repeated until learning is assured. They provide scope for improvisation, adaptation, and redesigning according to personal and situational needs.

The trainer or the facilitator has a wide range of critical roles in simulation sessions. One moment she provides expertise, the next she is theory-builder and teacher: she organizes and manages the session and facilitates its process. Both process learning and cognitive learning can result from a good simulation session. The most common shortfalls occur in the processing or debriefing of participants after a game or exercise.

Several steps can be identified for designing behavior simulations. Box 7.1 presents a set of thirteen and can serve as a checklist.

In-Basket Exercises: The most elaborate simulations "create" a complex work organization, rotate participants through key roles in it, and have them "deal with" specific situations of a kind they encounter in real life. Management trainees may work at an office desk with ringing telephones and full in-baskets. Participants have a number of intradepartmental and interdepartmental memos, letters, reports, forecasts, and other data on their desks, such as they might normally receive. They pose a series of problems to handle, perhaps a crisis which the officer they play must correct. They can use the channels of communication normally open: telephone, memos, and face-to-face meetings.

Box 7.1

STEPS IN DESIGNING INSTRUCTIONAL SIMULATION

1. Define instructional problems.
2. Describe the operational educational system.
3. Relate the operational system to the problem.
4. Specify objectives in behavioral terms.
5. Generate criterion measures.
6. Determine appropriateness of simulation.
7. Determine type of simulation required.
8. Develop specifications of simulation experience.
9. Develop simulation system prototype.
10. Try out simulation system prototype.
11. Modify the simulation system prototype.
12. Conduct field trial.
13. Make further modification to the system on the basis of the field trial.

SOURCE: P. A. Turelker, "Designing Simulation Systems" in *Introduction to the Systems Approach* (Englewood Cliffs, N.J., 1972).

The development of in-basket exercises requires familiarity with the roles participants work on and various styles of memos, letters, and telephone calls. Critical incidences, for inclusion in the "in-basket," spring from such familiarity.

Exhibit 7.2

SIMULATION METHODS: OUTLINE SPECIFICATIONS

	a) Role Playing	*b) Business Games*	*c) In-Basket Exercises*
Participant's role	Player/ observer	Player/colleague or competitor	Player

Exhibit 7.2 (Continued)

	a) Role Playing	*b) Business Games*	*c) In-Basket Exercises*
Data	Self-generated	Normal working data	Normal working data
Trainer's role	Organizer/ conductor of review	Organizer/ conductor of review	Organizer/ conductor of review
Time required	1 hour 15 min.	2 sessions	2 sessions
Trainer requirements:			
Ratio	1 to 20	1 to 20	1 to 8
Time for preparation	1 to 20 hours	High depending on materials	High depending on materials
Facilities required	Nothing special	Separate areas for each 4 or 5 participants	Real setting: e.g., desks, working telephones, etc.

The major problem in using any type of simulation method is to ensure that its drama does not become so intriguing that participants are seduced from the primary purpose: learning something for action. This purpose differs from others for which similar methods can be used. A passing moment's reflection about one such purpose may recapture the distinction and point of view that must be safeguarded. Psychodrama and sociodrama are also simulation methods. They are used in therapy to help disturbed people relive situations that upset them. The drama may lead anywhere. Its importance lies in the process, in the reliving itself. The purpose of simulation methods of training, on the contrary, is to offer opportunities for specific experiences. If they lead anywhere else, the trainers have failed.

Exhibit 7.2 summarizes the specifications of simulation methods of training.

3. Laboratory Training for Personal and Organizational Development

The purpose of laboratory training is to provide participants with an intensive experience of how they affect each other—and probably other people also—and how a group forms, maintains itself, and deals with relationship problems that are also characteristic of larger organizations. For intensity of experience and for clarity of data the training group needs to be small: twelve to fifteen. Some programs specify eight to ten. The laboratory is shorn of several key aspects of normal work (incidentally, also of key aspects of most other kinds of training). For instance, the group has no task other than to study its own working; attention to other data is regarded as misdirected. It has no hierarchical organization other than whatever the group constructs for itself; certainly the trainer will not assume leadership. It depends on immediate and clear feedback beyond any standards normal in everyday living and working. All this makes the experience for the participants very real and intensive. They are themselves; they are not "playing" at someone else. They work only on problems that they themselves initiate. The insulation of the setting from ordinary life is emphasized if the sessions take place in a soundproof room. It is then obviously a laboratory.

In terms of Lewin's three-stage model of learning, the unexpected behavior of the trainer and the other special conditions of the training laboratory make for rapid unfreezing. Figure 7.1 shows the process of laboratory training according to Lewin's model.

Figure 7.1

CHANGE MODEL OF LABORATORY TRAINING

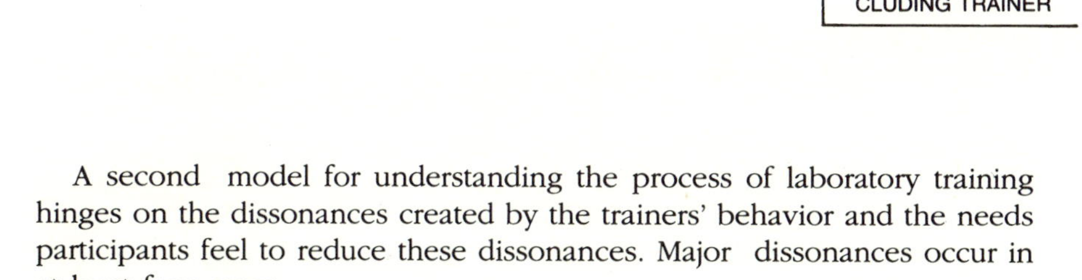

A second model for understanding the process of laboratory training hinges on the dissonances created by the trainers' behavior and the needs participants feel to reduce these dissonances. Major dissonances occur in at least four areas:

1. Between the participants' expectations of the trainers and the trainers' actual behavior. The trainers ignore all attempts to seduce, force, or otherwise get them to conform to initial expectations.

2. Between participants' concepts of themselves and their actual behavior and its effects in the laboratory.

3. Between participants' expectations of the group's reactions to them and how the group actually reacts.

4. Between the image of themselves participants wish to impress on others and the image others actually have or develop of them.

The trainers' role is to belie in front of the group the commonly accepted standards of hierarchical relationships and the neglect of the effects people have on each other's feelings. Their task is to show that these effects are worth studying, *can* be studied and taken into account, and lead to useful and acceptable feedback. They plug all avenues, barring one, for escaping from the discomforts of dissonance. The avenue left open requires participants to face both inner and outer realities and then to alter present habits if they produce undesired effects.

Shattered expectations and other dissonances make a training laboratory a disturbing and intensive experience. The same quality probably explains the high rate of retention of what participants have learned in such laboratories. Research findings with the U.S. Bureau of Naval Research place the retention rate at seventy-five percent, compared with fifty-five percent for visual material and thirty-five percent for lecture presentations. But such high intensity has a price. First of all, laboratories are best if full-time. Many participants cannot carry on with other work at normal standards while they are involved in a training situation as productive of anxiety and anger as a training laboratory usually is during its early stages. That is a major limitation of this training method. Other limitations arise with any attempts to fuse a training laboratory with other kinds of training in the same program. Both to attain and maintain the necessary intensity, laboratory training is best carried out separately or at the very beginning of a diversified program. The high level of motivation for learning that laboratory training usually engenders is likely to carry over to other parts of the program, but more of this later.

The severest limitation of this method is probably the shortage of mature trainers who are both skilled and experienced. Skill and experience alone do not suffice here. Or rather, since laboratory trainers are working in the delicate area of participants' perceptions, feelings, and reactions, only people with a fair insight into their own motivations and a large capacity for accepting others qualify as trainers. Even then training laboratories make heavy demands on the trainers' nervous system and sheer stamina. The learning that a training laboratory promotes is, of course, correspondingly exciting and satisfying to the trainer. Exhibit 7.3 summarizes the specifications of laboratory training.

Exhibit 7.3

LABORATORY TRAINING: OUTLINE SPECIFICATIONS

Participant's role	Him- or herself
Data	Generated by group itself, "here and now" feedback
Trainer's role	Nonauthoritarian, resource person
Time required	15 x 2 hours, preferably in a block
Trainer requirements:	
Ratio	2 to 12–15 or 1 to 8–10
Time for preparation	Very little.
Facilities required	Small room: tape recorder (helpful)
Special points	Requires rare training skill, may arouse high levels of anxiety which can affect activities running concurrently

4. Sampling Real Life: Incidents and Cases

We are leaving the realm of action, real or simulated. Participants can no longer talk with the people in the situation they are considering, for those people are not in the session. They cannot influence the situation, for it is over and done with. All they now have is a descriptive record in the form of an incident of a case. Any "life" such a record is to have for the participant must be breathed into it by them. They do this by "seeing themselves" in one or another person in the case, or in several in turn. As a result of this projection they experience the situation vicariously, as though they had been involved.

From this important point of view a case on audio tapes or on film has disadvantages. For the closer the case situation approaches reality, the more difficult it becomes for participants to identify with the people in it. They may become more conscious instead of differences in voice, looks, and surroundings, and fail to see the similarities in content and problems between that situation and their own. In learning, not the reality outside but the reality to the participants is the key factor.

One purpose of providing vicarious experience is to multiply, well beyond what they would meet in their day-to-day work, the situations and problems participants can be exposed to during training. Another is to present each sample of real life in slow motion, so that through its detailed study participants can learn the most from the data offered. The communication is clear. Data are limited—and precious.

The third purpose of the case method is to help participants develop the habit of taking more factors into account than usually done, to analyze them carefully, and to put them together in an integrated picture for guiding understanding and action. These factors include the personal feelings and relationships of the actors in the situation. Because the descriptions of people and situations are taken from real life and resemble people and situations with which participants are familiar, this method also promotes the exploration of one's own attitudes and relationships.

Cases provide all the data available to participants in advance of the session. Participants are expected to have prepared themselves thoroughly, to be familiar with the facts and with ways of relating them usefully. The incident process developed by Paul and Faith Pigors[1] does not assume preparation. The incident itself is only a very brief statement of the situation. Additional data are available from the "instructor" of the day, who may be a participant whose situation is up for discussions of their choice from among the issues seen in the case. This is a useful thing to practice. For the "instructor," i.e., the participant/instructor, the process provides additional practice in writing up an incident out of available data, making a teaching plan, leading the discussion, and observing the discussion process.

The trainer's role in the session is to help participants, individually and collectively to clarify their understanding of the people and the situations and what decisions, actions, and implications can be drawn. He or she then builds on the participants' contributions. By helping generalizations to emerge from the study of a particular situation, the trainer enriches the conceptual schemes with which participants will approach their work in the future. These functions are different from piloting a meeting through an agenda, chairing a debate on an issue, or lecturing on a concept. Trainers develop different personal styles of carrying out these functions. The point here is that they alter the traditional relationship between trainer and participant. This, in turn, affects other parts of the training program in which an altered relationship does not necessarily develop.

Both shortage of skilled trainers and an acute shortage of adequate teaching materials severely limit the use of these training methods in developing countries. These limitations are interconnected. Experience elsewhere suggests that case research and case teaching are complimentary skills and must be developed together. The orientation from which they spring tends to pervade the entire training program. Indeed, whole

[1] Paul and Faith Pigors, *The Incident Process—Learning by Doing,* Massachusetts Institute of Technology Series 2, No. 46, 1962.

institutions have based themselves on the use of these methods.

> Professor Pigors' courses at the Massachusetts Institute of Technology and the work at the Harvard Business School are prime examples. In India, the Indian Institute of Management in Ahmedabad has developed the case method into a major orientation and method. Its faculty members receive training in the method abroad and have developed several hundred teaching cases in various fields of management, which are used in their two-year degree program as well as in special courses.

In India, apart from very few and partial exceptions, only the words "incidents" and "cases" are familiar. They are applied to a wide variety of materials. Some are not teaching but research cases. They deal with historical themes, or the author's, rather than with detailed data of a particular situation calling for understanding from persons involved. Others are limited to the point of view of one person and hence their discussion is likewise limited to what this one person saw. Still others present the unusual or absurd when the need is for material that can increase skills widely needed for everyday operations. Yet others are merely illustrations of some principle, as though life were an illustration of principles rather than the starting point from which useful principles can be deduced. And much of the material is simply inadequate in coverage and quality so that no useful discussion of it results.

The development of material for incidents is no easier and perhaps even less advanced. Though fewer data are given to the participants in advance, the trainer must have full and complete material, even fuller than required for a case, in order to answer participants' questions. After the participants have become familiar with the method, i.e., after three or four sessions, the trainer can shift the burden of preparing incidents to the participants, which also has the advantage of involving participants in discussions of their own experiences. But even good material does not guarantee effective incident or case sessions. Few trainers habitually use such material. Hence the danger is very real that these methods will not meet the high expectations with which they were introduced. If these methods are used without the backing of adequate material, skill, and institutional support, they are likely to fail.

The minimum concentration of resources for using the case method is high. Trainers need time and funds for case research and case writing, and specialized training to become skillful case teachers. Enough incidents and cases must be available for a self-contained series of at least twelve sessions, not just one or two, a series being necessary to familiarize the participants with the method. Advance preparation by participants of cases for discussion must be rigorous and comprehensive from the first case and set high norms for the rest. Otherwise the session tends to become an abstract argument instead of a meticulous consideration of available data, and will engage only a few participants.

This difficulty in preparation is avoided in the incident method, which starts by questioning very brief data; in fact, this is the advantage the process seeks to explore. Either series must be long enough for the novelty of the trainer's functions and role to wear off, particularly their non-evaluative character. The reality of the data, the demands these methods make on participants to handle their considered points of view in open discussion, and the different roles of the trainer—all make the use of incidents and cases thoroughly desirable. But nothing less than the minimum material and skill will do for initiating self-generating programs along this line. Exhibit 7.4 summarizes the specifications of the incident and case method.

5. Individualized Training

Tutoring, individual practice of specific skills, and reading and written assignments are traditional methods of individual training. For the many tasks that involve a senior and a junior together, and for others involving just one person, this method simulates the work situation. Otherwise, it means one more step away from reality: colleagues, customers, citizens, and others are totally absent.

The greatest advantage of individual training is that it enables each participant to determine the speed with which training can proceed. The tutor adapts his or her activities to the participant's singularity is even more sharply marked. Not only competence but also motivation is tested, both quite exposed.

Exhibit 7.4

SAMPLING REAL LIFE: OUTLINE SPECIFICATIONS

	a) Incident	*b) Case*
Participant's role	Initiator/contributor/ leader	Initiator/contributor leader
Data	Specific life situation elsewhere	Specific life situation elsewhere
Trainer's role	During question time, resource person; then discussion leader	Listener/clarifier/ conceptualizer
Time required for preparation:		
Of one session	—	Session time x 2
Series of sessions		10 x $1^1/_2$ hours

Exhibit 7.4 (Continued)

	a) Incident	*b) Case*
Trainer requirements: Ratio	1 to 20-40	1 to 20-?
Time for preparing sessions	10 x 2 hours	10 x 2 hours
Facilities required	Circular/horseshoe seating arrangement; large blackboards	Circular/horseshoe seating arrangement; large blackboards
Special points	High initial cost of material: 2-4 weeks' highly skilled work for each incident	High initial cost of material: 2-4 weeks' highly skilled work for each case.

Until recently, social isolation and high cost have limited individual instruction to a supplementary method of training. The development of programmed instruction individualizes the simultaneous training of many participants in certain skills. The essence of such a program is that it takes the trainer's place in several important and time-consuming respects. Based on a meticulously detailed analysis of what participants are to learn, the duplicated program (rather than the individual trainer) confronts participants with a set of specified steps so designed and ordered as to make it possible that each will progress in the direction desired. Other directions are closed out. The program may be in the form of a teaching machine or a programmed textbook, video, or TV program; the package is secondary. In the words of Wilbur Schramm, the essential elements are six:

> a) an ordered sequence of stimulus items, b) to each of which a student responds in some specified way, c) his response being reinforced by immediate knowledge of results, d) so that he moves by small steps, e) therefore making few errors and practising mostly correct responses, f) from what he knows, by a process of successively closer approximation toward what he is supposed to learn from the program.[2]

Initially introduced in school education, programmed instruction found its way into industrial training. By 1965 industrial companies reported the successful use of programmed instruction in mathematics, statistics and computer skills, production, maintenance and other managerial activities

[2] Wilbur Schramm, "Programmed Instruction Today and Tomorrow," in *Four Case Studies of Programmed Instruction* (Fund for the Advancement of Education, 1964).

involving scheduling, basic science, and aspects of engineering services, as well as an increasing number of operator skills. Programs have also been developed and tried out in human motivation for supervision, and for imparting knowledge to salesmen and service representatives about a wide variety of new services and products.

One great advantage programmed instruction has over other methods is its flexibility, for participants, trainers, and also program administrators. Often individuals can work through programs on their own time, as well as at their own speed. They need neither to start nor to finish a program together with others. Experience in industrial settings suggests that the slowest learners take about twice as long as the fastest. When they work on individualized programs, the slow need not feel harried, nor the fast restrained by others. This flexibility is most advantageous in training groups which are heterogeneous in terms of specialization, for example, production engineers and marketing and financial executives who are all starting to learn general management. At any point in time some participants will know much more (in their specialized field) than the rest. Programmed instruction thus allows what in schools is termed remedial teaching: special programs to enable a portion of the course group to catch up with the rest.

A second advantage of programmed instruction is that it provides in private the step-by-step evaluation and feedback that most participants would find unacceptable in front of their peers and trainers.

A third advantage is the uniformity of training input that comes from substituting a program for a trainer or, more likely, for several trainers. When the same course is taught by several trainers, there will be almost certainly significant differences in content. It is difficult even for the same trainer to maintain consistency from one course to the next. Trainers usually have a general syllabus and a session outline. What they do within this outline is a creative, highly individualized act. Individualized programs, on the other hand, have been subjected to empirical testing on sample groups of the participants for whom they are intended. Rigorously modified step by step the programs emerge highly consistent with objectives and constraints. Research studies show that final examination scores are much more homogeneous in programmed instruction than in other training methods. Few, if any, participants fail.

The problem at this stage of the development of individualized training methods is to sort out the "fads" from what is sound and permanent. Many of the original claims made for programmed instruction are spurious. There is no indication that adequate individualized instruction requires either fewer or less well prepared trainers. As for the quality of trainers, the reverse is more likely to be true. This is because participants will have arrived at various stages of the program simultaneously and ask questions over a very wide field; also, to the extent that the participants feel stimulated by the program they may ask more sophisticated, broader, and deeper questions. For many purposes appropriate programs are hard to find, and a good one is difficult to identify without further testing under controlled conditions. This is a costly and time-consuming process. Moreover, a wide range of programmed materials are required to instruct participants of varying ability. The costs per program vary widely but are certainly high. They are usually economical only when the prospective training population is large and the training objectives stable. Several expensive skills go into making a program. One American company has reported $ 3,500 as preparation costs per instructional hour.

Some questions pertaining to what is actually learned from programmed instruction also remain unexplored. Clever participants seem to develop a knack of short-cutting the program. Others go through the program apparently satisfactorily but then cannot pass tests or answer questions on what they have read or accomplished. Apparently, the alleged reward from immediate feedback, which tells participants they have made the right response, does not suffice. While feedback and reinforcement in the usual social situation of trainer and participant may be less consistent and reliable, it appears more durable and carries other important values too. Complaints about boredom are the most common from participants in programmed instruction. That complaints about boredom are heard too about other training methods does not settle the matter for programmed instruction. In this case the complaints about boredom raise questions about the very basis of the method: higher motivation and truly individualized training. If these objectives were achieved, surely boredom would disappear. But it is difficult to know what "boredom" really describes. Does it describe, for instance, the relentless pressure participants feel to concentrate on a program that does not allow the luxury of "tuning out" they could enjoy in sessions using other methods?

A final thought: programmed instruction has a very great indirect advantage. It demands meticulous specification of training needs and definition of training objectives, and training sequences and methods related most carefully to these objectives. A similar degree of care should, of course, inspire all training efforts, irrespective of method. But often it does not. Here is a method wherein nothing less will suffice. This should be reason enough to believe that programmed instruction has much to offer India and other developing countries. Exhibit 7.5 summarizes the specifications of programmed instruction.

6. Seminars and Syndicates

The purpose of seminars, syndicates, and other general discussion methods is to provide participants with opportunities to exchange information, views, ideas and recollections of experiences. Through this exchange they stimulate each other's thinking, broaden their outlook, and also gain experience in the kinds of give and take that commonly occur in meetings of many types. This process develops tolerance for the views of others. The methods are most promising if the group consists of people who come from different professional backgrounds and functions but work in similar organizations and jobs. The understanding and tolerance developed is appropriate to general rather than functional management, and is useful in considering issues of broad policy.

> The Administrative Staff College of India, whose work is based on the syndicate method developed at the Administrative Staff College at Henley, U.K., pays major attention to the composition of syndicate groups. Each syndicate includes participants from public and private industry and from public administration. In terms of functions these people represent engineering and technologies, accounting and finance, personnel and marketing.

Syndicates and seminars differ from the discussion of incidents and cases in that they focus on wide topics and problems, not on a single concrete situation. Nor do they focus on a carefully specified problem or on taking action. Syndicates and seminars aim generally at widening the participants' horizons and providing opportunities for exercising the mind: reading, preparing material for discussion, and participating in and leading discussions.

The participants' role in these methods is an active one, if they choose. Studies have shown that in groups of more than eight some participants tend to be silent, yet most groups are larger than eight, at least ten to fifteen. These methods depend, nevertheless, on participants' speaking. It is common for participants to take turns preparing material for discussion and chairing the sessions. A trainer's role is correspondingly inactive during the sessions; she is there as a resource person. She may even sit apart from the group, thus signalling that the participants are fully responsible

Exhibit 7.5

PROGRAMMED INSTRUCTION: OUTLINE SPECIFICATIONS

Participant's role	Individual, wholly in charge
Data	Standardized programmed material
Trainer's role	To answer questions
Time required	Flexible
Trainer requirements:	
Ratio	1 to 20
Time for preparation	Little
Follow-up	None

Exhibit 7.5 (Continued)

Facilities required	"Programmed" textbooks, etc.; individual work space
Special points	Preparation of program is quite separate from its use. Its high cost, about one month's highly skilled work per instruction hour, is economical for training large numbers of participants

for the proceedings. Her active functions are mostly behind the scenes—helping compose the group, thinking of topics and assignments to give the group, and paying attention to participants who seem to experience difficulties with the method or group, and perhaps helping them in private.

The purposes of these methods of training also set their limits. They assume that participants can use on the job the general skills these methods help them to practice. They also assume that the decisions reached by the group at an intellectual level will affect participants' behavior. These assumptions may or may not be valid. The intended effects are so general that the methods cannot be assessed for effectiveness per se, i.e., separately from the effects of the training environment as a whole or from a wide range of background factors.

A serious drawback to these methods is that they run counter to some basic needs of developing countries. For instance, where motivation for development is slight or mixed, participants in a general discussion may settle for tolerance at the price of new ideas; they may accept verbal agreements at high levels of abstraction at the price of working hard instead to reconcile differences and to widen areas of genuine agreement. They may not learn to respect, and to live and work with real diversity. The preponderance of "perhaps" and "broadly speaking" in many documents emerging from seminars confirms one's fears that verbal subterfuges have been used by the group to avoid exploring areas of disagreement or even stating different opinions side by side, unresolved. Yet development depends basically on divergence—dissonance—followed by integration—collaboration (as does training). That these methods should be so widely used in developing countries and heralded as major advances is, therefore, disturbing.

The exception to this worrisome drawback is brainstorming. Brainstorming is the very child of novelty; new problems call for "creative" solutions. Nothing is taken for granted, least of all the relevance of past experience. The method deliberately provokes participants to breakout of habitual grooves of thinking, to come up with fresh approaches to the problem. There is no trainer. The atmosphere encourages divergence and unorthodoxy. The starkness of this goal is far reaching. Brainstorming frankly favors divergence. Perhaps this fact alone explains why it is neglected in developing countries, where new solutions ought to carry the highest premium. It is still rarely used, even though its immediate aim is limited to new ideas only, and not changes in behavior. Exhibit 7.6 summarizes the specifications of three methods for broadening the mind.

7. The Lecture

Of the six types of training methods discussed so far in successive sections of this chapter, four use data from real-life situations as they occur right in front of the participants in the field or in the training laboratory, or from situations specially set up or reported by an observer or trainer, as in simulation techniques, incidents, and cases. The fifth method, individualized instruction, standardizes (i.e., abstracts) data from real life for systematic step-by-step learning of certain types. It also takes participants out of the social context of most training events: away from other participants in tutoring, and in programmed instruction also away from the trainers. The latter method underscores that participants, in order to learn must want to learn, and that they will in the final analysis proceed with learning at their own speed. Motivation and speed are thus acknowledged to be at the participants' end of the training process. The sixth set of methods, various kinds of general discussion, reintroduce the social dimension but put the participants to work on general topics and problems, that is, 'on abstract data.

Exhibit 7.6

GENERAL DISCUSSIONS: OUTLINE SPECIFICATIONS

	a) Seminar	*b) Syndicate*	*c) Brainstorming*
Participant's role	Contributor/ chairman/ presenter of data	Contributor/ chairman/ rapporteur	Contributor
Data	General topic or problem	General topic or problem	New problem
Trainer's role	Very small, resource	Very small, resource	Stimulator of unusual ideas
Time required	2 hours	2 hours	1 hour

Exhibit 7.6 (Continued)

Trainer requirements:			
Ratio	1 to 12-15	1 to 10-15	0 to 6-8
Time for preparation	Little	Little	Little
Follow-up	Little	Little	1 hour
Facilities required	Circular seating	Circular seating	Circular seating
Special points	Tend to abstraction and verbal agreement		

The seventh training method, the lecture, also keeps the data abstract and also eliminates the social dimension of learning. For purposes of training, our only concern here, the assumptions of the lecture method are numerous. Five are listed below.

1. That participants are motivated to learn. If they are free to choose whether or not to come to the lecture, their coming represents some motivation although if the lecturer is famous, attractive, or has a melodious voice, the motivation may not be primarily for learning. If attendance is obligatory, as invariably it is in training courses, the participants' motivations are not known.

2. That the lecture and participants are on the same wavelength, which forms a basis for common understanding. This assumption underlies the lecture from beginning to end.

3. That the lecturer has selected a speed of delivery, a set of ideas, etc., which are necessarily the same for everyone but nevertheless yield useful results; that he or she can "feel" when the purposeful attention of the majority of the participants is engaged. The lecturer assumes that the participants are keeping pace.

4. That assembling participants in the same room and atmosphere with little or no interaction between them produces useful results; i.e., that the social dimension of training can be ignored.

5. That participants can by themselves, through reading and informal contact, build the bridge between the lecture and their work situation, and that intellectual understanding will influence action.

These assumptions are open to doubt, as already seen in earlier sections. No wonder the lecture is the most difficult method to use effectively. Yet, ironically, it is the most common and apparently durable of all the training methods.

As a training method, the purpose of the lecture is, in fact, specific and quite limited. In the continuum of knowledge, understanding, and skill or behavior, the lecture can focus on the second: understanding. When, through reading assignments and experience, participants have become fairly familiar with information about a subject, the lecturer can relate the facts to one another and fit them into a memorable scheme, an understandable whole, a thesis, a theme. This may be more memorable than, say, reading a book, because of the living voice and manner, and "the ambience" associated with the lecture. The lecturer can make facts "come alive," imbue them with vitality and significance.

The effectiveness of the lecture method depends, therefore, on its place among other methods in the same program. The lecture holds greatest promise when it is a response to questions raised by participants during previous discussions, fieldwork, or other experiences. The length of the lecture is an important factor in its effectiveness. Studies have shown that twenty to thirty minutes may be the maximum time a lecturer can effectively speak continuously and still hold attention. A lecturer can break up a longer period of time by using a blackboard or more elaborate audiovisual method, or by interspersing the lecture with occasional questions to the audience. But these details and devices must not diminish our awe of this most difficult training method in terms of effective use. The participants' role during the lecture itself is that of individual listeners, members of the audience. The trainer is activity personified; he or she decides the subject matter, lectures, and responds—or not—to the reactions of the audience.

The main attraction of lecturing as a training method is its deceptive simplicity and the control over the session it purportedly yields to trainers. Coverage and preparation of the lecture can be predetermined. Lectures can be scheduled weeks ahead. Participants may either take notes or be provided with duplicated summaries. Once prepared, a lecture can be repeated on other occasions or even delivered by a surrogate. Perhaps even more attractive is the predictable course of the session itself. Lecturers can "feel" satisfaction from their lectures. Thus lecturing holds first place as an established method of training. Other methods have to challenge its primacy. It usually does not suffice to suggest that they be compared to lecturing in terms of the purposes they serve and their comparative effectiveness and costs.

The simplicity of lecturing is deceptive, first and foremost, because what lecturers say is not directly related to what listeners learn. This relation, as we have seen, is anything but neat. Some participants will learn nothing the lecturer intended. More frightening, perhaps, is the readiness of others to accept the lecturer's theme as "gospel," rather than think it through and choose, discard, or vary it for themselves, i.e., digest it, make it part of their own understanding. The very qualities of a good lecture threaten its value as a training method. The more complete and logically consistent the argument, the more erudite its derivation, and the more appealing its delivery, the more it tends to be "bought" as the final answer, Q.E.D. The satisfactions participants derive from a lecture often differ from those derived from learning: a sense of being looked after by knowledgeable elders whose learning and performance they can never hope to equal, a sense of dependence.

The tested results of lecturing, therefore, encourage only its rare and deliberate use. It is effective at that stage of the learning process which seeks to increase intellectual understanding. For passing knowledge on, the lecture is inefficient. People remember only about half of the lecture's content immediately after delivery, no matter how carefully they think they have listened. Two months later they remember about twenty-five percent or less. Incidentally, those who remember the most are not necessarily the most intelligent.[3] An underlying fact is that people think several times as fast as anyone speaks. Their attention to a lecture, therefore, depends markedly on what they do with that "spare time."

Some studies have been conducted to elucidate what transpires in this "spare time." College students whose interest might be most directly intellectual were tested. The researcher played back tapes of classroom activity to group of college students and asked them to recall what they had thought about at the time. He found that students in lecture classes, as compared to students in discussion classes, reported significantly more thoughts classified as "irrelevant" and "simple comprehension," and significantly fewer thoughts classified as relating to "self," "other persons," and "problem-solving." In a related study, students were asked to rate ten academic activities in the order that they elicited "mental activity." Variability was high, but composite ranking remained fairly constant for groups of students over a twenty-year span: group discussion ranked second and lecture eighth.[4]

These studies were done in America. During a seminar in India twenty senior officers listened to the erudite head of their own organization speak for one hour. A quick check the very next day revealed that no one was able to recall with certitude more than one of the five policy points the speaker had made—this in a country with a tradition of oral communication.

As a method of changing action (the objective of training), lecturing is also ineffective. Two famous American sets of experiments—one concerned with changing food habits, the other with lessening labor turnover and other disturbances following production changes in a garment factory—have been duplicated in India, with similar results. Only three

[3] See Dominick A. Barbara, *The Art of Listening* (Springfield, Ill.: Charles C. Thomas, Publisher, 1958).

[4] Quoted in Norman E. Wallen and Robert M. W. Travers, "Analysis and Investigation of Teaching Methods," in N. L. Gage (ed.), *Handbook of Research in Teaching* (Skokie, Ill.: Rand McNally and Co., 1963), p. 482.

percent of the women in three lecture groups changed their food habits, compared with thirty-two percent in the discussion groups.[5] Labor turnover in the factory was almost eliminated through the workers' active participation in production changes.[6]

Development and utilization of a new skill calls for a commitment from participants. This commitment springs from the meaning a change in behavior has for them personally and the degree of consensus for change they see in their group.

Lecturing of itself addresses neither the individual nor the social dimensions of this process. It is proper, then, that "training" through lecturing should be renamed, in many instances, "orientation". This word limits its aim to the intellectual and the abstract. But "orientation" is also becoming a bad word. A change in words does not resolve the problem.

The central task is essentially no different for lecturing than for other training methods. One must specify the proper time and place for its use in the training process, through careful examination of the aims it can promote, and through an equally careful evaluation of the results. Exhibit 7.7 summarizes the specifications of the lecture method.

TRAINING METHODS COMPARED WITH OBJECTIVES, LEARNING PROCESS, AND FACILITIES

We have now examined seven major types of training methods and given examples of each. There are others—the workshop, symposium, demonstration, and panel discussion, to mention just a few. We trust the reader will have no difficulty in placing them under the appropriate major types. Several are normally used in conjunction with other methods and so appear under several titles. Demonstrations and an increasing range of audiovisual methods are among these.

The choice of training methods for a particular program depends, first of all, on a series of three comparisons. These have to be interrelated in the final choice in much the same manner that a craftsperson assembles a tool kit. The tool kit of training methods shows neither the sequence nor how frequently the tools will be used. Choice of methods is best addressed by looking back at the design of the training program.

[5] Kurt Lewin, "Studies in Group Decision", in Dorwin Cartwright and Alvin Zander (eds.), *Group Dynamics* (Evanston, Ill.: Row, Peterson and Co., 1956), chap. xxi.

[6] Lester Coch and John R.P. French, Jr., "Overcoming Resistance to Change," in Cartwright and Zander (eds.), *ibid.*, chap. xix.

Exhibit 7.7

THE LECTURE: OUTLINE SPECIFICATIONS

Participant's role	Listener/part of audience
Data	General, abstract
Trainer's role	Lecturer
Time required	20-30 minutes. One hour or more if audio-visual and discussion methods used
Trainer requirements:	
Ratio	1 to hundred
Time for preparation	Varies
Facilities required	Varies with size of session and subsidiary methods
Special points	Effective at understanding stage of the learning process

The three comparisons required in choosing training methods for a program are:

1. Methods compared with training objectives;
2. Methods compared with the learning process and its stages; and
3. Methods compared with available time, skills, and facilities.

Summary data for these comparisons are presented here in three exhibits.

1. Methods Compared with Objectives

Exhibit 7.8 refers to the nine training objectives listed earlier and evaluates training methods in terms of them.

The ratings are necessarily rough. A skillful, devoted trainer can deflect the tendencies of a particular method. Some contexts are favorable, others unfavorable. But even rough ratings indicate the major tendencies. Where widely varying conditions might make a rating misleading, we have left the space blank. Blank ratings may be regarded as promising, *if* certain conditions are present.

Simulation, laboratory, and case methods are promising on almost all scores. Simulation is low on exposure to new ideas. The laboratory method scores highest (five "V. Highs"). But its coverage is limited to personal and organizational behavior and so leaves thinking about the job as a whole uncertain.

Individual training, seminars, and other general discussions cannot meet a number of training objectives and, therefore, are limited to very specific uses. Seminars and lectures do well only for exposure to new ideas and studying one's job in a wider context. The "High" ratings for protecting participants and organizations against mistakes indicate that some methods are very distant from the work situation. It was this very distance that placed them in sixth and seventh place in our list of methods.

2. Methods Compared with Learning Process

Exhibit 7.9 rates methods in terms of the ten stages of the learning process. Although the stages are listed in sequence here, they overlap in practice. Once again, these ratings are only indicative.

Training in the field and by simulation, laboratory, case, and individual methods scores high in the five early stages of the learning process. In its limited field of coverage, the laboratory method is very strong throughout, except for conceptual understanding of a job as a whole. The general discussion and lecture methods do not fare well in this comparison.

3. Methods Compared with Facilities

Exhibit 7.10 summarizes the sectional tables of specifications for different training methods. All items except the first (participant's role) have a direct bearing on the skills and facilities required to use a particular method.

The data in this exhibit is important in that it relates what is desirable to what is possible or impossible for a particular program, or institution, or system. The limitations impinge particularly on three aspects: inadequate time for preparation and follow-up (field, simulation, and case methods), scarcity of suitable materials (cases and individual training), and scarcity of certain training skills (field, simulation, laboratory, and case methods). The time limitation is the easiest to remove. Much of it can be removed by planning further ahead. The rest can be translated into costs. But if costs were related to the results of training, the additional cost would prove a bargain in almost every instance.

The limitations of training materials are more difficult to remove because they are linked with the third limitation, the severe shortage of training skills needed for the use of highly desirable methods. In the case of diagnostic field training and laboratory training, the shortage is so critical that these methods have to be omitted from the tool kit for all but the

Exhibit 7.8

COMPARISON OF TRAINING METHODS AND TRAINING OBJECTIVES

	Training Methods						
	(1) *Field*	(2) *Simulation*	(3) *Laboratory*	(4) *Cases, etc.*	(5) *Individual*	(6) *Seminar*	(7) *Lecture*
1. Realistic and manageable part of job	High	V. High	High	High	High	Low	Low
2. Help with internalizing learning	High	High	V. High	High	V. High	Low	V. Low
3. Protection for participant and organization against mistakes		V. High	High	V. High	V. High	V. High	V. High
4. Learning to learn	High	High	V. High	High	High	High	V. Low
5. Exposure to new ideas and methods	High	Low	V. High	High	High	High	High
6. Experiments with behavior	High	High	V. High	High	High	Low	Low
7. Membership of new reference groups	Low	High	High	High	Low	High	Low
8. Step back to think about job as a whole	High	V. High		V. High	Low	High	High
9. Very intensive learning	High	High	V. High	High	High	Low	Low

Exhibit 7.9

COMPARISON OF TRAINING METHODS AND STAGES IN THE LEARNING PROCESS

	Training Methods						
	(1) *Field*	(2) *Simulation*	(3) *Laboratory*	(4) *Cases, etc.*	(5) *Individual*	(6) *Seminar*	(7) *Lecture*
1. Simulation by data, situation	V. High	V. High	V. High	High	High	Low	Low
2. Interaction and involvement	High	V. High	V. High	High	V. High	High	Low
3. Experience	High	High	V. High	High	High	Low	Low
4. Practice	High	High	V. High	High	V. High	Low	V. Low
5. Feedback	High*	High	V. High	High	V. High	Low	V. Low
6. Repeat practice(s)	Low	V. High	V. High	High	V. High	Low	V. Low
7. Repeat feedback(s)	Low	High	V. High	High	V. High	Low	V. Low
8. Conceptual understanding of job	Low	Low	Low	V. High	Low	High	High
9. Conceptual understanding of change process	V. Low	V. Low	High	High	V. Low	V. Low	V. Low
10. Creative experimenting	High	High	V. High	High	V. Low	Low	V. Low

* For diagnostic field studies the rating should be low.

Exhibit 7.10

COMPARISON OF TRAINING METHODS AND OUTLINE SPECIFICATIONS

	Training Methods						
	(1) *Field*	(2) *Simulation*	(3) *Laboratory*	(4) *Cases, etc.*	(5) *Individual*	(6) *Seminar*	(7) *Lecture*
Participant's role	Outsider	Player/ observer	Him-Herself	Initiator/con- tributor/leader	In charge	Contributor/ chairperson	Listener
Data	Situation	Partial sit- uation	Here and now	Description of situation else- where	Standardized programmed material	General	General
Trainer's role	Active guide/ resource person	Organizer/ discussion leader	Resource person/ consultant	Listener/clari- fier/theoretician	Resource person/ organizer	V. small/re- source person	Lecturer
Time required:	Heavy			10 x 3 hours	Varies	Varies	20-30 minutes
Preparation per session	Heavy	2 hours	15 x 2 hours	10 x 1 $^1/_2$–2 hours	Varies	$1^1/2$–2 hours	1 hour if sub- sidiary methods used.
Time requirements							
Ratio	1:15* or 1:5	1:8-20	2:15	1:20-?	1:20-?	1:-12	1:many
Time of preparation	V. Heavy	Heavy	V. Little	10 x 1 $^1/_2$ hours	V. Little	Little	Varies
Follow-up	Heavy						
Special points	Long lead time, expensive		Coverage limited to personal and organizational behavior; rare training skill; difficult effects on concurrent programs	High initial cost of materials and long lead time	High initial cost of materials; ex- pensive	Tends to verbal agreement	Tends to dependence
Detailed chart	p. 142–43	145–46	149	152–53	156–57	158–59	163

* Technique practice

fewest programs, certainly in developing countries, until more trainers become available. But cannot interested people learn these skills "on the job"? Not, we appeal, when these methods offer participants and organizations the least protection against mistakes. The first principle must be "risk no harm."

For most programs in developing countries the methods that sample real life (incidents and cases) must also be left out of the training kit. Lack of training skill per se will do no harm, but the material by itself, even if good, cannot make the method effective. And wasting the time of participants (and their organizations) and dragging the method into disrepute cannot be considered harmless.

So shortages in materials and skilled trainers generally force developing countries to use those training methods which, at best, are effective for very few objectives and at few stages in the learning process, namely, general discussion and lecture methods. Breaking out this discouraging situation is a two-dimensional task. One step is to stop looking at general limitations and study meticulously instead the methods that can, in fact, be assembled for a particular training program. The system may have trainers with such close relations with a work organization that diagnostic field training would surely lead to no harm. Others may have a knack for role playing. They might not be able to verbalize what they do, or why, but they are effective; so role playing can be included in the kit. A discussion serves objectives a lecture cannot serve, even if not particularly well led. So that can be included. It might be possible to include a series of cases or a training laboratory by borrowing materials and skilled trainers from another agency. The point is to augment the tool kit with desirable methods just as much as possible, recognizing that each carries clear minimum specifications for its use.

Another positive step is to use programs that do offer novel training methods to enable more trainers to acquire scarce new skills. Two ways are possible. Firstly, active trainers can be encouraged and helped to make the most of their new experiences, through review sessions with more experienced trainers and through faculty development programs. Secondly, training sessions can be used directly for developing additional trainers. For instance, many kinds of sessions would suffer no harm if additional trainers were invited to sit in and to take part afterwards in review and planning sessions. Breaking through the prevailing shortage of skilled trainers must, somehow, command first priority in developing countries. Some of the ways for doing this are detailed in the last part of this book, where the training system and its development are discussed.

Chapter 8

Developing the Group and the Climate

> No single thing is so important to every man as to have for neighbors intelligent, companionable persons.
>
> — BELLAMY

> A teacher will not be successful in instituting a plan... for achieving a given learning objective unless the social dimensions of the group are in harmony with it.
>
> — G. JENSEN

ALL TRAINING methods, even the most individualistic, have social dimensions, but in some these are more prominent and important than in others. For interactive methods they are both very prominent and very important. Supervised practice, as in a master-apprentice situation, is at least a dyad, and practice often proceeds in the presence of others. Social dimensions are also in play, though less obviously, in a crowded hall with a lecturer who monopolized the speaking, even in "individual" learning when participants learn from television, radio, or texts at home. Their role as learners, their honest application, preparation, and evaluation of progress, their expectations about guidance through the program and gains from success with it afterwards, are all largely social. Interactive training methods open learning most to trainer influence in these social dimensions, so we have drawn most of the examples in this chapter from programs and settings using these methods.

We start with a program that brings participants together in one place. The program is ready to begin. The participants have assembled. They have had available the general description of the program and the detailed time-table, at least for the opening days. For better or for worse, the main preparatory stage is closed. The might-have-beens no longer matter, whether in choice of participants, the composition of the training group, or the program design. These are now all fixed. The trainers' task is to do their best within the limits of the now existing program. As for second thoughts, well, they provide an opportunity for learning to improve future programs.

From the moment the participants arrive, a process starts that has little to do with program content—a social process. Participants explore who else is in the program and what they are like. This exploration extends not only to the other participants, but also, and very much, to the trainers. Participants have already explored these questions in their imagination and in contacts with participants of earlier programs. On the basis of hypothetical answers to these questions, they have built up some expectations. Now they watch for cues to check, elaborate, change, or confirm them. Early interactions always have such questions in the background. Even when the program of sessions begins, social questions, these and others, often demand so much attention that they crowd out other aspects, such as the content of an opening lecture or of early discussions. It is just as well, therefore, that trainers not expect much recall of the content of these initial events. It is better if the events are set up in a manner that promotes this essential social process.

In short, a new community is born—a training group. This group is of special importance in residential programs, with built-in closeness of living, as well as learning, together. But a group forms in any training program. With the possible exception of very spasmodic training sessions, the nature and direction of this group will affect the outcome of the training program. It is the trainers' task, perhaps the basic statement of it, to influence the social process in such a manner that the group will focus on the training objectives, and develop norms, relationships, and a climate that will promote intended learning.

The idea of such a task still strikes many trainers as very strange. For some, the formation of a training group is not something desirable and potentially valuable, but an inescapable evil. They see it as a nuisance, as something they cannot stop but wish they could. For others, the phenomenon only arises because of administrative convenience and economic necessity. They would much prefer a tutorial relationship. What a pity it cannot be had. Even to those who admit that a "good" training group has value, it still counts for little. At any rate, the social process is viewed as highly unpredictable and not open to deliberate influence. It is simply something with which they are blessed or lightly cursed, something they must live with either way, fair weather or foul.

In that last they are right: like the weather, groups are with us, like it or not. Trainers with a positive orientation toward participants see groups as serving a variety of functions: a retreat from everyday work and living, a setting in which to try out new ideas and be stimulated by others, an association allowing experimentation during training, and continuing contact. To this general orientation, however, only few trainers bring the skill necessary to actually handle participants in groups.

Sharply contradictory attitudes are reflected in prevailing approaches to participants in a group. Some trainers seem determined to keep them separate, to allow as few interactions among them as possible. Interactions beyond a minimum are classified as lack of discipline. The opposite approach, equally individualistic and once upon a time advocated as vigorously as the first, is to let participants go their own way. The idea here was that individuals know how to maximize their own growth. In either approach, when a participant's performance falls greatly below the trainers' expectations, the characteristic reaction is an exhortation to improve. If that produces no result, the trainers' simply discount their expectation of that participant. If, on the other hand, a participant excels, the trainers may hold him or her up for emulation. Both acts assume that the "failure" or "success" lie primarily with the individual participant.

Yet in their heart of hearts—we will return to the "location" of this knowledge in the next chapter—most trainers know better—and, of course, so do the participants. Experience throws up inescapable questions. How is it that trainer X gets cooperation and learning from a group that trainer Y finds so discouraging? How is it that trainer X achieves effective results with almost any group, and trainer Y with distressingly few or none?

The forces at work, complex though they be, can nevertheless be understood and influenced. The development of a training group is basically no different from the development of groups elsewhere, at work and in the neighborhood. Whatever its setting, a group passes through a set of phases, thrives on plentiful contact, selects its own leaders, diversifies the roles of various participants, and has characteristic ways of working and dealing with strangers without and strangers within. In the training institution, the trainers' behavior is undoubtedly the most important single influence. But even here, the trainers are not omnipotent—though some would like to think so. Nor are they important—as others fear or prefer. They simply exercise the most important single influence. Their task is to use this influence effectively for training.

THE SOCIAL PROCESS: THREE ASPECTS

Participants coalesce into an effective group as they share common objectives and develop common tasks, develop common ways (norms) of attaining them and generally dealing with the world, and build incr-easingly realistic relationships with each other. To be effective for training, the trainers' objectives, standards, and relationships must become part of this social system. Otherwise, the group develops apart, or in opposition to them.

We shall examine the development of tasks, norms, and relationships separately, even though in real life they overlap and intertwine.

1. Establishing Common Tasks

In the course of joint preparatory work and certainly in its program announcement, the system will have stated the training objectives in broad terms. Hopefully, the participants arrive considering these objectives worth their effort and time. If they have chosen to come themselves, this is indeed quite likely, and the size of the fee they or their work organization have paid is some indication of the importance they attach to this training. But often the first discrepancy occurs right here. Their organization, or their parents, may have volunteered them for the program. There is no knowing then what effort and time a participant wants to invest.

The most critical stage for establishing shared goals is at the very beginning of a course. Even great diligence during the pretraining stage does not eliminate differences between the announced objectives of a program and the purposes that participants hope to achieve through attendance. Discrepancies of this type are least surprising in cross-cultural programs. The extracurricular attractions of an international program are great, and applicants are especially inclined to put their qualifications for it into the most favorable light; and, from the other end, the system finds it difficult to make long distance checks on marginal applicants. Similar difficulties beset local programs, too, but at a lower key. A participant may arrive, for instance, fully expecting a technical rather than a managerial course, or at any rate so preoccupied with technical questions that he cannot focus his attention on managerial ones. When the discrepancy is wide, it might be better for all concerned if the system asks the participant to drop the program altogether or only try it for a limited period. The possibility of misfits is greatly increased, of course, if the system has represented its program for marketing, political or other reasons to mean all things to all people.

More commonly, participants project their own preoccupations into the general statement of objectives by the institution. Everyone sees there what she or he wants to see. One sees an opportunity in a junior executive course to learn about cost accounting, which is her work area; another to learn from the same course how to diagnose general management problems; another to learn to lead discussions, or to get some new product ideas, or to write reports; and yet another to meet interesting people. All these are apparently reflected in the same broad statement of objectives. They might well be. There can be no certitude regarding what a program will actually cover until the trainers have provided opportunities for the inclusion or rejection of personal objectives. Some individual goals can be incorporated, others cannot. The procedures used for this assessment at SIET Institute have been given in chapter 4. The training institution's concern with useful objectives can hardly be communicated more clearly than by accommodating those items and priorities in the program which participants have helped to determine through careful consideration.

Other critical stages in establishing common tasks develop from time to time during the program. A critical stage ensues whenever participants working toward what appear to be positive, clear-cut goals, find themselves confronted with severe and unexpected difficulties. Insufficient time may be the stumbling block, the need for information that is not accessible, or a procedure that does not yield the expected results. When a critical stage occurs either the task should be changed or steps found to surmount the difficulty. If neither is done, frustration, despondency, and other undesirable side effects result. Each critical stage gives the trainers an opportunity to show that they are committed to realistic tasks, not to some mechanical notion of training, such as covering the syllabus.

2. Developing Norms or Standards of Behavior

Just as participants and trainers bring various, unstated personal objectives to the program which need to be sorted and coalesced into common objectives and goals, they also bring with them implicit standards of behavior. If they come from various backgrounds or parts of the country, they discover that the standards they take for granted in their lives are not, in fact, the same for everyone. The queries and adjustments incumbent on this realization can be unsettling and difficult, but also valuable.

To these differences trainers add the standards of behavior they consider appropriate for participants in the program. Some of these standards are system-wide, others vary between trainers. Some may be greatly at variance with standards participants recall from school or college days, and which they assumed would apply again in the training situation. Examples of school and college standards often resurrected are: the trainers will lecture and the participants speak only when they permit; participants will take notes and be tested on their recollection of them; assignments are individual and competitive, and on no account to be shared; and that participants will have to "get together" outside, rather than in the program, and away from the trainers, not with them. Instead, the participants may find a situation in which the trainers seem to welcome questions at any time in a session, expect them to carry on lengthy discussions without them, and encourage both personal and social developments in their sessions.

If the system has clear-cut standards on certain issues, it may state them in advance hand outs to participants and their work organizations.

For example, the Administrative Staff College of India states in an advance circular that participants will not be admitted after the starting date, that they will not be released until the program is finished, except for quite grave unforeseeable reasons, and that no holidays will be observed other than Republic Day and Independence Day. Other norms are implied in its statement of training methods. For instance, participants will be expected to prepare material for discussion, to participate at their own initiative, and to take turns chairing the syndicate. The corresponding standards for the training staff are to observe and listen, and speak rarely.

Additional standards are communicated when participants arrive, through written rules or unwritten conventions. Examples are that participants wear suits, they rise when a speaker comes into a session, and all training staff are present at every general session.

Standards stated in advance are usually simple and soon widely associated with an institution. Even then, dilemmas still arise over the enforcement of a rule: to stop short of enforcement would render the entire system of norms untrustworthy and unsettle the training process; but enforcement risks offending someone, perhaps an important organization.

The rule of not admitting a participant late for a program is an example. Sending a latecomer back is embarrassing and can entail lasting anger on the part of his organization. In one case the anger became greater when two foreign participants arrived late and were accepted on the grounds that the rule could not be enforced in their case. The local organization sent no participant for the next six programs.

Most standards are too subtle to set and to share in advance. Standards, e.g., about the amount of work participants and trainers will put into a program, in sessions and by way of preparation, and what quality and time limits are acceptable, develop over time. Admonitions during the opening session "to work hard" are usually heard as noise, and a very patronizing noise at that. It is more useful for trainers to specify what they consider acceptable. They might say, for instance, that a particular assignment usually results in two or three pages of writing and that they will collect it first thing Friday morning. They may add that such assignments will be returned to the authors with comments within X days. The trainers may open such scheduling to discussion. They may even turn questions of how to deal with any laggards over to the group as they arise.

These are examples of standards the trainers' state. They are also very influential as a model, through their actions and their style. This is so in any culture, also appropriate. The training staff has organized the program. Participants expect them to know what standards are appropriate for it. They truly depend on the trainers to show them and to serve as guides to their own styles of action. This is quite different from dependence that is inappropriate and hinders development.

If the trainers encourage and help the group to set standards for itself, these will often be stricter than any they would have set and tried to enforce. High work standards confirm the group's interest in attaining the training objectives and, usually, that they value the trainers' contribution. Other standards delimit what participants will and will not talk about with the trainers present and how they keep in line those whose behavior is unacceptable.

Reasonable consistency of statements and actions by trainers is important to developing positive standards quickly. If trainers attach importance to participants' developing initiative and collaborating closely with others, they can foster their standard by showing interest in that kind of behavior from the very outset and then whenever it occurs. They also set an example by collaborating with participants. Many standards emerge in this informal way: listening carefully to others before speaking, giving opinions freely, answering questions thoughtfully; treating questions as genuine expressions of doubts to clear, not as challenges to be resisted. Indeed, it is often not wise to state standards explicitly before their clarification in practice; or to state them too sharply or highly generalized.

> In the opening session of one program the principal stated that the trainers would "always' make it a point to be helpful, that this indeed was their main standard of behavior But helpfulness is open to many interpretations and occasions developed during the course when participants accused trainers of having misled them. They did not see the trainers' behavior as helpful on these occasions and whipped them with the principal's opening statement.

Trial and error is normal in the process of setting standards. Participants, and trainers too, test out what behavior is acceptable and what is beyond the limits of tolerance. This testing can be a trying experience, but the price is small compared to the importance of the process. Training partly consists of, and partly depends on, enhancing generally accepted standards—of commitment, quality of work, ways of behaving with others. Trials reveal, above all, that this essential process is actually under way.

3. Building Realistic Relationships

Common objectives and standards are developed in the course of personal contacts and interactions. It is the trainers' choice whether to limit interactions or to multiply them. They can behave in such a manner that contact and interactions are limited during the program, thereby slowing the development of the group and also excluding themselves from it. This happens when the trainers' do most of the talking, take most of the decisions, and treat participants uniformly and as separate individuals. Or the trainers' can so behave that interactions are numerous, joint tasks and standards are established quickly, and they themselves are simply members of the group with particular functions and responsibilities. To foster this kind of relationship the trainers throw the program open to discussion, to collaborative work and joint decision making, and make themselves readily accessible to the participants. They can ensure that all participants center their attention on an issue from time to time and contribute their views and preferences to the common pool, and that these contributions influence joint decisions. Such comprehensive inclusion is especially important if participants vary widely in age, experience, status, and linguistic competence and the group comprises members who are traditionally quiet in mixed meetings, e.g., women or villagers.

To maximize interaction, the size and physical arrangement of the group are always important. The trainers cannot interact readily with participants lined up in rows facing them—the usual lecture arrangement. Horseshoe and circular arrangements are better, but limit the size of the group to about twenty. But twenty is still too large if all participants are to be actively involved. Groups as small as eight characteristically have one member who speaks less than five percent of the time; the number of silent members goes up as the size of the group increases. Trainers eager to foster interactions have many ways of subdividing a large group, into buzz-groups of three or four, for instance, for which participants need only shift their chairs slightly; or into small work or decision groups in different corners of the room or outside on the grounds.

Trainers can also speed group development if they encourage participants to sort out their different roles openly and to experiment with unfamiliar roles. For the silent to speak or the normally passive to take the initiative are common examples of such explorations. They are time-consuming but can lead to very worthwhile and far-reaching learning for every one present. The talkative learn to listen and the leader to accept another's leadership. Role exploration and differentiation are subtly linked to specific situations and tasks. In time, their complexity and sophistication can indicate the level of maturity a group has attained. In a very mature group, X may lead in case discussion, Y in fieldwork, W in the group's social life, Z in helping a participant who finds it difficult to actively participate in the group's activities. O may be characteristically active in opposing the trainers, and expressing group resentment to unreasonable pressure. When O does this, P may encourage others to join in, while V finally smoothens matters and states what is to be learned.

The trainers' roles are clarified through this same process. Such clarification is very important since it directly affects the participants' motivation, freedom, and resources to explore and learn. Only one trainer role is simple: the sturdy, authoritarian one. In this role a trainer can surely cripple the most significant motivations and learnings. When trainers decide to share authority and to encourage the development of the training group, this simplicity disappears and their own role becomes the great unknown in the group. Many other role explorations have to wait for its clarification.

> The sequence of stages in a training laboratory illustrates sharply the difficulties and possibilities contingent upon a trainer's refusal to be a traditional authority figure. At first participants see the trainer's attempt as a gimmick, a test. They try to force him back into the familiar authoritarian role. If he resists, they find surrogate leaders among themselves to reestablish the familiar structure. Several participants usually compete for this role. This competition leads to anger and to renewed appeals to the trainer to stop "the game"—and the pains of development. Only when his determination becomes clear and the various explanations for his obstinacy wear thin, does the group turn to discover resources within itself. Participants then begin to notice the varied roles that they and the trainer can realistically perform.

Similar but less dramatic, more open sequences take place when the trainer assumes the role of consultant in the field: "Why don't you guide us more?"; or of the discussion leader in a case session: "What is the answer?" (i.e., *your* answer); or of the resource person: "Why don't you just tell us?" When a trainer resists these attempts to push her back into an authoritarian stance, the struggle ends in liberation of the group, which enables it to take steps forward.

The roles a trainer performs are no more stage roles than those participants develop. In fact, the notion (hope?) that they are staged, that the trainer is "only playing" is among the last strongholds before liberation.

> Once a tradition-laden East Asian participant came up after a session to ask one of us a personal question: "Professor," *(sic!)* he ventured, "is trial and error your method of teaching?"
> TRAINER: "You are very uncomfortable with what has been going on. *(Pause.)* If you thought I had planned this chaos, you would be able to accept it."
> PARTICIPANT: "Yes."
> TRAINER: "Maybe you are not quite sure just now whether I, your professor, know what I am doing?"
> The man looked as if his heart had missed a beat, then he turned and literally bolted from the room. For two days he did not speak in a session. After that, he participated more than ever before, and became more freely personal and involved.

Carl Rogers has summarized a lifetime experience as a trainer in a few pithy sentences on just this point. They are given in box 8.1. We shall examine them more fully in the next chapter.

Box 8.1

THE TRAINER-PARTICIPANT RELATIONSHIP

CARL ROGERS

If I can create a relationship characterized on my part:

— by a genuineness and transparency, in which I am my real feeling;

— by a warm acceptance of and prizing of the other person as a separate individual;

— by a sensitive ability to see his world and himself as he sees them;

Then the other individual in the relationship:

— will experience and understand aspects of himself which previously he has repressed;

— will find himself becoming better integrated, more able to function effectively;

— will become more similar to the person he would like to be;

— will become more of a person, more unique and more self-expressive;

— will be more understanding, more acceptant of others;

— will be able to cope with the problems of life more adequately and more comfortably.

I believe that this statement holds whether I am speaking of my relationship with a client, with a group of students or staff members, with my family or children. It seems to me that we have here a general hypothesis which offers exciting possibilities for the development of creative, adaptive, autonomous persons.

SOURCE: Carl Rogers, *On Becoming a Person* (Boston, Cambridge: Houghton Mifflin Co., 1961), pp. 37-38.

To help participants see that the trainers are genuine, that they are truly not authoritarian, trainers may have to go through many trials and survive many traps expressly set to test them. They will be watched not only in the session but outside it, in their contacts with each other, staff, and family. Their role crystallizes out of the picture participants form and share of them, the total picture.

That the development of common tasks, norms, and relationships constitutes a process with a more or less set sequence underscores the importance of so constructing a program that it promotes early, plentiful, and significant contacts between trainers and participants. Informal and personal occasions help greatly in getting to know one another. As this process of close acquaintance gets underway, other developments also take place. Trainers need not hold back for want of being "copybook perfect." Who is? To the contrary, trainers' inconsistencies and errors, especially if openly discussed, have the advantage of making them more human to participants: fallible, doing their best, and engaged, like them, in the process of learning.

INDICATORS OF GROUP DEVELOPMENT

The development of common tasks, group standards, relationships, and roles are all aspects of the same social process. We have separated them here only for the sake of clarity. Sad to say, trainers face the entire complex process, indeed its trickiest states, right from the beginning of the program, at a time when they know the participants least, both individually and as a group.

Yet the early stages are the most important because they prejudice what follows. Progression in either direction, toward closeness or distance, shared or unilateral decision, becomes increasingly difficult to reverse. Very few training programs go on long enough to allow the trainers the one hundred days of honeymoon allowed an incoming political government. Their sensitivity and tools need to be sufficiently honed to pick up with minimal delay even tiny indicators of the social process and to merge them into a general running picture of the group's development. Their perception of the group guides the trainers' actions.

Data unroll before their very eyes and ears, if only they attend to them. They see facial expressions, ways of sitting, who sits by whom. They can hear not only words, but the feelings they convey. Before long, patterns emerge: which participants speak frequently and which are listened to, which seem to rub everyone the wrong way. Individual preferences also emerge.

> For instance, participant Rao seems primarily concerned with winning, with coming out on top. In a simulation game set up to practice understanding the decision-making process, he seems instead to concentrate on figuring out how to win. Having won, his interest seems to flag. Aruna, on the other hand, focuses on how people set about the task. The outcome of the game seems to interest her less than what she can learn that might be useful in decision-making situations in the future. Teja appears very impatient with the game but does not say so. Maybe he holds back from fear of what an expression of his feelings might bring. The three are learning different things. At least Teja may need the trainers' early attention.

The trainers' own interventions evoke answers, or silence, or argument. There are masses of data for the trainers to attend to, as well as they are able. They can see that a direction or evaluation from them will shift the participants' attention away from the group and the task to their wishes. Evaluations, especially if unexplained, tend to make participants close ranks. They cover up for each other and seem to pit their wits against the trainers rather than work with them. Presenting the group with a problem produces quite different results. The problem may consist of a description of what participants or someone else set out to achieve, how they set about the task, and the extent to which performance fell short of goals. Attention focuses on consequences and finding ways to do better next time.

In terms of content, a discussion may often lack logical direction. In fact, it may seem quite chaotic, with successive contributions apparently unconnected and awkward silences or outbursts occurring at odd times. Throughout all this trainers can watch for indications that the group is, in fact, passing through successive stages of the developmental process. Sometimes the indications are clear, sometimes quite obscure. But each stage does have characteristic indications for the trainer to note. Blaming others for shortcomings is characteristic of an early stage. Blaming oneself comes next. The third stage is characterized by disregard for scapegoats and more attention to learning how errors occurred and how to avoid them in the future. By this stage the group is fairly far along in working out initial relationships. But often the trainers' role has still not been resolved. They seem to embody the single best way in which the job should be done, and the group is preoccupied with discovering their secret. While "digging for old," the group also dispels the aura surrounding the trainers. In its place emerges the value of acceptable and contingent alternatives, which the trainers can then help the groups explore. Operating procedures are eventually viewed as the best-working-hypotheses-to-date rather than rigid rules. When this degree of adaptability surfaces in the group, it signals that participants have indeed attained considerable acquaintance with and closeness to each other and the trainers. As the saying goes in football, they are "played in." They know what to expect of each other.

Trainers can multiply their data by involving participants in making such observations and establishing what they mean. This has several advantages over keeping the observations quietly to themselves. They thereby signal their preference for freshness and openness in confronting all kinds of data. They provide realistic objectives: observation, listening, understanding the progress of a meeting, and seeing the effect people have on one another. They can ask participants to take turns in observing the group's development and reserve ten to fifteen minutes at the end of a session for the observers to report what they have seen and heard. Very simple typed up classifications are helpful in this exercise. After some practice with these, trainers can proceed to simple sociometric and role studies. A few questions can bring the relationship pattern out in the open: For instance, "To whom in this group do you go for help with work? With a personal problem? To whom do you look to take initiative in a work assignment? To ask questions in sessions? To organize a social event?" What participants learn from such studies is not so much the data—they are usually familiar with it in a general way—but that data such as these can be openly shared and discussed. The same data can then serve as a kind of benchmark against which to note progress.

In these ways, trainers can learn much that is new to them and important. Often it leads them to review their impression of the group and change their behavior. For instance, a bright participant to whom they have paid considerable attention emerges from the data as somewhat isolated from the group. Special attention from the trainers may isolate him even further, when the opposite is required. Or a participant with slovenly work habits ranks as very influential in the group. The trainers then need to consider how to sustain adequate standards of work in the light of this fact. A third participant, who is having difficulty with the work, also seems isolated. Is she having difficulty because of her isolation or is her isolation largely due to an inability to keep pace with the group? Either way, singling her out for individual comment would only increase her isolation and so perhaps, her difficulty.

In role studies, it is important to collect information specifically related to the training tasks. It is important to know which participants are most interested in X subjects or are the hardest workers. When those who are seen as working hardest and most effectively are also the lowest in social influence, trainers can anticipate major struggles in the group. If they at least enjoy the respect of other participants, and if the social leaders are also reasonably effective at work, both the training objectives and the social processes are well in hand.

THE TRAINING CLIMATE

Out of the detailed training situations and interactions grows a general training climate, an ambience, a tone. This general pervasive phenomenon can greatly affect the rate of progress toward program objectives and also the satisfaction trainers and participants feel in the process. A similar climate may pervade the entire system and all aspects of the program; we shall return to this important dimension in the last part of the book. Whatever the system-wide climate may be, trainers are responsible for creating, insofar as they are able, a training climate favorable for their own part of the program. This, in fact, is their continuous contribution to the climate of the system as a whole.

Climate, ambience, tone—whichever the word, the phenomenon it labels is pervasive. Also, it tends to perpetuate itself, carrying the quality of the relationships forward in the program. One trainer sets a task. The group accepts it eagerly, perhaps as a challenge, and works hard. Another trainer sets the same task. The group resists it, quotes the timetable against her, and appeals to the principal. One trainer makes a mistake, but is liked the better for it; he is human and accessible. Another trainer makes the same mistake and he is ostracized. When the climate is favorable, nothing goes wrong in the program; when the climate is sullen, it is almost impossible to do anything right. Trainers and participants approach new situations with expectations which then tend to fulfill themselves, either way, and so strengthen similar expectations for the next session. Unless something extraordinary interrupts the cycle, fair or vicious, it goes on and on, self-fulfilling and self-enforcing. To the degree the climate becomes "institutionalized" and is supported by enduring procedural and physical arrangements it is the training *culture,* at least in that particular system (or part of it). This cultural dimension of a training system will be in focus again in part III.

In earlier sections of this chapter we focused on the trainers' actions, one by one, serially, i.e., their behavior. Actually, the training climate is shaped more by the feelings that underlie behavior. The participants' feelings influence their understanding of the trainers' behavior and the meanings they attach to their actions. Feelings are expressed in many "languages"—behavior, words, actions, gestures, omissions — and tend to persist because they are deeply rooted in experiences preceding training. To mark this deeper understanding we will therefore continue the discussion in terms of feelings: the feelings the trainers express, the feelings they evoke in participants, the climate that results from their interplay, and the feelings carried forward to the next situation.

A favorable climate develops when a trainer moves close to participants as a person, cares about their needs and difficulties, accepts them as valued people, and is eager to share the tasks of constructing and running the best possible program. Participants respond to this with friendly feelings, feel free to express themselves openly and to explore new directions, and accept difficulties and errors as unintended. These shared feelings of freedom, closeness, and enthusiasm characterize the climate favorable to learning and lead readily to high endeavor and satisfaction, eagerness to collaborate, sensitive and perceptive giving of help, greater openness and sense of belonging together. These feelings are then carried forward. This scheme can be summarized in a flow diagram, as presented in figure 8.1.

With each input this climate affects all involved more deeply and becomes more firmly embedded in satisfying experiences and expectations. At best, trainers and participants engage in a truly joint

Figure 8.1
FAVORABLE TRAINING CLIMATE:
ROOTS AND EFFECTS

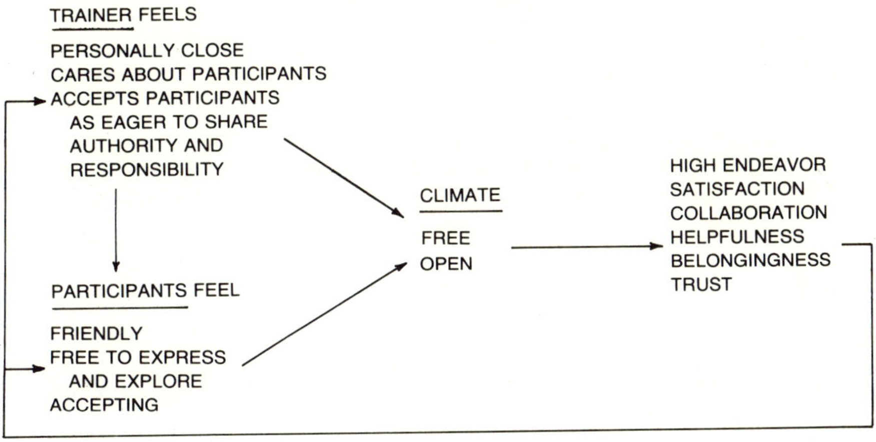

Figure 8.2
UNFAVORABLE TRAINING CLIMATE:
ROOTS AND EFFECTS

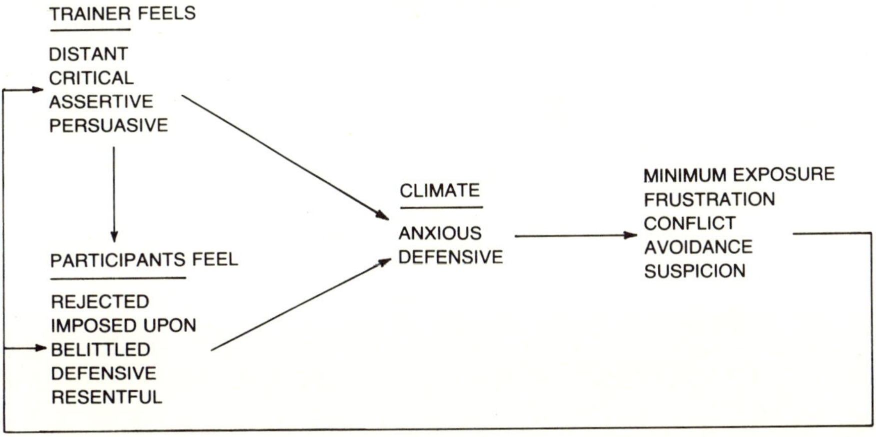

inquiry in which all persist in trying to find solutions to problems and carry through joint tasks. They see learning as the common quest and each contributes to its attainment. Learning to learn from others and collaboration with others are both necessary and fostered in the climate.

A climate unfavorable to learning is similarly summarized in figure 8.2

It is easy to see that an unfavorable climate interferes with training while a favorable one facilitates it. An unfavorable climate is full of interferences, static. Both trainers and participants wonder anxiously what each is going to do next. Participants direct attention from the task at hand to "keep their own ends up," avoid attack from others, and defend their self-image. It is a self-defeating pattern. Very different is the other pattern. In the freedom of a favorable climate, trainers can stimulate without dominating participants, encourage sharing without losing control, respond to individual needs but in the context of the small society formed by the training group, and allow the time and accept the angry feelings that come and go as participants veer toward self-motivated and self-disciplined activities. In this process all grow, trainers as well as participants.

Chapter 9

Trainers and Training Styles

> The shaman heals through the use of personal power, using craft, charm and cunning; the magician heals through his knowledge of archaic and complex rules, and his ability to follow ritual precisely; the priest claims no personal power, but achieves his healing capacity as an agent or vessel of an omnipotent authority; the mystic healer relies on insight, vision and wisdom, through which he cures the sick soul; the naturalist (the present-day physician) is impersonal, empirical, task-oriented.
>
> —Joseph Adelson

Learning takes place within an individual as a result of a confluence of diverse, intertwining, and occasionally opposing influences. It shows not in test performance—that may only show that the participant has memorized an approved response—but in action. It lasts. And it stimulates and supports further learning. The function of training is to entice the development of this mysterious process in participants, each and every one if possible.

To this task trainers bring, first of all, an adequate standard of competence in the field of training, be it health, accounting, or training methodologies. They have to be thoroughly familiar with the subject matter of this field. There is no substitute for this, not even, studies show, individualized programmed instruction. If this condition does not exist, the trainer is a nonstarter in this role. Training skill is no substitute for familiarity with the subject. Let us not belittle this: it is the minimum requirement, but regard it as the home base. We shall consider later how trainers can keep knowledge and familiarity with subject matter alive and up to date.

The first condition satisfied, we turn now to the trainers' actual behavior during training. This deserves attention at several levels. How trainers behave effectively in different kinds of training situations is open to observation, thoughtful listening, and understanding. This is one part of what participants do—pretty well perhaps almost all they do at the start of a program. So, in field training for example, participants can notice trainers making sure by their comments, and the manner in which they make them, that participants become aware of problem areas; then, as the trainers avoid giving ready answers, the participants work out satisfactory answers for themselves. In role playing the trainers leave all action to the participants, but ensure adequate time for preparation and playing, and stimulate an insightful discussion afterwards. In case discussions they again let participants carry the ball; they elicit contributions, state underlying assumptions, help participants think them through, and synthesize contributions into memorable conceptual wholes. In laboratory training they directly address the underlying relationships and personal issues that interfere with the group's progress.

Whatever the label of the event or the training method with which they start, trainers alter their behavior in whatever direction promises most learning. When a lecture or individual task begins to lose participant interest, they say: "Alright, we have sat long enough. Let's go out and take a look" (field visit, demonstration). Or, "You have been listening to me (lecture). Now let's hear from others" (discussion). Or, "This has been your experience. Now consider someone else's" (incident, case). Or, "you have been talking in the third person, about people. How about a little practice now in talking *with* someone, about something that concerns you" (role play, skill practice). Or, "We have done enough of this for now. Here is a reading (writing) assignment for tomorrow." A trainer is a craftsperson at work. Intent on the utility and elegance of the result, he or she varies the pace to achieve it, and thereby adjusts to the learners' best pace.

Circumspect timing of inputs of new data and different kinds of activities and concerns is one of the trainers' most delicate tasks. The process as a whole has proper "seasons." Certain times are ripe for disturbing and questioning—ploughing, others for seeding and fostering growth. This farmer's language presents a trainer's orientation and activities much better than teacher-talk about "making" or "requiring" people to learn. Notice the similes in Thelen's description of teaching: "The art of the sophisticated teacher manifests itself in the ability to capitalize on the wide range of natural tendencies that exist in the class: to work with them rather than suppress them and to teach...behavior through which [these] tendencies can be expressed."[1] It is no coincidence that medical analogies also come to mind, since the word "doctor" is derived from the Latin *docere,* to teach. Or "manage", which means "train by exercise." Craftsperson, farmer, doctor, manager—an effective trainer is apparently sibling to all these.

No description so far given in this book—neither of training event, nor method, nor a trainer's actions—has told us much about a trainer's effectiveness. What matters is not the event or the act but the meaning participants give it. And this meaning is largely derived from the social process

[1] Herbert A. Thelen, "Some Classroom Quiddities for People-Oriented Teachers," *Journal of Applied Behavioral Science,* Vol. I (July–September, 1955).

through which a particular training group develops its distinctive character and reaction. The shift away from trying to trace effective performance to the behavior and to character traits of the trainer—or leader—towards studying the partners in the learning process as they interact is quite recent.

> Literally thousands of studies have been conducted on teacher excellence since the beginning of the twentieth century. Investigators have looked at teacher training, traits, behaviors, attitudes, values, abilities, sex, weight, voice, quality, and many other characteristics. Teacher effects have been judged by investigators themselves, by pupils, by administrators and parents, by master teachers, by practice teachers, and by themselves. The apparent results of teaching have been studied, including pupil learning, adjustment, classroom performance, socio-economic position, attitudes, liking for school, and later achievement. And yet, with all this research activity, results have been modest and often contradictory. Few, if any, facts are now deemed established about teacher effectiveness, and many former findings have been repudiated. It is not an exaggeration to say that we do not today know how to select, train for, encourage, or evaluate teacher effectiveness. And many education researchers have abandoned the field of competence research as a simple-minded approach to a vastly more complex topic: the study of classroom interaction.[2]

We have seen that the nature, quality, and effectiveness of the interaction we call "training" depends heavily on the feelings trainers communicate to participants through their behavior. From this next deeper level springs the training "climate," a pervasive phenomenon that tends to feed and reinforce itself. So, for understanding the trainers' part, we have a layering, with behavior at the surface, visible; next knowledge, understanding, and skill, even social skill; and feelings next, determining the use to which trainers put the knowledge, etc., they have acquired. And beneath the feelings, whence *they* spring, is a trainer's "personality." Simply put, for trainers to project the kinds of feelings that evoke an effective training "climate", they must be genuine, "fit", and so project the people they are.

PERSONAL NEEDS OF TRAINERS

The kinds of feelings trainers must have to induce a favorable climate include an absorbing interest and excitement in the subject and work, eagerness to share the task and help participants grow into taking more responsibility for it; acceptance of participants as people with differing needs and personalities, and empathy toward them; and, finally, self-trust and confidence in others. As skill increases with experience and practice,

[2] Bruce J. Biddle and William J. Elena (eds.), *Contemporary Research in Teacher Effectiveness* (New York: Holt, Rinehart and Winston, Inc., 1964).

trainers communicate these positive feelings more effectively. But all the skill in the world is no substitute for the feelings themselves. If a trainer's interests and concerns lie in other directions, in research, for instance, or in promotion or power, any training will be unmasked. Devoid of personal roots, his training skill will soon be experienced by participants as manipulative, calling for submission or opposition, and as increasing their dependence on the trainer. At issue is the development of a personal understanding and trust between trainers and participants; and this is a matter primarily of feelings.

In an atmosphere of trust even an outrageous piece of behavior on the part of the trainee may "carry" the participants. A genuine gaff may even offer a bonus, increasing participant acceptance of the trainer as a fallible person doing her very best but not always succeeding. Once one of the authors found himself after the close of a training course in personal conversation with some participants whose travel plans had left them at the institution for an extra day. In the informal atmosphere he found it comfortable to inquire: "Why did you give trainer 'X' such a hard time?" After listening to their complaints, he added: "But when I made similar mistakes, you helped me." "Oh," came the rejoinder, "that's different. You like us." On the other hand, should a trainer fail to "come through" as a trustworthy person, even the most proper, correct behavior will simply confirm that he is a cold fish; and not just cold but dangerous as well, because he is so competent and inscrutable. In a recent survey of 1,000 college students in America aimed at eliciting what characteristics in their instructors they found most helpful, even a "steady temper" rated low. Top score went to enthusiasm.

Trainer's choice of events and methods in their work tell more about the people they are than about their intellectual assessment of the effectiveness of some events and methods compared to others. They settle on those that "suit" them, that they are more apt to be "good" at. Trainers who rely on lecturing tend to feel a need to talk, like order and neatness, both in their sessions and generally, are afraid they might lose control or show up unfavorably under questioning. Lecturing satisfies these needs. If a lecturer's table is provided, perhaps on a raised platform, it is not merely a convenience but also a welcome symbol of superiority; that is where she, the knowledgeable woman, stands, to whom all eyes are directed, who starts and finishes the session, allows or refuses questions, dispenses approval and disapproval. This kind of lecturer may not initially welcome this arrangement which segregates her from participants. But she is the party who chose a method that by its very nature increases social distance. Like the moat around an encampment, lecturing will indeed protect her from disturbing challenges. She is safe. If an institution has many trainers with such needs, good lecturing is likely to be the main avenue to promotion and all the advantages associated with it. In that institution young lecturers may well feel confirmed in using a method so nicely attuned to their personal needs and surroundings. They develop this skill through use, allowing others they might have to atrophy because they are less attractive.

Probably in no other dimension do training methods differ more, and more importantly, than in the degree of control trainers feel they need over participants. To this need is bent the traditional deference to the scholar, the wise elder, the priestly teacher. Trainers who set themselves up as the authority figure in control of a training event assume such deference is due them.

> One recent study describes a trainer who was preoccupied with "talking, whispering and horseplay" among participants. He tolerated such behavior up to the point where it challenged his authority, then took action to suppress it. What is important to note here is the point at which the trainer stepped in. It was not when the talking, etc., interfered with learning, but rather when it became a challenge to his "status."

The next step of this kind of trainer is to insist that his controlling is a necessary condition for effective training. Many trainers support this assertion in such vigorous terms that their underlying personal needs become plain. Others do not state it; they behave it. Their "discussions" tend to be series of dialogues between themselves and one participant at a time. They select exercises and games in which they can expect to shine and win applause. When participants have to struggle with a difficult learning task, they fall to lengthy explanations or shift to something else to restore comfort, often their own, at the cost of participant learning. When trainers have become accustomed to gratifying their personal needs through maintaining a central, controlling, dominating, distant role, they all too easily seek and find evidence to support their stance. If, as a matter of fact, participants do not take responsibility for improving the training situation, the trainers conclude there is no alternate method "whatever theory may say." Such trainers choose colleagues and successors to fit the same debilitating pattern: a vicious circle.

The relationship between personal needs and choice of training method and behavior is not necessarily simple and direct. It can be inverse. The same need for control may induce trainers to advocate collaborative and permissive methods. They may do so to avoid acknowledging to themselves and others their actual need for control. Thus they hide behind "permissive methods" and look to friendly human relationships for confirmation. Anxiety and lack of spontaneity earmark such trainers. Their heart is not in participation. They do not engage in it, but stand aside. If relationships do become friendly under these conditions, they are usually superficial and dependent. Moreover, they are achieved at the expense of the task.

The close link between trainers' personal needs, behavior, and the methods they select are no surprise. It is part of what makes much of the world go round. Industry, for instance, is full of managers who shape entire organizations so that they express and reflect their personal needs. We all experience satisfaction from congruence and seek it in many ways, for instance, by our choice of occupation. The same congruence, but in appropriate directions, likewise brings out the enthusiasm, care, and concern which produce an effective trainer. Truth and perversion are reverse sides of the same coin, here and in other areas of life.

What this realization ought to evoke is an adequate examination, at this personal level, of people to be selected as trainers. How does the applicant regard herself and where does she look for their satisfaction? As a scholar, primarily concerned with advancing her subject? As an administrator or organizer who looks for efficiency, perhaps power? As a public servant "able to do anything"? As someone continually learning, assisted by others?

We do not know to what extent the personality factors relevant to effective training are fixed by the time a person becomes a trainer. We do know that for many trainers in developing countries today, training was not their first or even their second choice. For many, it has been the only road open earning a "respectable" living or an activity seen as a step toward some other career. We also know that a developing society may quietly favor a particular pattern of training as a means of protecting itself against major change. It looks for trainees who conform to its self-image rather than for trainers who rock the boat. This cultural protection then exaggerates the inherent proclivity training everywhere has for starting off on the wrong foot. Participants feel most dependent on the trainer at the very beginning of training. The trainer, too, looks to the new group for reassurance and confirmation. The prevailing tendency, therefore, is to pattern the relationship on mutual dependence. This pattern is particularly difficult to modify afterwards. To this built-in pattern of training the world over, developing countries add a pervasive protective bias—all in the same unpromising direction.

To expect people who have not chosen to be trainers, and who value society's traditional deference to the teacher's status and functions, to do more than lecture and possibly chair a general discussion is both inappropriate and unfair. Their hearts cannot be in striving for more significant training. So it would be wrong, and possibly harmful both to them and to the participants, if they ventured into the more personal methods of training.

So far as reluctant (coerced) trainers are concerned, we have only one more thought to add. We doubt whether the costs of their inadequate or erratic motivation for effective training are comprehended, either by themselves or by others. These costs are great, economically and even more in human and developmental terms. If people in charge of training schemes continue to recruit these unsuitable people and saddle them with high expectations, it can only be because the same self-perpetuating defensive process described above is at work in them. After all, by definition development depends on people behaving in new ways. Trainers of these people must themselves be in the forefront to demonstrate essential novelty. We conclude that the development process would be better served if the training effort were limited to a scale that can be effectively staffed. We know trainers here and there, in several developing countries, who have the personal qualities required; surely there are many more who have the makings of effective trainers but require further self development, who need to nourish their inner strengths and to develop more skill in communicating their attitudes effectively. It is to them that the further professional training presented in these pages is addressed.

POWER AND INFLUENCE: TWO MODES

Of all their personal needs, the need for power may be the most salient and also the most treacherous for trainers. Their main task, after all, is to "move" individuals and groups in the program and, by implication, the larger communities and organizations they come from. Such "movement" should at least make participants more competent. Trainers look for indications that they are succeeding in this, otherwise their self-image is threatened and they feel "powerless." When they are lacking such indications they may short-circuit periods of uncertainty by settling for superficial acquiescence and rote learning. Power is a double-edged sword. It can be used to expand influence by making others powerful also. Or it can be used to shrink influence to a self-contained nugget in the trainer by making the participants feel increasingly impotent, ignorant, and abused. Either edge of the sword tends to hone itself and becomes more and more difficult to blunt—short, that is, of a crisis in relationship.

Two bases for the power trainers exercise can be usefully distinguished. One base fosters coercion, a reliance on formal authority and force. Formal status, threats of punishment, and the trainers' proximity to higher authorities are examples of overt signs of coercive power; manipulation of emotional relationships and reliance on charisma are more covert signs. Or power may have a persuasive, sharing basis and rely on helping others to think and make choices, thereby encouraging participants to become powerful too.

Another useful distinction can be drawn between the kinds of behavior that influence participants directly and those that influence them indirectly. This is the difference, for instance, between telling the participants precisely what to do and simply describing a task they have to accomplish. For example, if a trainer says, "please stop talking and listen to me," things happen along several important dimensions: he takes responsibility for a task yet to be specified, sets a standard of behavior, centralizes authority in himself, and restricts interaction between participants. On the other hand, if a trainer says, "there is just one day left before your plan for fieldwork is due," she points toward the task and also her standards, but hardly interferes with the relationships and roles already operating in the group. Direct influence narrowly limits the acceptable range of participants' activities on the task, setting standards, and developing relationships, all three. Indirect influence expands the range of possible activities in all three spheres. In short, by direct influence trainers inhibit the development of the group. By indirect influence they foster it.

The foregoing are generalizations from a major series of studies by Ned Flanders. The kinds of statements that characterize direct and indirect influence are presented in exhibit 9.1. Although these studies, and several others referred to later in this chapter, were carried out in settings of formal education, their findings point also to group development in training settings.

Exhibit 9.1

COMPARISON OF KINDS OF STATEMENTS BY TRAINERS WHICH HAVE DIRECT AND INDIRECT INFLUENCE

Statements of direct influence are those in which trainers	Statements of indirect influence are those in which trainers
— Express or lecture about ideas or knowledge	— Accept, clarify and support the ideas and feelings of participants
— Give directions or orders	— Praise and encourage
— Criticize or deprecate participants behavior with intent to change it	— Ask questions to stimulate participation in decision-making
— Justify their own position or authority	— Ask questions to orient participants to the task or to the topic of discussion

Not that there is a single pattern of influence that trainers should strive continually to maintain—even if they could. There are situations in which indirect influence is less appropriate than direct influence. Moreover, an identical act of a trainer may appear highly directive in one situation but indirect in another. What studies show is that a below-average proportion of direct to indirect influence over an extended period of time will establish more desirable participant attitudes and superior patterns of work. Participants working with more directive trainers, on the contrary, tend to

(a) imitate the trainers and use more direct influence in their interaction, even in the absence of the trainers; (b) have less positive attitudes towards the trainers, the group, and the learning tasks; (c) demonstrate less spontaneity and initiative and make fewer voluntary social contributions and (d) be more easily distracted from the task and respond with greater compliance to, as well as rejection of, the trainers' direct influence. Independent studies using different research techniques in a laboratory situation have shown similar results, adding that these participants reported doing less assigned work and less extra work.

Flanders relates these generalizations about direct and indirect influence by the trainer to three situations common in training: when the task is not clear, when it is clear and attractive, and when it is clear but unattractive.

Box 9.1

TRAINERS' BEHAVIOR AND PARTICIPANT DEPENDENCE—FOUR HYPOTHESES

NED A. FLANDERS

We will arbitrarily assume a particular structure of goal orientation and deal with situations in which, first, goals are ambiguous; second, goals are clear and attractive; and third, they are clear and unattractive. We will further assume that just two conditions can exist for each social structure: the structure of authority is either centered in the teacher or distributed rather evenly among students, and social access is either free or restricted.

Hypothesis One: When goals are ambiguous, direct influence by the teacher increases dependence by centralizing the authority structure and/or restricting social access.

Hypothesis Two: When goals are ambiguous, indirect influence by the teacher increases independence by decentralizing the authority structure and/or freeing social access.

Hypothesis Three: When goals are clear and attractive, direct influence will tend to increase dependence, and indirect influence will tend to decrease dependence, but only to the extent that the student cannot see the relationships between the teacher's comments and the clear goal.

Hypothesis Four: When goals are clear and unattractive, direct teacher influence is necessary to sustain work by restricting social process and centralizing authority, through a system of rewards and punishments, producing high dependency.

SOURCE: *The Dynamics of Instructional Groups* (59th Year Book of the National Society for the Study of Education [Chicago: University of Chicago Press, 1960]), Part II, pp. 206-11.

Box 9.1 states the four hypotheses he has formulated. They are of particular interest to us because everyone is concerned explicitly with the effects of trainers' behavior on one of the two basic themes of development, namely, the importance of reducing tendencies toward inappropriate dependence. Indirectly the hypotheses also address a second theme, the need to encourage innovation and divergence. Divergence is conditioned by independence and interdependence. Of the three situations the first, lack of clarity about the task, is intrinsic to the development process. Uncertainty again and again besets a society as it gropes for the directions and steps singularly appropriate to its development.

1. The Trainers' Behavior When the Task Is Not Clear to Participants

Even in a well-prepared program the training task is not clear on two occasions, as we have already seen: right at the beginning of the program, when expectations remain to be sorted and common tasks established; and again from time to time thereafter, when the task goes out of focus because it looks too taxing, or because it cannot be achieved at this time for some reason or the other. In these situations participants are likely to develop great dependence on the trainers.

Trainers can find many reasons to justify their inclination to exercise direct influence at these times. The participants want it; they obviously do not know what to do or how to proceed. The temptation then is to restate the task for them or give them "a little guidance." Or, trainers may succumb to the same temptation, but from a conviction that the participants do not like the task and will have to be forced to do it, or that they are incompetent, lazy, and contrary people. Without thinking further, the direct approach of simply giving the assignment or "telling them what do" looks very appropriate.

Irrespective of their motivation, trainers may at times get caught in the following sequence: (1) decide that participants are confused; (2) guess at the cause of their confusion; (3) then, acting on this diagnosis, proceed to give information, direction, and perhaps criticism. They expect that this direction will help the participants get on with the work. In fact, what they have done is strengthen participants' habits of looking to authority figures for indications of whether they are doing well or badly, and their expectation that they will be told what to do the next time, too, and the time after; and suppress their imagination and initiative for seeking solutions to problems themselves. The reaction of participants to this tripartite sequence of trainer-behavior would be directly contrary to some increasingly common and important training objectives: skill in situations of increasing complexity; independent operation; and initiative, imagination, and flexibility.

Studies have shown that trainers inclined to direct action give twice as many directions as indirect trainers and on the average, criticize eight times more often. Many trainers seem to think that plentiful criticism is the best way to make participants "tough." Studies do not support this hypothesis. To the contrary, they show that indirect trainers are far tougher because they put participants in the position of facing the consequences of their own ideas, opinions, and decisions. These studies further show that, far from helping, criticism and threat of criticism interfere with many kinds of learning. They evoke childhood fears of change and lead to preoccupations with immediate and simple steps at the cost of perceiving the complex tasks of reality. What many participants learn from frequent criticism is either to worry or not to care. Any pressures from trainers to show results also need to be timed very carefully, if they are not to vitiate learning in areas particularly important to development.

To exercise indirect influence when the task is not clear, trainers can ask participants to choose among alternatives. If these need to be clarified first, trainers can participate in that process. This is a demanding task and they can expect many attempts, some subtle, some angry, to give the job back. Holding out against these pressures from participants can be time-consuming and hard on the nervous system, and nothing tangible may be perceptible for some time. All this calls for a high degree of flexibility in the program, which puts pressures on other trainers also, as well as administrators.

Then comes the breakthrough. The participants face the task of choosing, perhaps of clarifying the task, and establishing roles. They practice diagnosing problems, setting up alternatives, and choosing among them. Irrespective of the particular outcome, these skills occupy an important place in the objectives of many programs. In short, trainers have to make up their minds at a particular moment whether participants now need greater or less freedom in order to go on learning. A predominantly indirect approach will increase their freedom to choose, while a more direct approach is likely to restrict it. It is important to stress that the distinction we are making here is not between active (= direct) and passive (= indirect). Indirect influence may come from quite active behavior. Active guidance by trainers may well be essential when the task is not clear and when the deterioration of activities indicates a need for help. The point is that trainers need to be active in helping participants to understand their difficulties and deal with them, and also in seeing that this understanding does not come from mere reiteration of the task. Neither does understanding come if the trainers guess at the difficulties and proceed on their own assessment. Even if their assessment were correct, the participants would still not understand their dilemma. Certainly if the trainers proceed by direct action, they increase the participants' dependence.

2. The Trainers' Behavior When the Task Is Clear and Attractive

This is the situation that all trainers try to set up and maintain. The participants work and see themselves advancing toward the objective. No problem arises so long as the trainers' behavior is perceived by the participants as helping them with the task. They may influence directly through giving information, directions, and criticisms, or indirectly by asking questions or expanding a participant's idea. The trainers have the opportunity to help broaden the participants' perspective of a problem, challenge their understanding, help them evaluate their procedures, and get the most out of this particular task. When the task is clear and attractive, the effects of direct and indirect influence are quite different from the effects in the other situation, when the task is in question.

An area of doubt arises in this favorable situation only when the trainers' influence, direct or indirect, seems to the participants to be neither logical nor relevant to the task. Much then depends on the participants' general assessment of the trainers and their relationship with them. Participants may see incongruous behavior on the part of trainers as simply an error to be ignored. They may wonder about it, wait and watch, and so give the trainers extra attention. They may see it as a kind of trick, something to test them. In short, when the meaning of the trainers' behavior is not clear to the participants, the effect on them is similar to the effect of the trainers' behavior when the task is not clear, i.e., the first situation. Direct influence here, also, will increase dependence and indirect influence decrease it.

3. The Trainers' Behavior When the Task Is Clear but Unattractive

Most trainers see this as a standard situation for direct action. Trainers in that situation use their authority "to see the task through." The tools for this are rewards and punishments. The rewards can take several forms. They can break the unattractive task into pieces and intersperse them from time to time with other tasks that are attractive, with rest periods, or with jokes. This is a kind of sugar coating; the task remains bitter. Moreover, even if accomplished in using these tools, by doing so they increase participants' dependence on them. Even if they manage to jolly the majority of participants along somehow, usually a few remain who resent the task, resent the trainers for imposing it, and resent them even more for their attempts to lighten it. By tuning into the underlying anger, these participants often acquire sufficient influence to spoil the task and any learning from it.

A safer and more effective approach is to share with the participants the task of finding out what is wrong, i.e., to use the indirect approach.

This requires asking questions, encouraging participants to express their opinions, exploring with them the implications of doing the task in various ways or not doing it at all, and other feelings expressed by the participants related to learning tasks. Trainers who possess the skills necessary to manage such procedures help participants reassess their own goals and make new plans for achieving them. The procedure strengthens the participants' commitment.

Trainers afraid to subject tasks to such a review lest the situation become unmanageable or the tasks formulated by the participants bear no relationship to the objectives of the program, either grossly underestimate their influence on the participants' activities, or are unsure themselves about the value of the task. Experiments with leaving participants wide open choices of program content and methods are entirely reassuring on this point, and in line with the results of similar freedom in other settings. The same indirect approach holds good in dealing with individual participants who experience difficulties. By asking questions, clarifying opinions and feelings, and helping participants reach their own assessment of difficulties, trainers and participants together are ready to examine different courses of action. Taking into account the likely demands and consequences of each, they can settle on the action that looks best.

We have looked at three common situations that arise in the course of establishing common tasks. Establishing tasks is itself only one of the three dimensions into which, for clarity's sake, we have chosen to divide the social process of developing the training group. The trainers' behavior affects all parts of the process similarly.[3] When, to the contrary, they use indirect influence in any of the three dimensions of the social process, they thereby develop shared responsibility for the task and at the same time increase interactions, distribute authority, and foster independent and collaborative standards of behavior. The characteristic effects of the prevalence of either kind of behavior on the part of trainers can readily be seen even in a single session and even by an outsider. The prevalence of direct influence surfaces as dominance by the trainers or by one or more of their favored participants; dependence on certain participants who lead the class; silence among large segments of the group during discussions; fixed and limited roles among group members; and disruption and breakdown when the trainers are absent. Expressions of semi-reverence toward the trainers and their abilities, combined quite possibly with expressions of resentment against the institution, can be expected outside the session. The prevalence of indirect influence by trainers, on the other hand, had a different set of indicators: spontaneous interaction among

[3] When trainers rely on direct influence through making decisions themselves, imposing discipline, and regulating other critical aspects of the task, they thereby also restrict interaction among the participants, centralize authority, and foster standards of submissive and rebellious behavior.

participants; possible difficulty in identifying the trainers or the participant leaders; low predictability as to who will take what role and high predictability that a particular role *will* be taken at any particular time; high commitment to decisions made by the group; strong feelings of responsibility for group action; and a feeling of ease and comfort whether trainers are present or absent. Outside the sessions much of the discussion may still center on the training tasks.

TRAINERS' "REALNESS" UNDER PRESSURE: THREE DILEMMAS

Any basic flaws trainers' have will show up under pressure, when they react spontaneously, "from the gut," from the depth of the people they are. Pressures of time, for instance, and sheer quantity of work are most common. We will focus on the last few minutes of a session.

Time is running out and the trainer has another two or three major points to make. But participants are busily following up an earlier thought. The discussion is lively. It is drawing in some who have not spoken earlier, and now speak haltingly and rather slowly, and not very directly to the point, perhaps. What does the trainer do? Does she "round off" the subject at the cost of interrupting a learning experience? Let the participants continue what they are doing? Or refocus the group on the main training objective? For instance, by stating the choices now left open to the group in terms of the little time remaining. It is a spot judgment, and despite the best intentions in the world, subject to many errors. But the very manner in which the trainer proceeds, in whatever direction, reflects her feelings and speaks about her as a person. In such a situation, one trainer may reassert himself quite roughly, as if the discussion had not taken place or had been an undesirable interlude. Another does nothing; perhaps she has lost sight of the objectives of the session or fears the group's displeasure if she reminds them. A third reminds them, but gently. He acknowledges that the current discussion may be more important and that "rounding off" might yet be done, say during the break, or by making some other time available.

In observing the trainer's reaction, a useful summary question may be: Where does he focus most of his attention? On the subject "to cover," the relationships among participants, bringing one or two "slow" ones along, their relationships with him, his relationships to colleagues and principal? The trainer who experiences the pressures in this quite common situation as a challenge to her authority will look for ways of dealing with them in a manner quite different from a trainer who sees them as arising out of the participants' endeavor to learn and, perhaps, out of his own human limitations.

It may be useful to list, with a brief comment on each, three dilemmas built into most training situations which bring pressure to bear on the trainer.

1. Participants' Expectations Versus Trainers' Intentions

Participants carry a burden of history, in the form of expectations, when they first meet the trainers. They have some picture of "a trainer" long before they actually meet. Getting to know them is bedeviled by interpreting their current behavior in the light of memories of other trainers. Whether these interpretations are rosy or black, they are certainly limiting and, from the trainers' point of view, chancy. The new trainers are classified in advance, cast for a part they cannot know, and one which may differ for various participants.

An informal opening through which a trainer intends to communicate friendliness and closeness may strike some participants as a sign of incompetence, others as lack of authority, yet others as a challenge promising fun, and others as fearfully vague and threatening disaster. Participants whose expectations are violated by this initial informality will react suspiciously: "What does this mean?" "Can I trust her?" Or, at a different level? "Can I trust myself with her?"

> Trainers need only to reflect on their experience of simply asking a new group: "Are there any questions?" Their intention may be to ascertain how well they have been understood. But no questions are forthcoming. Or the few questions that are asked give no answer to the initial question, really. They have learned from experience that some (unknown) participants hesitate to ask for fear of appearing stupid or unprepared before him and the others; others (unknown) do the same, to avoid the charge later of "playing up" to the trainer; others again, to avoid the risk of ridicule. For all of these participants silence is simpler and safer. Those who do ask questions (both they and their motives unknown) may be seeking to assume leadership in the group, or to show the trainers what "good students" they are.
>
> A similarly wide range of reactions may greet a suggestion that the trainers threw in to stimulate thought and make an idea concrete. Many participants immediately conclude that this is not so much a suggestion to examine as a hint, something to be implemented or opposed.

The pressures out of this discrepancy between participant expectations and trainer intention can become so great that trainers sometimes exclaim, "my group seems determined to misunderstand and misconstrue my every action!" So, what does a trainer do now? Vent anger on the participants? Ignore the pressure and "battle on"? Or look for ways to understand these misinterpretations and give participants a better chance to understand him?

Two conditions make the pressures that arise from such a dilemma very difficult to tolerate. One obtains when participants did not come for training of their own choice, indeed would have preferred not to come. This negativity not only clouds their expectations, but generates a dislike so pervasive that no trainer can do much to counter it. The other condition obtains when one trainer behaves in a manner strikingly different from other trainers working in the same program or elsewhere in the same institution. The signals the participants receive are then confusing and arouse their suspicion. They may feel treated as toys to be played with, or perhaps experimented upon and manipulated.

2. Individual Versus Group Needs

Participants differ in interests, methods of work, speed of learning, and interpretation of the trainers' behavior. But except for minor modifications, the trainers' actions have to be the same for all. To whom then do they pay most attention and address their endeavors? The talkers or the non-talkers? The quick or the slow? The agreeable or the attackers? It is all too easy to be mesmerized by the obvious, often clamorous, needs at one extreme or the other. Many trainers find it difficult indeed to forego the clamor and challenge, and deal with the less stimulating but often more numerous assortment of participants in the middle. It is all very well for them to acknowledge the satisfactions they find in working with the bright and the agreeable and the dislike they feel for those who tax their patience or get their goat. Such extremes challenge them as people and bring their own needs—to be liked, to succeed, to defend themselves—into sharp focus. But the primary needs, in terms of participant learning, lie elsewhere.

3. Consistency Versus Flexibility

The widely varying and changing needs of individual participants call for flexible behavior on the part of trainers. Like skilled craftspeople they seek to respond appropriately to the immediate situation, taking into account as best they can its multiple moving facets. Participants, on the other hand, look to trainers for consistent behavior, preferably faultless! That way they know how to deal with them and what to expect. They can make of the trainers all-knowing gods (or devils), best kept at a comfortable distance. The trainers' flexibility and humanity are disquieting to participants with this attitude, denying them the certainty and security they wish and to which they feel entitled. Common reactions are accusations of favoritism, incompetence, and manipulation to retain power.

Trainers know all these dilemmas from experience. They also know (or can find out) how to reduce the pressures. They can bring conflicting expectations out into the open and make common plans; offer participants paired suggestions to choose from instead of just one; work in small groups to handle individual variations in learning; deal with specific individual needs outside the session; state and restate the orientation and objectives of the program; encourage clarification of doubts about their behavior—and so on, down the list of all the desirable behavior we have described in various parts of this book.

The difficulty lies not in knowing, but in doing and in acting quickly when the occasion arises. Then again, not in doing so much as in feeling like doing—in the trainers' dispositions. If their disposition is not in line with effective training, then they add a fourth dimension which really *is* unmanageable: trainer needs versus participant needs. We suspect that it is this basic dilemma, and the pressures arising from it, that many trainers seek to resolve through authoritarian, distant, and impersonal behavior, and by choosing training events and tools in the reverse order of effectiveness: abstract when something situational is needed, distant instead of personal, individual instead of social, and a focus on outward behavior instead of on feelings.

Training in developing countries is beset by these dilemmas—magnified. Trainers in such countries have to be exceptionally strong and able people if they are to be effective at levels of training that make a difference in development. The experiences and expectations that participants bring are, by definition, sharply at variance with effective training for the future. They place trainers firmly in positions of authority and participants in positions of dependence. These expectations resist major modification, partly because dependency needs are deep-seated in the participants' personalities, and partly because they continue to govern so many important relationships. Participants are accustomed to the satisfactions of dependent relationships at work and in their families. In many settings they themselves are in authority with others dependent on them, or can look forward with assurance to the time when such will be their position. Any rebellious feelings they have had against people in authority, perhaps even expressed in action, have not taken them far along the road of personal and social development. They are commonly what psychologists call "counterdependent"; the focus of attention for their feelings is still the trainer vested with authority.

Effective training in such a situation depends on creating opportunities for participants to experience pressure from many sources, live with intense personal and social demands, and to make individual decisions under these conditions. Lectures and general discussions offer little along these lines; they promote conformity or intellectual debate without testing disagreements in action. Training, on the contrary, must provide opportunities in which participants can practice differing from others and collaborating with them across these differences. To be effective in these directions, trainers need, first and foremost, to possess these very qualities and be able to demonstrate them. They must feel this personal freedom and interdependence themselves so that they can express these feelings in the ways they behave with participants and in the kinds of training events they organize.

Trainers express this freedom at the personal level through what Carl Rogers calls their "realness", and interdependence by responding to others in the ways we described in the last chapter under "indirect training". Roger writes:

> Learning will be facilitated if the teacher is congruent. This involves the teacher's being the person that he is, and being openly aware of the attitudes he holds. It means that he feels acceptant toward his own real feelings. Thus he becomes a real person in the relationship with his students. He can be enthusiastic about subjects he likes, and bored by topics he does not like. He can be angry, but he can also be sensitive and sympathetic. Because he accepts his feelings as his feelings, he has no need to impose them on his students, or to insist that they feel the same way. He is a person, not a faceless embodiment of a curricular requirement, or a sterile pipe through which knowledge is passed from one generation to the next.[4]

The basic importance of a trainer's realness is confirmed by a growing body of studies based on elaborate recordings of discussions and statistical correlations between predicted and actual ratings. Denial by trainers of their own feelings is accompanied by lower effectiveness.[5]

Helping trainers learn to accept their own feelings more fully and so become more real can be attempted through programs of laboratory training and various kinds of counseling. Especially valuable for developing trainers is psychoanalytically-based work, such as "study groups" pioneered by Tavistock Institute of Human Relations in England since the 1940s and introduced into India and other developing countries. They focus steadily on the group leader and examine issues of authority and dependence, which are particularly intricate and urgent in developing countries. Competencies in interdependent relationships and collaboration can also be for trainers: first, practice in accepting, clarifying, and using the ideas participants offer in planning the work and diagnosing difficulties; second, increasing trainers' recognition of acts that restrict participant reactions and those that expand them; and third, developing trainers' understanding of theories of instruction that they can use to control their

[4] Carl Rogers, *On Becoming a Person* (Boston, Cambridge: Houghton Mifflin Co., 1961), p. 287.

[5] John Withall and W. W. Lewis, "Social Interaction in the Classroom," in N. L. Gage (ed.), *Handbook of Research on Teaching* (Chicago: Rand McNally and Co., 1963), pp. 683-714.

own behavior as they guide communication in practice.[6]

To sustain self-development and resistance to dominant pressures toward familiar authoritarian and directive patterns, trainers, need above all regular reliable information about their own behavior and its effect on participants. A sympathetic colleague can be an excellent source for this type of information. If colleagues pair up and take turns providing this information to one another, any threat implied by such checkups can be greatly reduced. Not evaluation, but information about interactions is required. The question is not what should have happened but what in fact did. This kind of sharing engenders self-improvement.

Training trainers for greater effectiveness means, then, changing the authoritarian image tradition has instilled in the trainer to an image of a resource person capable of helping participants in the process of learning. The new image is usually not one that trainers have experienced. Neither have they received such help nor given it, at least not consciously. In the absence of personal experience, the new image is likely to have little meaning for trainers. Even apart from feelings they may have about helping others in ways denied them, there is also the difficulty that the new approach to training has no model. Technical assistance personnel could model the needed attitudes and personal disposition; this would be a strategic contribution. Without *some* variant (deviant) to attract attention, trainers cannot point either to themselves or to some immediately visible figures as exemplary. Thus, the ideal they work toward with participants' potential remains remote: a developing society, something largely intangible and difficult to describe.

The new approach demands from the trainer great acumen, sensitivity and adaptability, and continuous application. The only reward it promises is the personal satisfaction that comes from greater effectiveness. In the institution and program in which they work, the rewards of status and reputation will almost certainly continue to run in the traditional direction of subject knowledge, research, and publications and, no doubt, for quite some time to come. Status and recognition for more effective training lie far in the future.

TRAINERS' ROLE: THREE HIDDEN FUNCTIONS

Training oriented as here incorporates three functions in the trainers' role in addition to the well-recognized one of conducting training sessions. Each of these functions is complex and none fits readily with the others. They are: providing guidance and support to individual participants—mentoring; designing and helping to implement organizational

[6] Ned A. Flanders, "Teacher Influence: Pupil Attitudes and Achievement" (mimeographed; Minneapolis: University of Minnesota, 1961).

change strategies to provide scope for trained personnel—intervention; and preparing and running an entire training program—a managerial function.

The mentoring function has been neglected in recent years, even denied, on the grounds that it tends to confirm participants in their dependencies on the trainer. So trainers would rather not risk incurring this price plus the certainty of heavy additional work. But there are usually some participants in programs who feel drawn to establish a special relationship with a particular trainer, as a means toward greater exploration and learning. This can be a legitimate and healthy dependence and the chosen trainer can participate in it with excellent results. First of all, trainers need not fear that all participants will want mentoring, an overwhelming task indeed, only just a few. Secondly, they can ensure that the dependency is not unduly prolonged. With wise handling, both parties, mentor as well as participant, can benefit from this special relationship, which is honored throughout history and in every land. Sufficient caring is a trainer's basic qualification for this function, expressed in part in a careful preparation and review, perhaps with collegiate help. Certainly, the mentoring function in training deserves renewed attention today.

Trainers also have the function of intervening in the participant's work organization(s), to ensure that newly gained competencies will be effectively used there. That such interventions may be critical for their success as trainers is a recent recognition, superceding earlier assumptions that organizational contexts would obviously favor the use of new competencies—why send participants for training otherwise?—and that participants could by themselves make any changes necessary. Today, if the trainers' help in this direction is rejected, their training system ought to reconsider future admission of people from that work organization for training. Conversely, in the course of their work with participant organizations, trainers also learn what to incorporate in order to make training even more effective.

The third additional function, at least of fully competent trainers, is to plan, organize, and run effective training programs. Staff, materials, facilities; participants have to come together on schedule and within budget limits. There may be fieldwork to arrange and support staff to supervise work preparatory to future programs, even while current programs are under way. These "housekeeping" chores are often belittled and left to others while trainers seek to concentrate on "more creative" tasks. They may begrudge the time spent on management. Their disinclination may also mask low competence and inexperience in this aspect of training. But direct familiarity with the management function, achieved and maintained by including its practice in the trainer's role, is their opportunity to appreciate the immediate context of training and key colleagues working in it. It also provides an opportunity for freshening their appreciation of issues they deal with in training sessions from the point of view of participants, who are practitioners eager to improve their practice. Furthermore, managing the different aspects of training and integrating them effectively generates fresh creative ideas and field data for the training program.

TRAINERS' STYLE: UNIQUE, APPROPRIATE, FLEXIBLE

Trainers have the personal task of dovetailing very diverse functions and making them distinctively their own. In carrying this out, they develop their own style, one that suits them, one that they find effective. Lists of discrete behaviors of more or less effective trainers—until recently the preoccupation of researchers—describe the essence of style no better than assorted notes convey the nature of a song. Two general points emerge from these studies. First, training goals and the styles through which trainers promote learning vary widely. Some trainers state their primary goal in terms of developing self-awareness; others in relating the subject to practical problems; and others again in increasing the participants' urge to study. The trainers' primary direction of interest varies, accordingly, toward the participants, the subject, and the process of training. In action, some trainers express their opinions, others do not. Some address the participants as a group, others address mainly individuals. Some exercise much control, others little. Through it all, participants may or may not learn what is intended.

But diversity of goals notwithstanding, uniformities in style are quite striking. In a study comparing seven training styles of "effective trainers," the word "responsive" accompanied every mention of control or control sequences. All the trainers studied were "relaxed, accepting," even the "businesslike" ones. The "businesslike" trainers, just like the others, presented differed in frequency of interaction but all interacted in an indirect manner. All these trainers, regardless of their style, were very flexible and able to vary their roles and methods to suit changing needs. Such flexibility derives from feeling at home in both one's personal style and the situation. To summarize, effective trainers range markedly in style and behave far more flexibly than ineffective trainers.

"Realness", that a trainer's style rings true, or fits, is therefore the basic hallmark of an effective style. That trainers, to use a contemporary idiom, "have their act together" makes them credible to participants in what they say and do across different concrete situations, and hence also makes them reliable and trustworthy as instigators of new thoughts and as guides. "Unreal" trainers, on the other hand, no matter how clear their exposition of a topic, leave participants floundering—unsure what to believe or disbelieve, to try or not to try. Hence participants often settle for similar make-believe behavior, e.g., rote answers, or simply tuning out.

Explorations and development of one's style is a slow, maturing process, which begs trainers to come to grips with the personal dimensions of their needs for power and influence and determines the extent they will or will not exercise those needs in the role of trainer. Helping younger colleagues make progress along this difficult path may be the richest contribution experienced trainers can make to them, to a system, and to the profession.

The second general point emerging from studies on trainer behavior pertains to varying specific behavior to suit different situations. This is the contingency approach to the matter of appropriateness. For instance, emphasis on task performance is often appropriate when the situation is confusing prior to mastery of some concept or skill, while emphasis on process learning is usually more appropriate when the situation is otherwise structured and/or the participants have matured as a group. Experienced trainers will deliberately use both sequentially in order to move the group in a desired direction.

Contextual appropriateness in turn requires adaptability. Trainers have ready access (at most times) to a wide variety of tools—concepts and skills—in their bags of experience and can move between them to suit the fluid situation in session as well as the differing needs of individual participants. In the terminology "Transactional Analysis" an effective trainer may have all ego states—Parent, Adult, and Child—in play at one time or another, in OK (or not OK) ways. OK denotes trainer behavior that helps participants mature and become better able to cope with their lives and their circumstances.

Different styles, methods, and events can be accommodated in the same training program. They need not be confusing to participants and certainly make the program more stimulating. More importantly, the variety itself communicates, first, that different kinds of behavior can be equally effective in a situation as long as the behavior is genuine and/or second, that participants have the very personal task of developing styles of behavior of their own, styles which truly express the person each is. What does confuse participants and can seriously disrupt a training program is a mixture of genuine and "pseudo" trainers. This leaves participants wondering in which direction to look and to proceed. When subject to the conflicting pressures that markedly characterize developing countries, they are very apt to conclude that they are being manipulated, teased rather than trained. An experience of this nature is almost sure to freeze them in their traditional rigid patterns. Training in such cases is a waste, or worse. A consistently "real" training environment, on the other hand, is supportive. Participants feel certain of a genuine response, and see the effects of their new behavior. They develop personal styles which, like the trainers', will surely be more varied and more flexible than the styles they came with. This is the direction of effective training for development.

Chapter 10

Posttraining Support for Improved Performance at Work

> If the Atlantic could have been crossed as easily as it can be today, most of the Pilgrim Fathers would probably have returned.
>
> —MATTHEW MILES

THE PROGRAM has run its course. The participants are leaving, on their way back to their jobs. They will now "show what they have learned." If the program was full-time and residential, going back to work is a major event. If it was long and located far away, perhaps abroad, everything conspires to magnify the changeover. But in a very real sense every training program, even one just around the corner and part-time, takes the participants "abroad."

Kenneth Benne labels participants according to the manner in which they return from training and characteristically set about the problems of transferring what they have learned to their work situation. These are: the easy convert, the tourist, the expatriate, the missionary, the self-mystic, and the learner-critic. Benne's classification is presented in box 10.1. The learner-critic is the most promising model.

Participants may be assumed to have come to the program with well-ingrained tendencies to behave predominantly according to one or the other such model. The program sought to affect these tendencies, to strengthen the effective ones and to modify the others. So when participants go back to work in their organizations, not only they, but also the program is under test. If some programs fail through not taking participants "abroad," many more fail, or substantially fail, through not equipping them adequately for the return. Or, more accurately, shortcomings during the earlier pretraining or training phases show up now, at the posttraining phase.

REDRESSING FOUR COMMON IMBALANCES IN TRAINING PROGRAM

Matthew Miles attributes difficulties in the posttraining phase to the

Box 10.1

THE TRANSFER OF LEARNING: SIX MODELS FOR MAN IN TRANSITION

KENNETH D. BENNE

The entry into the Laboratory culture and the reentry into the back-home culture present similar problems to the person. He brought certain established behavior, attitudes, ideas, loyalties with him that were relevant to his memberships in back-home groups. These have been challenged in the training culture, have confronted him with *personal emergencies*. As the emergencies have been resolved here, behavior, attitudes, ideas, etc., of the person have undergone certain modifications. Therefore, he is returning as a somewhat different person and is therefore faced with a reentry problem. The incongruence between the two cultures has to be reduced by the person.

There are certain models of man in transition which give us a picture of how the problem may be solved.

1. *The easy convert:* He has been passive in the Laboratory culture, taking it in with no struggle or fight. When he goes back home he will quickly put on the old shell, and no one will see any difference with him. He will continue to behave in the groove with no change.

If, however, we take the view that the two cultures are different and that the person has had involvement in each, then conflict is inevitable. The conflict may be resolved in several ways:

2. *The tourist model:* He has been a visitor, inspecting what goes on in the training and returns home with a kit of techniques and papers but no real change inside.

3. *The expatriate model:* He left home and deeply involved himself in the Laboratory culture. He may feel unhappy when he goes back home because "things don't happen there the way they happened at Bethel."

Neither the tourist nor the expatriate models forecast change in the person in the enduring back-home situation. Three models admit the possibility of transfer of learnings to back home. These are:

4. *The missionary model:* He came to change and may be overeager to spread changes to others back home.

5. *The self-mystic model:* He changed but cannot explain what happened to him. It was "a terrific experience". He may communicate and transfer learnings after more time has passed and he sorts things out.

Box 10.1 (Continued)

6. *The learner-critic model*: He has taken a tough-minded, reality-testing attitude toward the Laboratory culture. He has continuously compared and contrasted the two cultures, accepting differences and resolving conflicts in his overlapping membership roles here and back home. He is the best bet for transfer of learnings.

Some suggestions for enhancing the learner-critic function (which to some extent is available already to all of us):

THE LEARNER-CRITIC MODEL

1. Stay marginal or in transition as far as possible so both cultures are available and valued.
2. Accept the greater potency of back home because of its demand and enduring satisfaction.
3. Be critical of back home and a deeper student of that culture—risking negative reaction of colleagues and work through resistances.
4. Accept the potency of a new culture—Bethel—as a reference group against which you can rehearse the application of ideas and behaviors back home.
5. Meet the honestly expressed needs for change back home by making your learnings available to others for them to test as you tested them when learning at Bethel.
6. Accept yourself as a person with more autonomy and spontaneous competence as you contact puzzling human phenomena, diagnose them, act to change them and be ready to receive feedback.

SOURCE: Theory Session of National Training Laboratory for School Executives, July-August, 1961, Washington, D.C.

failure to redress four imbalances in many training programs. He calls these input overload, unrealistic goals, alienation, and linkage failure.[1]

1. Input Overload

The program stimulated the participants so much that they came to the end of it too excited for their own good, or for the good of their organization. This overload may have come about through several kinds of

[1] Matthew B. Miles, "On Temporary Systems," in Matthew B. Miles (ed.), *Innovation in Education* (New York: Teachers' College, Columbia University, 1964; pp. 437-90.

errors on the part of the trainers. The trainers may have attempted to cram too much into the program. This is very common. Or they may have scheduled a major group task so late that participants could not "decompress" before the end of the program. Programs that build up a late assignment into a dominant indicator of the program's overall success or failure often suffer from this weakness. To make sure participants return home in top form, trainers deliberately tend to hold the assignment until the last possible moment—a report of fieldwork, for instance. They then go on to mistake the level of excitement generated at the end of the program for a true measure of the success of training.

2. Unrealistic Goals

The second imbalance may have occurred when setting the goals of training. In their initial enthusiasm, participants, severally and jointly, set themselves goals that are excessively high. And even though these unrealistic goals were unattainable all along, the trainers failed to dislodge them from the participants' minds.

The freer the training, the more prone was it to develop this imbalance. In the freedom to explore and learn the limitations in various work situations, a kind of hothouse atmosphere ensues in which realistic goal-setting is difficult. Trainers may have exaggerated this tendency by not controlling competitive goal-setting; perhaps they even welcomed it. In the process, their attention was diverted from the realities of actual work situations. The characteristic list of requests from participants at the end of almost every program indicate at once the eagerness and the anxiety they feel about implementing the goals they have set for themselves. A standard request is that their superiors be trained "so that they will understand us." Another is for some kind of continuing association of participants as a separate body of trained people. A third is for continuing live contact with the trainers and the institution.

If unrealistic goals still loom at the end of the program, one of two things happens. Looking back, some participants may sense the lack of realism in the goals, feel they are returning to work unclear about what they can usefully attempt to do, and so entertain doubts about the practical value of the training program as a whole. Others, who take the unrealistic goals back to their work, are bound to fail and to become disenchanted.

3. Alienation

As participants have drawn closer to each other during the training program, they have also separated themselves from colleagues who stayed behind at work. The separation is widened (except in remedial training) by the new things participants have learned. The gap is particularly noticeable if it occurs in the realm of attitudes and values: to the extent, for example, that participants have become far more egalitarian, open and trustful among themselves, colleagues at work may appear very different, less enlightened. This is a first step to alienation. Any alienation left unresolved at the end of the program will interfere with even the most realistic plans participants have made for communicating their learning to others. Often it heads them into general resentment and isolation at work. This unintended and unexpected result can be most painful and disillusioning.

Compared to their necessarily improvised, untried, and tentative attempts to change things, existing methods of working, sanctioned and supported, appear wonderfully solid and invite continuation. Why try to change them when only anger results? Sooner or later, the initial impetus of training wanes, and the participants doubt the utility or wisdom of continuing to wander in the wilderness of novelty and pioneering. Response from all around urges them to forget their training just as soon as possible. The crudest example of alienation is the plight of many participants in long overseas programs who, when they returned to their home country, felt like fish out of water and hence departed again. Some have clung to an indefinite idea of trying to return again later, but the second try usually looks more difficult even than the first.

4. Linkage Failure

The very detachment which made the training program clear, fascinating, and productive may have blinded participants to what they will be up against when they return to ordinary life. There the simplicity of the training situation is replaced by role conflicts, work pressures, and vested interests. If important sections of the work organization did not approve of the training in the first place, or if participants committed themselves to a program without their organization's active support or even approval, then the problems of effectively linking training and work are bound to be acute. Even without these additional complications, there is a built-in linkage problem. In the first place, training programs imply some inadequacy on the part of the work organization: a need for change, a defect of routine mechanisms, some inadequacy that prevents the exploration of ideas and behavior beyond the organization's normal tolerance. If training has succeeded, these challenges invade the organization itself through the returning participant: a Trojan horse of unknown contents and implications is present in their very midst.

Changes derived from the training program, therefore, despite appropriateness and quality, do not determine the prospects of successful innovation of and in themselves. The organization's preparedness also matters greatly. But even when preparedness is assured, the adequacy with which participants have been helped to anticipate and to cope with the strategic problems they will encounter at work matters even more.

The following extract from a letter illustrates well the frustration of a participant who had just returned to work and encountered organizational unpreparedness and also in his own skill:

> The last four to five months are enough to make me fed up with the things here. What a difference! During the training both Roy and I were working like mad people. Work and work and work, and what a joy! And here—as soon as I reached I got the first sad taste of inaction. As I have sinned in going for training in the first place... I have none to blame except myself—for interpersonal incompetence. We take sessions on temporary systems, we talk about "linkage failure." We talk about back-home job reorientation. That's it. Cognitively we all are experts. But when it comes to experiencing and action, we are no better than laymen.

Each of the four common imbalances discussed above has its roots way back in the program or even in the pretraining phase of training. They were noted in the training strategy and in the overall relationships between the work organization and the system. Figure 10.1 shows the effects of the four imbalances in the training program on the participants and their organization back home.

For future programs a training institution can iron out such imbalances in approach and methods. For instance, it can take steps to increase the organization's awareness, as well as the participants', of the difficulties to be faced at the end of the training program. It can adjust the program to a volume and rhythm that will enable participants to deal with the difficulties of transfer. It can make structural changes in its program to avoid disabling alienation; for example, the institution can split a long continuous program into a series of shorter separate programs, or it can strive to build quickly minimum concentrations of trained participants in the organization, perhaps at several interrelated levels. Such steps show an institution learning from its own experience. Systematic evaluation of current programs can help it learn, as will be seen in chapter 11. Right here we are concerned with a program that has just finished, whose participants are returning to work. If there are imbalances in the picture at this moment and the participants beset with difficulties as they journey homeward, the institution's hands are fairly empty. For better or for worse, the participants must proceed substantially on their own. Only when the imbalances are moderately low can an institution carry out posttraining functions.

Figure 10.1

FOUR COMMON IMBALANCES IN TRAINING: EFFECTS DURING THE POSTTRAINING PHASE

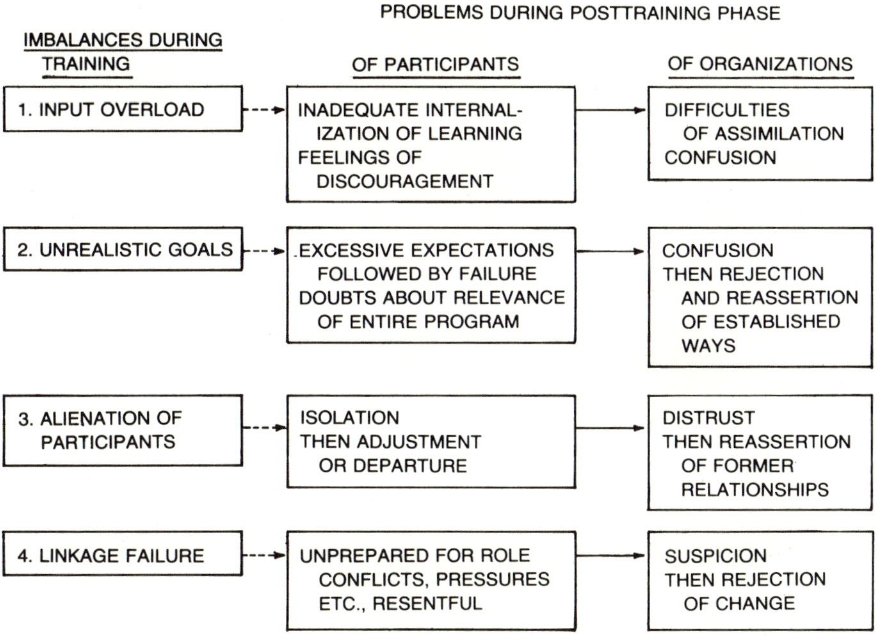

SUPPORTING INNOVATION AT WORK

The problems, great or small, which returning participants face as they attempt to work on their jobs with new skills and attitudes are intrinsically difficult. Basically, they are the same problems encountered in innovation anywhere. Dealing with these problems involves a chain of three sets of activities: first, stimulating and ensuring sufficient interest on the part of colleagues; second, helping colleagues evaluate the proposed change as an idea; and, third, trying an acceptable change in actual practice. However good the training program has been, and however able the participants, the training will be effective only to the extent that they and their colleagues at work engage in this three-pronged process. The work organization can ask for system resources to help in its implementation. That is ideal. Regardless, the system should be so concerned with the successful use of its training that it goes ahead and provides whatever support and services it can, at least to its erstwhile participants.

Back at work, participants are the key figures in the process of change. They must interest others, stimulate them to assess the new ideas, try them out, and proceed to develop ideas of their own. With their return to work, their immediate colleagues and others to be affected by changes, therefore, become the learners and the participants the quasi-trainers. Has the training program prepared them for this task? Perhaps it has, through involving them in planning and running various parts of the program, and through exercises simulating their role as change agent back in their organizations. Does their place in their organization offer a fair chance to work as a change agent? A negative answer to this question should have excluded them from the program in the first place. It means that they may not even receive a hearing when they return.

Even when they are sufficiently well placed, the change agent's role is still formidable. They lack experience of it. That they return to an organization to which they have belonged, have been an insider, holds some advantages. It also adds some complications to the task of introducing changes. Thus one thing is certain: participants on returning to work need access to all the experience, wisdom, and help that the training system can offer. These are rightfully theirs by virtue of the agreed purpose for which they have been trained: to effect change on the job in their organizations.

Ten percent of total training budgets is a reasonable proportion to earmark for costs of contact between the training institution and the work organization before and after the program itself, and two-thirds of this may have to be spent on supportive follow-up activities. In developing countries where governments often cover all training costs, including participant travel, living costs, and allowances, and disperse these funds directly to the training units within each ministry, this allocation seems a simple matter. But the logic of it is deceptive on two counts. Planners are allergic to budgeting for activities that cannot be programmed rather precisely in advance, yet follow-up is too large an item to include under "contingencies" and is also far too vulnerable in that category to misspending. Provision for follow-up support is, therefore, usually inadequate or absent. A more basic objection, one that applies to all one-way financing of training through the training system, is that it shields the work organization from the thorough planning or commitment of its own resources to put training to the best use.

On the positive side, when training has addressed realistic needs at work and been promptly put to use, even simple follow-up visits by training staff can quickly surface opportunities for helpful organizational interventions. Trainers can be encouraged and funded to pursue these and, in addition, can pass their development experience in one organization on for learning by others. Many official and unofficial agencies welcome opportunities to fund promising "learning systems" or chains that are based on actual experiences that have already proven useful elsewhere.

> In one province in Indonesia the new training team working in the health sector surfaced ten action projects in its first half-year of working together. Two of these projects developed further the following year into learning systems

comprising a series of districts, and one project directly affected polity formation at the national level.

If the organization has carried out its particular responsibilities during the training period of its staff, much work will already have been done to arouse interest among the participant's colleagues in the impending changes and to assess their likely implications. This is a follow-through of the work initiated during the pretraining phase when the selection, preparation, and dispatch of participants for training became a part of the organizations' commitments and plans to change. While the participants were in training, the implications of consequent changes were further examined in the organizations, and preparations made for their return. If all is well, the organizations have looked forward to their return and are thoroughly ready to forge ahead.

At worst, an organization's interest in the change has evaporated, perhaps even disappeared, altogether. Maybe further examination revealed the prospective change as not so desirable after all, or the idea was overtaken by unfavorable events. This can happen even with the best will in the world, especially when general conditions alter as precipitously and unpredictably as they often do, not least in developing countries. Failure of organizational interest in change is one of the wastes that must be expected even in sound training. The usual situation lies between these extremes. The institution had some contact with the work organization while the training program was in session. It is aware, in a general way, of the organization's receptivity for change and the kinds of problems likely to confront participants upon their return. It will have included in the program some preparation for them in handling these eventualities. So they arrive back at work with the realistic encouragement of trainers and some access to training resources.

What participants commonly find is that their colleague's interest in their training and the changes it portends have been stifled during their absence by more immediate preoccupations. Their return constitutes a reminder. Dormant interest is rekindled and refocused now that they are back. The time has come to put change into practice.

Help from the system at this stage can range widely in content and assume manifold forms. Most important is continued contact with participants and their organizations. This is important in itself, and also as a basis for other services.

Continued Personal and Organizational Contact

Three degrees of closeness and continuity in the continuing contacts between the training system and the participants' organizations can be distinguished. The closest leads participants, colleagues, and trainers to do some work together right on the job. The introduction of a change thereby becomes a collaborative effort backed by additional professional resources. The linkage is complete and maximum resources are available when the most difficult action takes place.

An example of such collaboration occasionally occurs in the intensive plant counseling of the Central Small Industries Organization (CSIO) of the Government of India. The scheme of intensive counseling is itself an outgrowth of SIET Institute's field training. The counseling team at work consists of one or two SIET Associates working together with colleagues to make up the necessary assortment of disciplines. SIET Institute undertakes to attach one of its trainers to such a team for up to one week. He or she works along with the team in much the same relationship as she worked with the participants during their in-plant study in the training program, as consultant and resource person. At other times, extension officers of the CSIO collaborate with SIET trainers on a demonstration or training program. The Associates take the lead. The trainer joins them for planning, evaluation, and sometimes for part of the program itself.

The second best contact, running far behind the ideal, is direct contact with participants at a distance. The system can encourage participants to get in touch whenever they encounter difficulties they think a trainer might help remove. During the training program trainers may have avoided personal counseling because of the inordinate time it takes and because it might conflict with some types of training events. Postprogram requests for counseling do not hold these risks. They tend to come from few participants and can be safely encouraged.

A high proportion of requests are for further information on matters mentioned during training which became real and urgent only after the participants returned to work. Requests we ourselves have received refer to teaching cases used during the program that later proved directly relevant to a participant's situation or arose from readings taken back with them. Others, the most desirable but also the most difficult to meet, asked for contact in person over problems on the job.

Counseling can be of direct help in one kind of situation. When participants, facing a sudden heavy increase of pressure on the job, know what to do and use their enhanced skills only to find it inadequate, they then have the unsettling experience of having done everything correctly but with the wrong result. Trainers may then be of help in reassuring the participants that their specific steps were not at all at fault, but rather their assessment of the situation as a whole was. Miscalculations of the scale and speed at which colleagues will become involved in changes are the most common error; unaided, participants may well slip into despondency that could have been averted.

The third degree of contact between participants' organizations and training institutions is yet another step back from giving concrete help on the job. It is exemplified by general refresher courses. These may be located in an organization, some town, or back at the institution. The Administrative Staff College of India recalls the participants of a particular course for a week's program around two years or so later. Other agencies organize events for participants of several programs who work in the same organization or live in the same locality. It is important to safeguard the working purpose of such events against the very natural tendency to convert them into wholly social reunions. Provision in the programs for several informal contacts between participants outside working sessions usually resolves that problem.

Posttraining contact between the system and participants and their organizations is readily acknowledged the kingpin of adequate follow-up services but, in fact, is rarely attempted in a systematic manner. It is one of the crucial areas in training where good intentions often idle. If personal contact does occur from time to time, it usually is a by-product of some other training consultation or research project, or of a brief evaluation visit to collect information on how actively and successfully the alumni are working as a result of their training (e.g., for inclusion in the section on evaluation in the system's report to the funding agency). Meetings with associates tend to be short and mainly social, with superior officials formal and ceremonial. They are pleasant but lead to no significant support for participants on the job. Sometimes, too, instead of personal involvement in a job problem of a participant organization, the trainers conscript willing participants to organize or administer a local program of the agency. In fact, examples of sound, sustained contact are very hard to come by. This wide discrepancy between professed intent and action is another weakness of training strategies that limit their vistas to the beginning and the end of the formal training programs and barely have in peripheral vision those who came to the programs or what they accomplished afterwards. Yet helping participants and their organizations to implement changes following training is too important and far-reaching a matter to leave so unplanned and so unattained.

Supplementary Services

Regular follow-up services of most institutions are limited to the issue of periodic news sheets and encouragement to new and old associations of participants. When rooted in continuing contact with participants and their organizations, they serve a useful function, and very economically so; unrooted, they soon atrophy for want of substance or may even do more harm than good.

In countries with little professional literature and few journals of their own and in which participants—and trainers—are often widely dispersed, periodic newsletters have obvious attractions. But few have continued after the first issue or two. Even those eagerly proposed by participants at the end of a program and organized as a collaborative venture between participants and trainers contain almost nothing that originated with the participants. They are continued with increasing grimness by the system itself for a while, then stop. Associations of participants, too, tend to be short-lived since few have a realistic base in their organizations or localities. Those that do continue do so because one or two people strain to keep them alive—often for mixed reasons. If the participants value the association for its exclusiveness, they perpetuate the damaging separation of those who have been trained from those who have not. Before long, the association becomes predominantly social and thus avoids the difficulties (as well as the possible advantages) of associating with colleagues for the explicit purpose of evaluating progress toward work goals, and of giving and receiving professional support.

As part of a systematic set of follow-up services, similar newsletters and associations can have genuine value. Newsletters can include descriptions of participants' work activities, problems encountered, and experience gained. Some associations have expanded an erstwhile newsletter into a full-scale journal appearing regularly and containing, in addition to the usual personal and institutional news, professional articles and new information.

The NTL Institute in Washington, D.C., USA, for instance, provides all participants in Management Work Conferences with a one year free subscription to its journal, *Applied Behavioral Science*. Participants and their organizations are free to continue this subscription thereafter if they wish.

Similarly, there are associations of participants that serve as effective contact points with the system and become a local clearinghouse for participant experiences and for professional contact and consultation.

For the training system, developing posttraining contacts and supplementary services is part of its primary task. This point must be stressed, both for clarity and for economical use of its resources. These contacts and services are required for performing the original task effectively and efficiently. This is the objective, not courtesy or good fellowship. The same criterion sets the limits of what is required. Posttraining services need to be developed and sustained sufficiently for the task, no more, no less. Which services are required can only be ascertained through sound evaluation of the training process and its results.

Chapter 11

Evaluation of Training

Plenty of people can draw, but you....have observation.

—JOHN MILLAIS TO BEATRICE POTTER

I have tended to agree with the Talmudic doctrine which teaches that the human foetus becomes a viable creature only when it graduates from medical school.

—GERALD WEISSMANN, M.D.

BARELY LAGGING behind the massive increases in training efforts and expenditures since the 1950s have been the efforts and expenditures involved in their evaluation. By the early 1970s evaluation had generated its own literature of journals, books and, above all, manuals, a field for specialized research, doctoral dissertations, and a growing body of experts. By the late 1970s the time gap between training and its evaluation had vanished in many places; policy makers and funders of training, disillusioned by past performance, pressed for assurance of better results in the next budget period, often in advance of the events to be approved and funded. All parts of the present book are evidence that for actually improving training—resolving issues of training strategy, program staffing, organization and management, choices of methods and materials, follow-up, participant selection, and pre- and posttraining work with client organizations—evaluation has so far been of little help. References here and there to exceptions to the rule serve to emphasize this sad but true generalization.

Ritual elements still predominate in the evaluation of training, with their own logic and rich elaborations. They seek to propitiate the powerful providers of training funds with reassurances that escalating training budgets can indeed be justified, that controls on expenditures are in place, and that weeding out of worthless training does occur. Since training's lifeline depends on these assurances, how and on what bases they are offered, and how evaluation procedures actually affect training plans, are less important considerations. In many places system administrators have assumed primary responsibility for evaluation. To ensure that the data, conclusions, and funding recommendations carry the extra weight associated with independent study, they call on special staff and outside experts to do the evaluation. These outsiders intrude with ***their*** agenda and particular pressures on trainers trying to cope with the ongoing work of training. Distant at best, adversarial and potentially destructive at worst, such evaluators are hardly receptive to useful information for evaluating training. Their obligatory reports are glutted with basic descriptive information about participant numbers, curricula, and program duration on the one hand, and data on proper housekeeping of allotted staff and funding on the other—the type of data policy makers and administrators consider routine—and heavy, too, with generalized judgmental comments. Such reports are usually light on insightful pointers to better policies and practice.

Evaluation by practitioners and academically inclined researchers (also proliferating) has likewise been largely ineffective, but for other reasons. Much of it resembles in-program monitoring in that it presents program structures, participant composition, and other key components as given. That is quite appropriate to monitoring, to putting immediately available opportunities to best use while a program is going on. It is inadequate for evaluation, however, for it avoids the very dimensions which ought to be assessed after training, such as how far a program actually met the needs of the organizations, how adequate were the trainers and other resources made available, and how far this training contributed to developing the new capabilities in the training system itself which longer-term plans call for. These kinds of questions, central to the evaluation of training, cannot be addressed by evaluating this or that part of a training program in isolation; the interrelation of key components and their effective focusing on projected goals is essential. Yet practitioners and researchers tend to comment no more concretely on this dimension than administrative evaluators do from their different perspective. Numerous other evaluations by practitioners and researchers mainly detail refinements of conceptual and methodological tools of training and of evaluation itself; they often suggest elaborations far in excess of the resources and contextual conditions which actually exist.

In short, administrative evaluators scrutinize training from the outside, mainly for indicators of good or bad housekeeping, and do so without much help from practitioners. Practitioners and researchers, on the other hand, tend to evaluate only the internal dimensions of training, looking little or only vaguely at the purposes of training and how it might be better related to them. These unhappy generalizations, by and large, are even truer of training in the public services than in production and sales organizations, and of training for better policymaking, management, administration, and supervision than for higher technical competencies.

TWO SETS OF ISSUES FOR EVALUATION

To contribute significantly to a better fit between training and the realization of its goals, evaluation should be addressed to two kinds of issues. Practical measures are needed for assessing the effectiveness of training and for assessing the commitment particular constituencies intimately involved in the training enterprise make to it, each and together.

Measuring Training Effectiveness and Identifying Constituencies

If, as we maintain, training aims at definite changes on the job in an organization, then two criticisms must be leveled against the evaluations of training attempted to date. First, the usual rough and ready "measures" of training simply do not suffice. One, the "number trained," tells nothing at all, even about the participants' learning. They may have learned very little or next to nothing. They may even have learned just the opposite of what was intended, for instance, that training is a hateful experience and a waste of time, or a time of rest, or an avenue to high status. If so, the training experience has done damage, and the participants may have carried away a jaundiced view of future training opportunities for themselves and others and a negative appreciation of the training institution and its courses. Without doubt, this dismal reaction will be shared with friends and colleagues. Other commonly used statistics, such as length of training, session time for certain topics, categorical or total expenditures, likewise tell next to nothing about the value of training. Such parameters merely justify faculty strengths and training budgets; they do not measure the effectiveness of training.

Measurement of participant learning at the end of a program appears more promising but risks other kinds of confusion. These measures look specific and can usually be quantified. Their precision helps trainers cover uncertainties they feel about the effectiveness of their activities. Was it worthwhile? Did we do our job well? Sure, Rao is now able to handle the machine, Aruna can now do a cost study, Sarwar can now speak before a large group. Before-and-after tests prove it. Ergo, these three trainees have learned something—true enough, but not what really matters. Even if these were things that Rao, Aruna, and Sarwar needed to learn, these tests cannot show whether they can use the new knowledge and skill on their jobs and will make them truly part of their competencies through practice. To realize this objective, Rao's, Aruna's, and Sarwar's new behavior has to be accepted by the people with whom they work, in particular their immediate superiors and colleagues. Measures of what they know and what they can do at the end of a training program simply do not incorporate such indices.

To round out the list, a third common parameter should be mentioned and peremptorily thrown out: that participants praised the course and were tearful at parting. Emotional partings are quite common. Feelings expressed there have many sources, and cannot be reliably traced to satisfaction with the quality of the program. Furthermore, current satisfaction is no guide to the effectiveness of the training back on the job.

A second line of thought also flows readily from our understanding of the aims of training: evaluation and ensuring consequent action cannot be the training system's task alone. The effectiveness of training is determined by all three partners in it: the participants, the system, and the work organization, just as the strength of a chain is determined by its weakest link, so the least contribution from any one partner becomes the maximum overall level of effectiveness possible. By no means can every weakness or failure in training be attributed to the system, nor assessed or removed by improvements in its program. Perhaps a participant was simply not up to the challenge, albeit his organization is itself too weak to use well-trained participants. Possible causes of failure of training are numerous.

Starting with the training program itself as the most obvious and also accessible component to evaluate, the following sections focus in turn on issues and practical ways of evaluating the more basic dimensions of participant learning, the training objectives themselves and the worthwhileness of the whole training effort. In this sequence the organization's role in evaluation escalates and with it also the quality of collaboration required between the system and the organization. The notion of worthwhileness embodies long-term strategic considerations by the organization and often also by public policy makers, planners and providers of funds; the role of the training system in evaluating worthwhileness is to furnish information.

Evaluating Training

1. Evaluating Programs: The System's Particular Responsibility

First we concern ourselves with questions that most directly call for evaluation and action by the training system. They comprise two categories. One: What can the system learn about the effectiveness of that central phase in the change process in which its responsibility is largest, namely the training program? Two: How can the system best help the other partners evaluate their parts and improve them, so that the training process *as a whole* becomes more effective? An example of the second would be inadequacies in the participants, which may be remedied by renewed attention by the organization to selection procedures and to preparing candidates for training. Even these two sets of questions can only be explored adequately if the system collaborates closely with participants and their organizations.

Exhibit 11.1

EVALUATION BY TRAINING SYSTEM: FIVE SETS OF OBJECTIVES AND THREE MAIN QUESTIONS

Objectives	*For Whom*	*When*	*How*
1. Evaluating the Training Program			
To improve the program as a whole	System and trainers	Concurrent and end of program	Questionnaire, feedback and discussion involving trainers and administrators with participants
To improve major components of the training program	System and trainers	Before and after the inputs	Questionnaire and scales, feedback and discussion involving trainers and participants
To increase the effectiveness of specific modules or sessions	Particular trainers	End of module or session	Module or session evaluation scales, checklists, feedback to participants
2. Evaluating the Training Process			
To improve the training climate	System and trainers	Concurrent	Interviews, open reviews, critical incidents, feedback and discussions with participants
To improve the training methodologies	Trainers	End of program	Questionnaires, interviews, discussions among trainers
To improve effectiveness of the trainers team	Trainers	End of program	Discussion of trainers team and participants

Exhibit 11.1 (Continued)

Objectives	*For Whom*	*When*	*How*
3. Evaluating the Training Program			
To improve training facilities	System	Concurrent and end of program	Questionnaire and feedback
To improve contextual factors	System	Concurrent and end of program	Questionnaire and feedback
4. Evaluating Training Outcomes/Impact			
To increase learning by individual participants	Participants	Concurrent	Objective tests, skills tests, analysis of assignments
To increase use of learnings in work performance	Work organization	After 3 months periodically thereafter	Task analysis, analysis of diaries, critical incidents, interviews of participants and their role sets
To contribute data to organizational effectiveness	Work organization	After 3 months, periodically thereafter	Unobtrusive measures of conflict, collaboration, productivity, motivation, etc., including customer reactions
To help the organization change	Training systems and work organization	Once every 3 or 4 years	In-depth action research and consultation

Exhibit 11.1 (Continued)

Objectives	*For Whom*	*When*	*How*
5. Evaluating Posttraining Factors			
To maximize cost effectiveness of training	System	Once every 3 or 4 years	Cost-benefit analysis, human resources accounting
To ensure posttraining support at work	System and work organization	Once a year	Questionnaires, interviews, feedback, discussions
To identify helping and hindering factors	System and work organization	Once a year	Questionnaires, interviews, feedback, discussions

Exhibit 11.1 shows five sets of objectives for evaluation by the training system and three major questions for each: For whom is the evaluation? When should it be done? and how? For evaluating the total training program the basic question is, simply, to what extent did the program achieve what it set out to achieve? This is a larger-scale version of the question that trainers ask of every session, module, and larger part of the program. The program started with a set of objectives, namely, that by its end the participants should know X, be able to do Y to Z standard, and have developed an outlook on A. Now that the program is over, to what extent, in fact, did it succeed in these terms? How far has participant learning in fact carried over into improved performance at work? Evaluation at the very end of the program reveals what new knowledge, understanding, and skill participants gained during training. The same kind of data at various stages of the posttraining phase shows how stable these gains are, and to what extent they have survived transfer to the work situation.

A comparison of repeated ratings can yield four different results:

1. If the ratings consistently lie within a satisfactory range of performance and show improvement when repeated, this means the program was sound; that both participants and their organizations were ready to use the training; and that participants learned enough during training to keep on improving their performance through practice on the job.

2. If the ratings tend to decline with repetition, this means participants and their organizations found the training less useful than expected, or that participants did not have sufficient training during the program and/or support on the job to carry on successfully.

3. If the results show a sharp drop at first and then rise, this shows that the transfer from training to action was unexpectedly difficult, but that, participants and their organizations have overcome the difficulties and are making headway.

4. If the results show a sharp drop and stay down, this means the organizations and/or the participants were not prepared to make the change on the job, or that the training objectives were not realistic.

Such results are clearly important to the system as a guide to further action. In most cases detailed study will be required before strategic difficulties can be located and their strengths assessed. For instance, results (2) and (3) suggest linkage problems in the transition from training to work situations. More adequate support for participants on the job may obviate these in future programs. But their removal may also call for more time and rigorous work on back-home problems in the training program itself. Results (4) and possibly (2) suggest renewed work on the original training objectives.

Impact evaluation (set no. 4 in exhibit 11.1) is still "touchy" that training systems and work organizations usually settle for opinions about impact—a very indirect and erratic guide—in preference to collecting "hard" data about actual performances. This preference for "soft" data cannot be attributed to excessive methodological difficulties. More likely the two constituents quietly collude because impact is the sum of training plus organizational preparedness and support, and so raises questions about both the system and the organization as well as their collaboration. So the constituents reinforce each other's reluctance. In fact, the impact on individual performance, immediate work group, and units can be measured quite economically, if a major change strategy is in focus, so can the impact organization-wide. Measures can also be developed for an organization's growing capacity for further developments in the future.

The National Institute for Inservice Training (Pusdiklat) of Indonesia's Ministry of Health had seven objectives for impact evaluation four months after its second Advanced Program for Management Trainers (APMT). While that program's impact on current work performance was in central focus, the objectives included reference back to the first program, to future advanced programs, and also to developing future systems capacities for consultation. The objectives were:

1. To have a second round of impact evaluation of APMT-I to assess both stability and snowballing of the changes (benefits) and their synergistic contribution to the benefits from APMT-II.

2. To assess the impact of APMT-II on individuals, systems, and their interlinkages.

3. To assess benefits from the two-week International Mid-Career Program for Developing Individual, Team and Organizational Competencies (Phase 1 of APMT).

4. To assess the impact of APMTs on (a) individuals (b) organizations and (c) training strategies and systems, as well as major factors contributing to variations in the impact.

5. To assess the impact of APMTs on the effectiveness of building internal consultation resources in the health system.

6. To make suggestions for better utilization of graduates of APMT.

7. To make suggestions for planning the strategy and design of APMT-III.

Creative approaches to the choice of impact measures and processes for collecting data can make impact evaluation both sound and economical. This, in turn, calls for creative approaches to collaboration between the three constituencies in training. Trainer consultants can take the lead in both. They can propose extracting an indicative set of impact data from routine records, such as production, inspection, and cost figures, and keep the costs of collecting primary data low by judicious sampling of data for indicators that are not usually collected, e.g., process indicators. Exhibit 11.2 shows the impact outcomes and the simple indicators used for evaluating the same Advanced Program in Indonesia presented in exhibit 11.1.

Critical incident methodologies can play an important part in impact evaluation, especially to highlight the range and qualities of change. Each incident describes an actual situation, e.g., task, territory, technologies, time; lists the people involved—the participants returned from training and also others involved in the situation; details actions and events in which the participants played a focal role; and assesses consequences. Written, or recorded live in discussion, incidents can be collected from sets of colleagues of the participants at the same, higher, and lower levels in the organization and analyzed to show impact on the planned development(s) for which training was to be used.

> For example, analysis of critical incidents collected from participants of the second Advanced Program for Management of Trainers in Indonesia, from their superiors, and from their colleagues, indicated significant impact on participant interpersonal competencies (increased openness, sensitivity, emotional control, and self-confidence and also professional competencies initiative, collaboration, innovation, and responsibility). Analysis of the same critical incidents also showed impact on four major organizational dimensions: stronger teamwork, higher mutual support, onward team development, and demonstrated initiative.

Simple content analysis of critical incidents can also be used to indicate training impact on individual performance. Grouping such data according to work teams, departments, and finally the organization as a whole can yield information about impact on those systems.

2. Evaluating Participants: A Primary Responsibility of the Work Organization

When training objectives have been clearly formulated in terms of changes to be effected at work, the work organization is in the best position to evaluate the effects of training on individual participants. The question remains, what is such evaluation for? The organization may use it for the same legitimate purposes that trainers did during the training program itself: to provide participants and trainers with information about progress toward various training objectives and about any difficulties that require attention on the way. This involves feeding the evaluation results in the first place back to the participants, and proceeding together with

Exhibit 11.2

IMPACT OUTCOMES OF PROGRAM FOR MANAGEMENT TRAINERS AND THEIR INDICATORS

Outcomes	*Indicators*
a. Individual participants only in Phase I:	
1. Personal and interpersonal effectiveness	Initiative taken Consideration shown
b. Individual participants in full APMTs:	
1. Personal and interpersonal effectiveness	Initiative taken Consideration and help
2. Professional competencies	Training designs Training methods used
3. System competencies	More teamwork
c. Organizations sending participants:	
1. Higher credibility of the training function	Competent persons nominated
2. Greater acceptance of APMT alumni	More consultation with them
3. Greater interest in competence development	New training program
4. Greater demand for APMT alumni from outside	Requests received
5. More innovation in training	Analysis of curricula
6. Greater recognition and use of training center	Training center data on programs
7. Stronger training team	Reconstitution of teams
8. Development of training system	Current systems
9. Greater organization learning	Use of experiences
d. The Center (Pusdiklat):	
1. Higher involvement in project activities	More meetings on project issues
2. More open communication	Mutual consultation
3. Increased participation in project inputs	More participation
4. Stronger linkages with provinces	More visits for consultation
5. Establishment of resource network	Intern network
6. Multiplication of gains across provinces or /diffusion function	Inter-province
7. Greater problem-solving actions	More task groups
8. Higher credibility of Pusdiklat in the provinces	More demand by provinces

SOURCE: Pusdiklat, Ministry of Health, Government of Indonesia, 1986.

them in the implementation of any requisite action. An increasing number of organizations have set up individual evaluation procedures for these purposes and in this manner. Regular personnel evaluation and merit-rating schemes are examples, especially when coupled with personal and career counseling.

For these purposes the system can help the organization develop regular rigorous procedures for collecting data from participants and from their superiors, colleagues, and subordinates. It can also help in analyzing the results.

If, on the other hand, the work organization uses evaluation for other purposes, and keeps data hidden from participants, the system had better stay away—even though prevailing traditions may be to the contrary (perhaps especially then). Nothing so inhibits participants from developing a free and close relationship with trainers as the idea that the system may be reporting on them to their organization. Instead of exploring new methods, participants will rein themselves in and shrink from taking the risks of learning; they will also be preoccupied with pleasing the trainers to ensure as far as possible a good report. Ethics apart, this price is excessive. Such limits and preoccupations are wholly inimical to every phase of the training process. Even so, private communication between the training system and the work organization about individual participants is still common, directly in line with the general tradition of confidential reports. Instead, the system should announce publicly that it will not provide confidential information about participants to anyone, their organizations included.

There remains the help that the work organization may rightfully expect from the system to decide the most suitable placement of a participant after training and the specific support participants may need to carry through the planned changes on the job. This is reasonable enough. Especially if the training has been residential and long, trainers may have come to know a participant so well that their comments and advice may be of direct help in settling such questions.

Some systems have formulated two principles in handling requests for information about participants from the organization. The first is to become involved only in those cases in which it can contribute information and clarification that others cannot give. This principle eliminates many requests that could be answered far better by participants themselves or their colleagues in the organization. The other principle is to inform the organization that the system will deal with its questions in collaboration with participants themselves. Participants thus know and concur in any information and suggestions passed on to their organization. Some organizations have welcomed this procedure, other have dropped the request.

For designing situation-specific instruments and processes for collecting

Box 11.1

OPERATIONALIZING TEAM BUILDING

Development of the training team [team of trainers] should reflect the following aspects

1. Cohesion: The trainers function as a strong team, supporting one another; each member feels his/her views and concerns are considered by others; and each member backs the group decision.
2. Collaboration: Most work done by trainers (teaching, special assignments, preparation of material, preparation of reports, etc.) is done by didactic or 3- to 4-member groups. Members feel free to volunteer, ask for, and respond to requests for collaboration.
3. Collectivity: Most significant decisions (training strategy, training programs, training responsibility, special assignments, training structure, etc.) are discussed and taken by the team.
4. Comprehensive Training: The training team pays attention to pretraining (assessment of training needs, and enhancing motivation for learning), training (linking training with specific action improvement, e.g., through action-specific measurable objectives and modules), and posttraining (follow-up and evaluation) dimensions.
5. Material Output: More and more training materials (modules, reports, cases, role-play scripts, teaching notes, conceptual notes, transparencies, video scripts, etc.) are produced by the individuals and teams of trainers.
6. Creativity: The trainers, individually and teams, use a variety of approaches and methods for pretraining, training, and posttraining work.
7. Problem solving: The major problems faced by the training section are brought to the training team for discussion, generating alternative solutions and recommendations for action.
8. Synergy: Trainers collaborate to supplement each others' competencies, to be able to produce a greater impact of training effort.
9. Individual Functionality: Individual trainers continue to be more functional and effective in their behavior.
10. Improved Trainer Behavior: The trainers individually function in a more balanced way, using their potential for the development of participants.

SOURCE: Report on Impact Evaluation of Second Advanced Program for Management Trainers, Pusdiklat, Ministry of Health, Government of Indonesia, 1986.

evaluative data for any purpose, operationalizing the gains expected from training can be a very useful start. In fact, in choosing one or more standard instruments off the shelf this is a necessary safeguard. Box 11.1 shows the dimensions, operationalized for evaluating a team-building program for trainers.

Evaluation of participants as individuals and in work group and teams is also a basis for reviewing the criteria by which participants are selected for training programs. It can reveal that a particular program is of greater profit to participants who already have substantial working experience or bring basic competencies, e.g., in mathematics. Other programs may be more suitable for those with less. Detailed evaluation of participants can reveal repetitive patterns of difficulties, point to a more precise delineation of population for certain types of training, and separate certain groups into some programs or combine groups for others. Finally, participant evaluation can guide decisions about support for returning participants and their colleagues anywhere in the organization.

Box 11.2

TRAINING OBJECTIVES VERSUS ORGANIZATIONAL DISPOSITION

E. A. Fleishman, E. F. Harris, and H. E. Burtt

An evaluation study of a supervisory training program in a large American company shows clearly how a major discrepancy can arise between the objectives of the program and the training needs and possibilities on the job. The objectives of the program were in the general area of improving human relations among the workers and between workers and management. Specific objectives included reducing conflict and promoting greater job satisfaction. By these routes greater efficiency was to be achieved. Foremen were to be the change agents for these improvements. The program was to train them for this function.

Preliminary studies established two clusters of supervisor behavior which could serve to evaluate the training in terms of its objectives. One cluster included kinds of behavior that could be classified as "considerate" attention to workers as people, listening to personal problems, helping and the like. The other consisted of behavior that stressed formal relations, written rules, and keeping to production schedules. The authors formulated these objectives into two operational criteria. One they called "consideration"; the opposite they called "initiating structure." Factorially sound and highly reliable instruments were developed for measuring leadership attitudes and behavior in terms of consideration and initiating structure.

From these instruments, applied before and after residential training, clearly favorable training results were established. The foremen showed significant decreases in initiating structure and corresponding increases in

Box 11.2 (Continued)

considerate attitudes. But when the same instruments were used again later, after the foremen had returned to work, they revealed the opposite result: trained foremen tended to be lower in consideration and higher in initiating structure than did the untrained foremen. A check with workers under these foremen confirmed these results. Clearly the effects of this human relations program were not stable.

The general interpretation of these results was that the program succeeded in making the foremen more considerate but that it at the same time separated them sharply from the workers. The foremen themselves became more aware of belonging to the management. Singled out for special training in a program that was obviously expensive, they concluded that they had definitely crossed over to the other side. Certainly the workers saw this as the main meaning of the supervisory training program. The result was that the more considerate attitudes that showed up in the immediate posttraining questionnaire were off-set by the foremen's tendency back at work to assume more determined leadership roles. The discrepancy between these two evaluations at the end of the program and later on the job illustrates well the danger of relying only on the first when the acid test of effective training is the second.

The authors then correlated the "contradictory" results with the "climate" set up by the foremen's superiors. The correlation was direct: trained foremen who continued to show more "considerate" attitudes on the job were those whose superiors were "considerate." The others dropped the considerate attitudes they had gained in the training program in order to conform with superiors who were strong in initiating structure. The implication of this for a more effective training strategy would be to provide training for the foremen's superiors and perhaps of *their* superiors also.

The authors also took a second look at the training needs of different jobs in order to establish whether more considerate attitudes in fact produced greater efficiency. This reexamination led to a useful distinction. In production divisions where meeting time schedules and production targets produced great stress, foremen with the highest proficiency ratings showed more initiation of structure. In the service divisions, on the other hand, where these stresses were not so prominent, the higher proficiency ratings went with more consideration. This finding suggested differentiating between training objectives for foremen in production and service departments and changing the criteria for selecting participants.

The results have wider implications. They call for formulation separately of long-range and short-range objectives of training. The relative importance of work satisfaction, freedom from conflict, speedy technological change, and immediate efficiency need to be decided in the work organization. "Perhaps immediate efficiency," the authors conclude, "may not be so important as a long-time balance between efficiency and morale."

SOURCE: Summarized from Edwin A. Fleishman, Edwin F. Harris, and Harold E. Burtt, *Leadership and Supervision in Industry* (Columbus, Ohio: The Ohio State University, 1955).

3. Evaluating Objectives: A Primary Responsibility of the Work Organization

If objectives are inadequately formulated in the first place, even a "good" training program has really no chance to be effective. Faulty job analyses have sometimes led to such results. Or participants are shifted from job to job so frequently that no one job analysis or training can be relevant to their future work. This is the position of many government officers who are considered interchangeable. They may be sent for specialized training in one field only to find on their return that they have been posted to another. These are instances of training failures due to the absence of objectives rooted in definite plans for changes on the job. In other situations the process of change falters through inadequate organizational commitment and support.

The study summarized in box 11.2 describes a situation in a large American company in which discrepancies between training objectives and organizational readiness for changes led to some surprising evaluation results. First of all, the evaluation instruments used at the end of the training program yielded diametrically opposite results when used again sometime after participants had returned to work. End-of-program evaluation is obviously not an adequate final evaluation of training impact. Second, wherever ratings remained steady, the participants' new learning was supported by their superiors. Third, when training needs were reviewed again after one round of training, production and service departments were poles apart in their assessments. The same training had, therefore, not been effective in both.

This program suffered from incompatible training objectives, a weakness common to many programs. Behind this weakness lies confusion between lists of wishes and realistic policy. In this instance, speedy technological change, freedom from conflict, and immediate efficiency were all among the objectives. But no detailed thought had been given to the question of how they might be fitted together. The work organization required a deliberate policy for this to guide the establishment and revision of training objectives.

Where overall policy is realistic and clear, regular and frequent evaluations followed by marginal adjustments usually suffice to keep training objectives aligned with shifting needs. This assumes a close relationship between the training system and the work organization.

The burden of drastic changes is particularly heavy for developing countries: changing tasks, changing situations, and changing divisions of functions. Training needs in those countries are therefore especially difficult to define, let alone keep up to date and embodied in organizational policies. Well-designed and operational evaluation procedures are then particularly important to help bridge the gaps that surely occur between needs and policies and between training objectives and training needs.

To bridge a gap of any sort, something has first to exist on the other side. We have seen training systems struggling to evolve sufficiently clear training objectives out of inadequately defined needs. Either of two results has invariably followed from putting the cart before the horse. In some cases the key relationship between the system and the organization deteriorated. The system, as it were, was caught in quicksand, and its later struggles to put the relationship and the training objectives on a sound footing simply sunk it further. Its every move led to accusations that the system was improperly usurping functions and overstepping its responsibilities. If the system replied that it could not mark time while the organization caught up with neglected responsibilities, successful in-fighting rather than effective training became the dominant objective for action.

In other cases the training system has taken an early hint and withdrawn from any attempt to evaluate overall training objectives, limiting evaluation instead to meeting the training objectives within the confines of the formal program. The question of their efficacy for the participants' jobs and the organization was left to them to pursue or not, as they wished. The usual result of this very understandable reaction is uncertainty and low morale among the trainers. They can never be sure that their devoted and diligent efforts have had any value in practice.

In short, evaluation of training objectives is the responsibility of the work organization in the first place. The system can contribute procedural expertise and consistent and sustained interest. Collaborations between the organization and the system ensures rapid use of evaluation results in the selection and preparation of participants, in program designs, and in preparing the organization for change.

4. Evaluating the Worthwhileness of Training: A Primary Responsibility of Policy Makers and Resource Providers

Training strategies and programs are instituted to yield benefits in excess of costs, that is, benefits to the work organization and to general development. However crude and nonspecific the calculation on which training was originally approved and funded, policy makers and providers of resources expect to be convinced soon after its completion that the training achieved the goals defined, and kept its costs within the limits set for it. Careful housekeeping and accounting of training expenditure are important, and definitely the responsibility of the training system to document. But evaluating the worthwhileness of training involves far more.

Much more difficult to assess are two other sources of cost/benefit consequences which are essentially related to training outcomes but arise outside training per se. One of these is the costs of developing the other components for the changes in which the newly trained people are to be used. These other components—technical, managerial, organizational—are often complex and intricately interrelated, and estimating their costs accurately in advance is very difficult. And even well-calculated bases for training decisions are subject to sudden shifts in general conditions and often invalidated. In the early 1980s, for instance, the sharp escalation in costs of investing in new technologies and expansion led in many countries to drastic revisions in training plans that were not related to the quality of training or its specific costs. Other contextual costs had simply become too high to continue developments at the originally planned speed and scale that training was to serve; many programs were cancelled altogether and the costs already incurred written off. Estimates of these kinds of costs, their reassessment in terms of later eventualities, and revisions in training plans are all in the domain of policy makers.

A second and rather different dimension in evaluation for which policy makers have first responsibility concerns the adequacy of training plans, programs, and performance in the light of longer-term developments, e.g., in technologies, or scale and location of services, or building the basic capacities for undergirding the next strategic steps in development. The computer "revolution" is a dramatic case in point. For this, cost estimates as well as training strategies and designs can only be very rough and eventual benefits mere conjecture. In past decades the rapid expansion of training and its rising costs often crowded longer-term needs off stage, with the result that training systems have again and again been pressured into offering "crash" programs to catch up with needs only lately recognized. The costs of such programs, far higher than warranted in the normal course of events and often distorting the cost of regular training programs running concurrently, should be debited to myopic policy making. But the training system is usually the scapegoat; its performance "fell below par." In projecting future needs, suggesting appropriate strategies to meet them and evaluating the contributions made by training programs, those persons and institutions expert in developing new technologies and visualizing "futures" might well be valuable contributors.

For the orderly identification of constituencies to involve in evaluating training in all its essential dimensions, the schema Delbecq and Van de Ven developed for program planning in general may be particularly useful.[1] It distinguishes four constituencies; service acquirers, technical experts, resource providers, and service providers. This is also the order of their recommended involvement. First, come the acquirers of training, i.e., the work organizations undertaking developments for which training can

1. Andre L. Delbecq, and Andrew H. Van de Ven, "A Group Process Model for Problem Identification and Program Planning," *Journal of Applied Behavioral Science,* Vol. 7 No. 4, 1971, pp. 467-90.

serve them and their participants in a training program. To classify needy organizations as acquirers, rather than, say, recipients, conveys their assertively active role in ensuring that they will get the training they need and pay for. When it comes to evaluation, work organizations and their participants are then, properly, also first to assess to what extent the training they acquired met expectations and was worth the costs. Not all they wanted, or still might want after the initial experience, may in fact be feasible, at least not at a manageable cost.

The second constituency in Delbecq and Van de Ven's schema is the training system in its role as expert in the technologies of training. In this role the system can help map realistic options and establish the costs of the training that an organization wants. The providers of funds and other resources, the third constituency, are approached next. They consider the options identified as technically and economically feasible for meeting the organization's needs. This third constituency usually comprises officers higher up in organizations, funding agencies and government. These resource providers consider the options in the light of alternative uses for the resources available and ensure that the training proposals and the developments in which training is to play a part fit into the overall plans and priorities. When outside funding is involved, the proposals need to fit into that agency's plans as well. The decisions taken by system policy makers and resource providers are the ones the fourth constituency, the providers of training, are then asked to implement.

In a book primarily for trainers and training systems, to propose a sequence in which trainers and training systems in their usual role come last in developing and also in evaluating training is not likely to be popular. Yet, it makes good sense that these practitioners work only on programs which command sufficient organizational and financial support to succeed. Evaluation efforts are best expended on programs decision makers have decided to continue.

ROLE OF THE TRAINING SYSTEM WITH EVALUATORS FROM OTHER CONSTITUENCIES

Although other constituencies are responsible for major decisions that follow evaluation, such as whether to continue a training strategy or program and, if so, on what scale and with what priorities and modifications, the training system, in fact, has a most important and active role at every stage. It transposes the evaluation needs of an organization and its participants into dimensions, methodologies, and processes that can yield significant information. It does this anyway for itself, to make sure that any future work with this organization is soundly based. But the organization commonly also expects the system to provide technical guidance and data collection, and to help with data analysis and the formulation of conclusions and recommendations for action. Organizations often rely on the system to energize evaluation efforts, as well as guide them, and to ensure that all constituencies carry out their parts completely and on time, and to interlink them into a usable whole.

This helping role differs markedly from attempting to do the work of other constituencies for them, as emphasized already in connection with setting training objectives and evaluating them.

In the evaluation of training objectives (primarily the responsibility of the work organization), the training system can contribute methodological and procedural expertise and consistent and sustained interest. Collaboration with the organization can ensure the rapid use of evaluation results in selecting and preparing new participants, in program designs, and in preparing the organization for change. Organizations often need help also in developing regular and rigorous procedures for collecting data from participants and from their superiors, colleagues, and subordinates. System personnel can help with this, with analyzing the results, and with working out procedures for their communication and implementation within the organization.

Finally, the system has another two functions in helping other constituencies carry out *their* parts in evaluating training. First of all, it can create opportunities for several constituencies to prepare, then meet together so that the articulation of various components can be expedited; furthermore, different constituencies can learn to appreciate each other's points of view, concerns, and appropriate roles and functions in the joint effort.

A workshop organized by the Education and Training Division of Indonesia's Ministry of Health in December, 1983, is an example. Its purpose was to evaluate preservice training of nurses for the national health service which required a very large number. Previously, program design and evaluation had been conducted only by the nursing facilities together with international nursing consultants. The Division's new director decided instead to invite three other constituencies to prepare data and to take part in the evaluation, in the hope that such collaboration would influence the strategy as a whole. The three additional constituencies were: service acquirers of primary health care (drawn from an intensive field study area in a large province), technology providers (professional staff from the Research Division of the Ministry who had conducted studies of nursing values commissioned by the Training Division); and top-level officials in the Ministry responsible for developing policies and approving funds. The service acquirers and researchers prepared working papers for discussion. The three-day workshop was formally opened and closed by the policy makers and resource providers from the two ministries of the government directly involved in consequent decisions. The results of the workshop were fed directly into the official plans for 1984-85 and the national Fourth Five-Year Plan (1984-89).

The other function that the training system is in the best position to perform for all constituencies is to scan the entire field of training evaluation periodically and to alert policy makers in particular to structural and procedural deficiencies that require rectification. Regulatory requirements may need to be added or amended, new resources provided, or new evaluation opportunities used. Microcomputers, for example, can be used for quick local feedback, while serving to keep evaluation economical.

PART III

Training and Training System Development

Chapter 12

The Training System

> The object of...ideas as a whole...is to provide us with an instrument for finding our way about this world more easily.
>
> — Hans Vaihinger

> Above all, a concept should be robust : robust enough to survive mistranslation into various languages, to survive distortion by political pressures and interservice rivalries, to survive drowning in floods of emotion engendered by...crises and catastrophes.
>
> — Freeman Dyson

By using so broad, generic and, in this context, unfamiliar a word as "system" to designate the partner responsible for identifying and organizing training and resources and for providing the actual training and associated consultation that a work organization and its participants need, we have alerted readers to prepare for complexities. Now, starting the practical study of it, "system" also offers three important pointers: a system has many components; these components are interrelated and cohere; and a system has boundaries, a position in an environment, and connections and transactions with this environment that matter greatly. Clearly these pointers to the nature of a training system raise concerns far beyond the usual ones of sending some staff to a training course somewhere, "leaving" training issues to "the training people to get on with since that is *their* business," expecting a new worker or trainer to "pick up" a particular set of competencies by simply being "put with" an old-timer, and other standard but costly simplifications.

To visualize training resources as a system is a useful first step — so long as it is not also the last! Figure 12.1 shows the basic model. The "import," "conversion," and "export" subsystems in it represent the more commonly used "inputs," "throughputs," and "outputs." Trainers are quite familiar with these concepts, and also with "boundaries," "environment," "linkages," and "feedback loops." Many have become quite adept at converting lists of items for program planning or evaluation into system diagrams. It is the onward steps that are wanting. Once the diagram is drawn, energies often flag. As if they were an end in themselves, this labeling and diagramming are commonly used to wall off rather than to open up the business-like consideration of practical issues. And so the language of systems, which should help trainers "find their way more easily in a complex world," is often used instead to strengthen their protective shield against the world's realities.

Figure 12.1

SIMPLE MODEL OF TRAINING SYSTEM

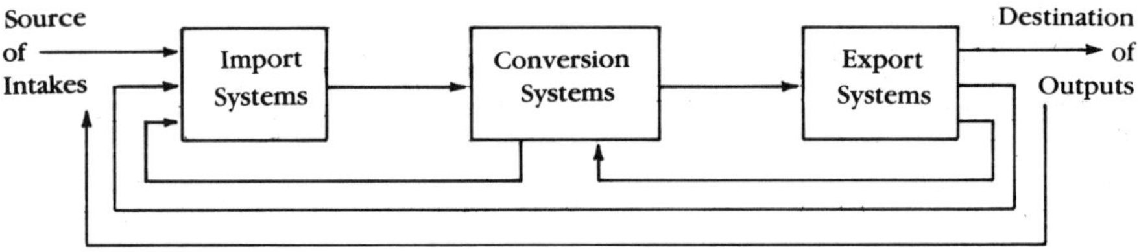

Adapated from *Systems of Organization* by E.J. Miller and A.K. Rice (London: Tavistock, 1967), p. 160

Those realities are complex, as we have seen, but not endlessly so. Earlier chapters have laid out sets of training modalities and orientations to inform choices of training strategies as well as sets of training methods and settings, each with resource specifications. The occasions and agenda for contacts between system staff and work organizations have also been identified, both at programmatic and policy levels. These are the categories from which to choose particular blocks for the construction of resource systems to meet a particular set of needs.

The environment to which the system relates can also be identified. Only those parts of it that are importantly connected to the particular "task, territory, technology, and time" concern the system sufficiently to warrant attention and proper linkages. These four "Ts", which the Tavistock Institute uses for delineating primary tasks, can also be used for identifying the parts of the otherwise limitless environment that are, in fact, *relevant* in a particular case. Other classifications are also available. True, a system and its environment become more complex with every traditional task, territory to be covered, or time frame to be addressed. But if developed step-by-step, even a large system can be quite manageable.

Longer-term issues and policy dimensions gain prominence as the system enlarges. Examples of special importance and urgency in developing countries at macro-levels are such conflicting issues as raising the general quality of training across many programs while simultaneously developing new kinds of training capacities and rapidly increasing their volume. Starting specialized training institutions while keeping existing institutions closely linked to operations is also a problem. As the system expands, so does its relevant environment. At national levels it includes, for example, professional associations and specialized research centres.

> In a major review in 1983 of its "existing internal training system," which then included three staff colleges, thirty-eight training centers, and a regular "relationship nexus" within the organization that included a deputy managing director and chief general manager, the State Bank of India developed preparatory papers on all the above issues in "a futuristic time frame." This frame took into account the Bank's expansion rates, especially of rural branches, "emerging" positions and roles, technological changes, and other considerations. The report based on these papers and their discussions stressed training as a "planned organizational intervention" and proposed means for making the identification of organization development and training tasks into a "continuous process." The "important areas of concern" identified ranged from the need for better "synchronization of organizational growth with the development of the individual employee... through career development" [to] "modifications of the structure" of the system in the light of these considerations.

While each component of a training system can be conceptualized in systems terms and these components built into an overall system diagram that incorporates the same concepts, there are important practical differences between systems of different sizes. It is only when all resource components needed for an actual training effort are assembled and synchronized for particular purpose(s) that the training system for it can be solidified. Successive drafts can be tested against particular pertinent questions and the constituent parts and the design refined accordingly. Questions about the macro-system are of a different order since they concern overall capacities and leave no scope for shifting resources away from one program or institution to another. For instance, will the nationwide system, perhaps augmented for a while with regional and international resources, yield training (of *all* required kinds) on a sufficient scale, and/or will that output be sufficiently well-paced and coordinated to meet the requirements of the planned projects, expansions and technical and administrative improvements? Can it sustain this level of effort? Are the estimates sufficiently feasible for coping with the imminent retirement of the "independence generation" of experienced administrators (which is predictable) and concomitantly for accommodating turbulent (i.e., unpredictable) changes in the environment? These are the types of questions that system development is meant to address at higher levels in developing countries. That complex scene characteristically includes pressures to develop training capacities in several major sectors at once; to compete for the very same handful of trainers that private enterprises try to attract with better salaries and conditions; to develop training capacities in widely-scattered provinces while simultaneously strengthening nationally acceptable standards of training; to multiply training opportunities even at the cost of purpose and quality; to shift experienced trainers away from training into training administration (or more distant tasks still), and from outlying places—but close to the action—to headquarters positions; and to train the work force for foreseeable changes in service needs while also multiplying and improving the quality of the same work force for current basic community services.

At the levels at which these concerns have to be included (and then parceled out to lesser systems), training system development is not only larger in scale than simply using systems thinking for developing a component, or a system at program level, or a temporary system, but its complexities are of an entirely different order. In line with this, a *readiness* to approach the development of a training system as a working proposition, for practical elaboration, improvement and confirmation over time, is of paramount importance in developing countries. Under such conditions the proper use of systems concepts and diagrams is as checklist and general map—to ensure that all essential components are accounted for, can readily attract necessary attention, and are also plausibly interrelated for charting the territory that lies ahead. Practical considerations will also limit further elaboration of conceptual components and their interrelations in terms of the available capacities for collecting and analyzing data, and putting these (or about to be available) results to use in influencing and managing the necessary relationships. The territory itself, full of concrete, stubbornly intricate, and often divergent, if not directly conflicting issues, remains yet to be entered and explored. This step can in turn, guide the further clarification and development of a training system, and the direction for the next steps.

SYSTEM GOALS AND APPROACHES TO SYSTEM DEVELOPMENT

Training system development is anchored in its goals—the intended outputs—and it is the acquirers of these outputs who are primarily responsible for seeking them. The patterning of roles and relationships is already familiar: establishing training needs—the work organization; taking decisions about training strategies and resources—the resource providers; and developing a training program to meet those needs—the training system. The temptation that full-time trainers and training institutions must resist—to put forward goals of their own—is likewise familiar. They must constantly remember that their goals are based on extrapolations of past performances or even, merely, past aspirations. No matter if they are better based than that, direct advocacy of a system's goals circumvents the proper trainer functions of helping organizations improve their own processes of goal-setting and of responding professionally to questions concerning technical feasibility, strategy options, and the resources needed for attaining the stated objectives.

A particularly important professional function is to ensure that enough resources are provided for system maintenance and longer-term development so that current activities, however pressing, do not exhaust current system capacities—a constant peril in developing countries. It is important that a line be drawn between providing information to assist in processes of decision making (a proper function of the training system) and taking responsibility for decisions of policy priorities and resource allocations which fall within the purview of national, provincial, or other, broader bodies.

When it comes to establishing the boundaries of the training system, including some sectors and institutions and excluding others, and settling directions and time frames for capacity development, responsibilities are more evenly shared and the processes involve more negotiation between the partners. Differences arise because the training system has to develop internal cohesion and its own capacities for boundary management, and trainers as a cohort have to assume responsibility and feel committed to the results.

TASKS OF THE TRAINING SYSTEM

In the classic system diagram the tasks that the system exists to perform fall inside a box in the middle, between "inputs" entering from the left and "outputs" going out on the right. When properly performed, managed, and coordinated, the tasks result in the system's coherent contribution to achieving the goals that users — organization, province, or region — have set for it.

The tasks can be classified in many ways. We have grouped them below under eight essential functions.

1. Building and Maintaining Support

For its very existence and continuation a training system has to merit and keep the support of the organizations that use its outputs. Without active support from the top policy and decision makers in the organizations, training—even good training—may be confined to areas of minor impact, and resources allocated for it consequently remain small and uncertain. For an initial trial period such limitations may serve both system and organizations well by keeping risks low. These risks include unexpectedly heavy demands on organizations following effective training. But if sidelining continues beyond the initial trial, the system risks dismissal or irrelevance. The more far-reaching the development(s) to which training is to contribute, the more important the system's tasks for ensuring support.

The first strategic objective for building support is to involve all levels and parts of the organizations that are prospective users of the outputs, will be involved in their production, and/or will be affected by them. Even the initial list of these, which can be extrapolated from the training needs and strategies for meeting them, goes far beyond the top group who decide whether or not to go ahead with a development at all and the initial levels of effort and funding for it. After policymakers have given training the green light, others in an organization have to be effectively involved in selecting participants, providing space, organizing opportunities, and perhaps arranging equipment, for practice. At every stage staff groups have the power to facilitate, delay, or even effectively negate essential steps in the implementation process, whatever the decision at the top. Modifying existing norms of training and effecting work and organizational change usually involves yet other people. The training strategy may call for new criteria for the selection and subsequent placement of participants at higher production levels and more collaborative work arrangements. Support from leaders in these matters is therefore important. Such changes are usually easier and more pleasantly achieved if knowledge about them has already engendered goodwill in the organization; a general atmosphere of goodwill generates support all around. For thinking through the complexities, for resolving doubts at the inevitable times of perplexity, for coping with stresses which change efforts invariably encounter, and for sharing and learning from the ongoing experiences, trainers and system leaders often look for intellectual and emotional support from professional colleagues.

The theory of institution building classifies linkages according to the types of support that a system needs: enabling, functional, normative, dispersed, and collegial. Figure 12.2 reproduces a typical pattern of linkages (for the first four types) for new institutes for population studies and training in academic settings.

Adequate support building, therefore, goes far beyond the initial green light and funds. Aside from the purposes of linkage, it is also important that all eventual users and supporters know they are included in the vision, even if the initial steps involve only a limited set of actors and are

Figure 12.2

PATTERN OF LINKAGES FOR DIFFERENT PURPOSES: AN ACADEMIC CENTER

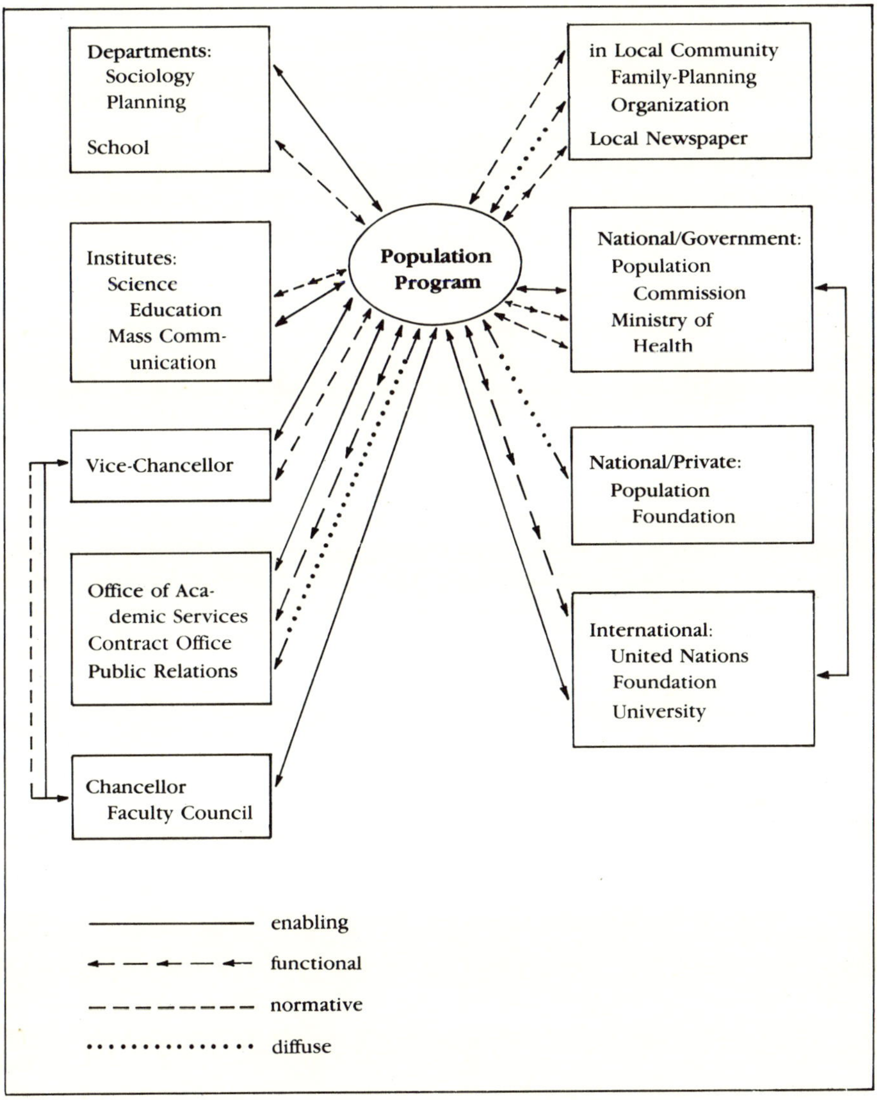

Source: Rolf P. Lynton, *Building Population Programmes in Universitites*, Carolina Population Center, University of North Carolina at Chapel Hill, 1974, p. 59.

heavily influenced by immediate tactical considerations. This means projecting the pattern of support required far into the future. By its pattern of linkages and manner of developing them a system makes its mission concrete, communicates it to its environment, and also establishes its own distinctive style of working and public image.

Detailing linkages goes hand in hand with using them. In each category specific units and contacts can be identified and used in the course of organizing meetings, distributing documents, announcing programs, etc. Establishing ways to keep this information up to date and serviceable deserves early attention, otherwise these tasks tend to become quickly unmanageable.

Building continued mutuality into all relationships is particularly important for maintaining support; all partners need to gain, and also feel that they are gaining, otherwise support wilts. System supporters for enabling and normative purposes are at greater risk of neglect than those involved in the more frequent and often discrete functional and collegial linkages. Maintaining top-level support exemplifies the difficulty. Whereas functional linkages are needed and used frequently, and many transactions are directly associated with payments or other benefits to these supporters, top-level support is an obvious and powerful need only at the time of annual budget appropriation or some emergency. But policymakers are amiss if such highly active occasions are the only, or almost only, contacts they have with the system. It is very important that the system find additional and more mutually satisfying ways to keep in touch. The least step is to provide policymakers with information on a regular basis that shows the training system effectively busy on priority developments. When major system developments are proposed and examined policymakers can be heavily involved in thorough reviews.

The following record, made by the head of banking institute, is an example of a thorough review by top-level policymakers initiated by the training system. "In 1983, on the eve of the establishment of...the second apex-level institution for training and development of the State Bank Group (India), a document was presented to the Top Management Group...and a two-day seminar organized at the new Staff College with the following objectives:

1. To have a review of the Bank's Training System in its retrospect and prospect.
2. To have an in-depth and meaningful in-house debate on the critical areas of the Bank's Training System.
3. To discuss areas of expectations, concern, and action.
4. To crystallize thinking on the Bank's Training System so that it remains continuously attuned to the needs of the User System.

5. To have a productive exchange of ideas for providing direction to the future course of the Bank's Training System—an enabling mechanism for sustaining growth and promoting organizational excellence.

As a result of an in-depth debate that was highly participative in nature a number of action points have emerged on which we are working at present.

Building organizational support at working levels is also very important, especially wherever trained people are trying to work more effectively and need their colleagues' collaboration to make improvements. Working support goes far beyond fostering an atmosphere of general goodwill at the work place. It is very concrete, and often quite pedestrian and routine. Occasionally it requires a training system to organize specific programs in conjunction with formal training in order to address this need.

In 1983-84 the Bank of Baroda (India) decided to relocate training programs in industrial relations for zonal managers from training centers to the zones themselves, to build more of the programs around issues specific to the zone and to involve zonal executives in the programs given the managers. A member of the core faculty writes:

The decision to do this programme on location was based on the feedback from managers that their effectiveness in managing IR at the branch level depends on the quality of support from zonal authorities. It was, therefore, decided to conduct this programme right at the zone so that it could address the specific needs of the zone and also involve zonal executives.

We have conducted ten such programmes ... Very important (feedback shows) is that before such a programme is launched, we diagnose IR problems of that zone with the help of personnel and trade unions. The programme is designed in the context of this diagnosis. On the last day of the programme is a four-house interface session where the entire zonal team, including personnel specialists, participate and answer the queries of branch managers. Here, during this session, managers raise a variety of issues and quote instances of inadequate support. Later on such issues are thrashed out and, where policy matters are involved, they are referred to higher authorities.

2. Building Training Competencies and Overall Training Capacity

Increasingly competent planning and running of training sessions and programs is the most obvious outcome of this task. But the task also covers system-wide aspects of training development. Trainer development for institutions will be discussed in chapter 13. At the system level, overall and for all kinds of training, consulting, organizing, and administrative functions, it involves, for instance, recruiting and building trainers into a coherent staff and making additional trainers available through networks of resources so that both immediate training needs and also broader needs, e.g., for organization development, can be met. The training system's credibility with its constituents rests largely on its displaying the capacities to manage itself well within its own boundaries. Internal management includes program planning, budgeting, and accounting; facilities and materials management; and the management of personnel careers and system change. Increasing competence in training organization and program implementation, in turn, builds the staff's confidence in their system, which probably raises competencies further.

3. Developing Training Materials

This task supports competency building and also reflects it. The most useful materials are developed from within the work settings in which training is needed (see the reference to materials development for industrial relations training in the Bank of Baroda above). The production of a steady flow of fresh training materials is characteristic of strong training systems. Another part of this task is to arrange ready access from larger systems to any additional materials needed, and to commission the development of new materials in the larger system when this is appropriate.

4. Building Internal Structure and Process, and Developing Policy

Developing its internal working and the requisite underpinnings for firming up arrangements and routinizing activities wherever possible is another task of a training system. This task, too, often tends to be postponed, purportedly to that day (which never arrives) when pressures for current activities lessen. One result of postponing is the great waste of time and other resources that occurs as people try to cope somehow, *adhoc* and again and again, with aspects of system's operation that could be routinized. Other results of the failure to carry out this task are the high sense of uncertainty in many systems as to how or whether "things work" and the low morale such uncertainty engenders. This task, like others, requires resources. Five percent of the time of system heads and their management teams may serve as a working estimate for it.

5. Strategic Planning

Strategic planning is commonly crowded out, a forgotten function, by pressures from current programs on scarce trainers and weak systems. But without it, systems deteriorate fast: resources are wasted, morale plummets, and training becomes the activity of a few idealist and of many who have failed at other work. Strategic planning starts—but does not end—with using projections of training needs for mapping the system required for meeting these needs. This already goes beyond the mechanical scaling up of numbers in work force plans (such as Indonesia's decision to increase nursing positions in the public health services by 220,000 in fifteen years), and dividing projected recruitment among existing and planned training centers, and even beyond using such estimates for extrapolating trainer recruitment and development needs. Estimates—numerical and others—are needed for all system components and all relevant parts of the environment.

It is useful to go down the list of all components inside a system and its relevant environment and map what would be needed by each in an effort as large as the projected scale. Right then constraints on one or two components might rule out the initial goal, e.g., the rate at which new trainers can, in fact, be found and developed, the capacity of the system as a whole for collaborative work, or the capacity of the service organization to place, absorb, allocate, supervise, and manage recruits (which will often scuttle initial recruitment plans). Funding usually receives the most attention but other constraints can be far more stubborn. Subjecting all components to systematic review in relation to projected training needs can identify those which are in fact *strategic*. Plans can then be made to concentrate efforts and other resources particularly on these. Even then *some* component(s) will set limits to realistic goals.

Mapping and initial planning for components individually and in subsets is followed by two further steps. One is to fit the pieces together into an integrated system under the projected conditions. This produces a composite map of a situation (B), which can be compared to the current situation (A). Strategic planning is complete only when a path has been worked out by which the system will move from A to B and when the decisions, resources, and other external and internal support required for this movement are, in fact, in hand.

6. Networking Training Resources

Another task of the training system is to make the best use of the resources available for training, both inside and outside the immediate system. Crossing its own boundaries in order to secure additional trainers, materials, and other resources which it cannot provide from within, or provide as well or as economically, leads to the identification, development, and management of external networks of training resources.

This task, focused as it is outside the system, is least familiar. It runs counter to strong personal and traditional inclinations to reserve resources for internal use only, as if for oneself or for one's family, and to regard their use by others as a weakness, as giving resources "away." In this perspective, calling on outside resources is a regrettable necessity to be terminated just as soon as internal resources can be built up. The perspective for building strong systems is quite different. The strongest systems make the fullest and most systematic use of outside resources. Having decided on their own areas of strength and built these up, they then value the flexibilities and economies of drawing on special strengths elsewhere. They also value the stimulation and assurances that come from working with competent colleagues in other systems.

The second important part of this task is networking within the system itself. It is characteristic of training systems in developing countries that trainers and other resources are either too centralized to be in effective contact with provinces, regions, and local situations where training is needed, or so dispersed and isolated that individual efforts yield little result and slowly peter out one by one. Clustering and networking address these needs.

> Since August 1983, the Indonesian Ministry of Health has operated a strategy of building training capacity at provincial level through a series of steps:
>
> 1. Select 3, then 3 more provinces (out of 27),
> 2. Compose any initial provincial "training team" that includes promising and available "trainers" from related ministries and service and educational agencies, private as well as public, i.e., begin the external network.
> 3. Make a series of technical inputs to this provincial team and develop action projects for putting the new techniques to use. Selected central staff join as active participants, i.e., develop the internal network.
>
> In six months the core training team of six in one large province developed a network of fifteen additional trainers. Networking is also supported by special funds for provincial team meetings and for joint field activities and materials development. A periodic newsletter from the center adds to regular communication between all team and network members across the country. By early 1984 direct contact between provinces and occasional work together on provincial programs had also begun.

Improved information gathering and management, the development of resource pools of trainers and materials at various levels of the system, and ready access mechanisms are important components of this task.

7. Action Spin-offs and Boundary Management

Training efforts that are well meshed with training needs tend to spark onward actions. These may require further supportive activities on the part of the training system and/or surface-related training needs beyond those planned and provided for originally. Such spin-offs are a good indicator of effective training and will bring training more organizational support.

> The development of training capacity in the initial Indonesian province sparked eight action projects in the first six months, of which three became major multiphase strategies. One of these called for an additional three weeks of senior consultation time. The other two required consultation time and, additionally, funds for provincial officials to participants in a series of local learning opportunities. Together, these two action projects cost half as much again as the initial year's work in the province.

Spin-off action projects and other consequences of effective training present dangers which good boundary management can contain. "Successful" systems, especially in understandably success-hungry developing countries, are at a high risk of being overwhelmed and washed away by the overloads organizations urge on them in the wake of successes. Weak systems have the opposite tendency, likewise destructive: they risk insulation and atrophy for lack of contacts across their boundaries.

To cope with the risks of success, two lines of action have yielded promising results. One is to seek a fresh clarification, together with policy and decision makers of organization(s), of the system's primary task, to sort fresh demands into priorities and sequences, and to attempt only as much and as many as do not endanger the performance of the primary task. Agreement with work organizations along these lines is very important, otherwise pressures on the training system will continue and the organization(s) feel deprived each time the system rejects an attractive project. The next line of action is to ensure that these clarifications and decisions are translated into mutually acceptable work plans and carefully matched with additional resources.

8. Monitoring and Evaluation; Appraising and Controlling Performance

Each task to be performed by a training system has a purpose, and its performance can be assessed in terms of both outcomes and the processes by which they were attained. Regular monitoring yields the data the system needs to improve its immediate functioning, structure, and, looking forward, further development. This task, important to carry out routinely for all tasks, also addresses the often intricate interrelationships between particular tasks and the performance of the system as a whole. The basic training system model presented earlier in figure 12.1 is elaborated in figure 12.3 to show its eight tasks and the linkages with its five basic constituencies.

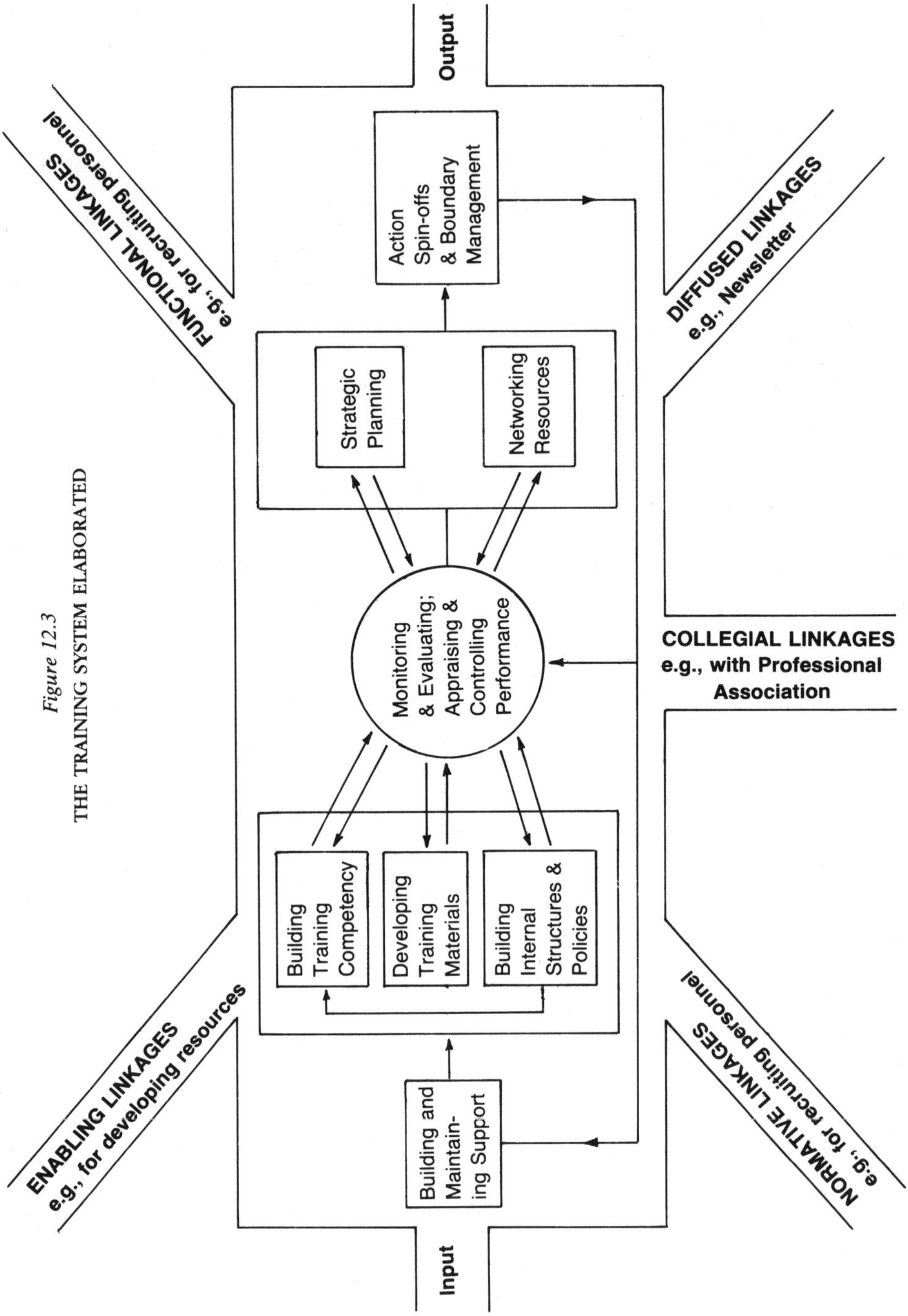

Figure 12.3
THE TRAINING SYSTEM ELABORATED

THE DYNAMICS OF DEVELOPING TRAINING SYSTEMS

There is no one way to develop a training system—training is too dependent on time and local circumstances and on the needs and resources of the work organization, all of which vary widely. The rigorous formulations commonly found in systems literature, comprising tidy and complete steps in one direction, may hide this main point, and by their apparent clarity and finality, confuse newcomers and discourage them. A six-point list of this type is given in box 12.1; it is useful as far as it goes, but that is not very far. To the overriding generalizations that there is no one way to begin, and that several starts may have to be explored before one works, three other operational steps may be added.

Box 12.1

ACTIVITIES IN TRAINING SYSTEM DEVELOPMENT

The process of training systems analysis essentially involves a series of carefully sequenced activities as follows:

1. Formulate a clear and unequivocal definition and specification of the system under consideration to include the need for the system and the delimitation of its boundaries.

2. Develop lucid and functional descriptions of the components of the system and the ways in which they interact.

3. Determine and define the system objectives in terms of optimal system operating performance and output.

4. Identify and specify the criteria to be used for evaluating the congruence of system objectives, performance, and output.

5. Identify and select alternative groupings of system components for evaluation in terms of practicability, desirability, and cost benefits, and determine the trade-offs involved.

6. Test selected alternatives to collect data upon which decision makers may base their choice of the configuration of system components for implementation.

SOURCE: Summarized from W. R. Tracey, *Evaluating Training and Development Systems* (New York: Amocam, 1974).

The first practical step is to work on training systems development alongside contributing, through training, to alleviating some severe pressures that organizations are experiencing, e.g., a severe shortage of nurses in the health services, patently inadequate supervision of costly materials or technologies, a major shift in technology. Second, no matter what the specific need, and the contribution training can make to meet it, several systemic tasks will certainly surface and demand attention quite quickly as training starts. Support building, trainer competence, resource networking, materials development, and presently, of course, monitoring performance appraisal and control — all predictably appear early. Only just behind (or remaining hidden just below the surface) will be the other tasks of renewing systemic structures and processes and of ensuring that the new work is part and parcel of deliberate strategies and plans. This emergence of systemic tasks can be counted on no matter what the starting point, because the tasks are closely connected.

The third (possibly discouraging) practical generalization is that none of the eight tasks is ever finished and "laid to rest." A cyclical pattern seems inherent: one or two tasks move to center stage, are reworked to a new level of performance, then give way to the next in line. Later, each comes full circle again (and again) for renewed attention, maybe in a fresh sequence and at different levels of system performance. This spiral pattern is true for each task and also for developing the system as a whole. Nothing seems to be gained by hurrying to the "next task" before the current one has been sufficiently accomplished; only then is attention to the next fruitful.

We hypothesize that the upward spiral of system development can continue until it exhausts the readiness of an environment to accept and support it. The immediate and most powerful environment of training is, of course, the work organization but broader culture supports and hindrances to further development may also set early limits, such as the traditions and tolerances of a country's civil service. Until these limits are reached performance levels for each task of a training system and the constituencies with which it is linked can continue to spiral upwards. System malfunctioning and disintegration may likewise be cyclical, but downwards.

> The initial six months of work in 1983 on trainer and training system development in the health services of a large Indonesian province showed such a cyclical pattern. Figure 12.4 shows the sequence in which tasks received primary attention and also the time spans for which they held it. The figure is only illustrative; we expect system development elsewhere and at other times to show variations in sequence and time spans. But these will indeed be variations on the basic theme of system development proceeding in cyclical, spiral patterns.

The judgment of when "enough" progress with a task has been made

Figure 12.4

TRAINING SYSTEM DEVELOPMENT IN A PROVINCE IN INDONESIA

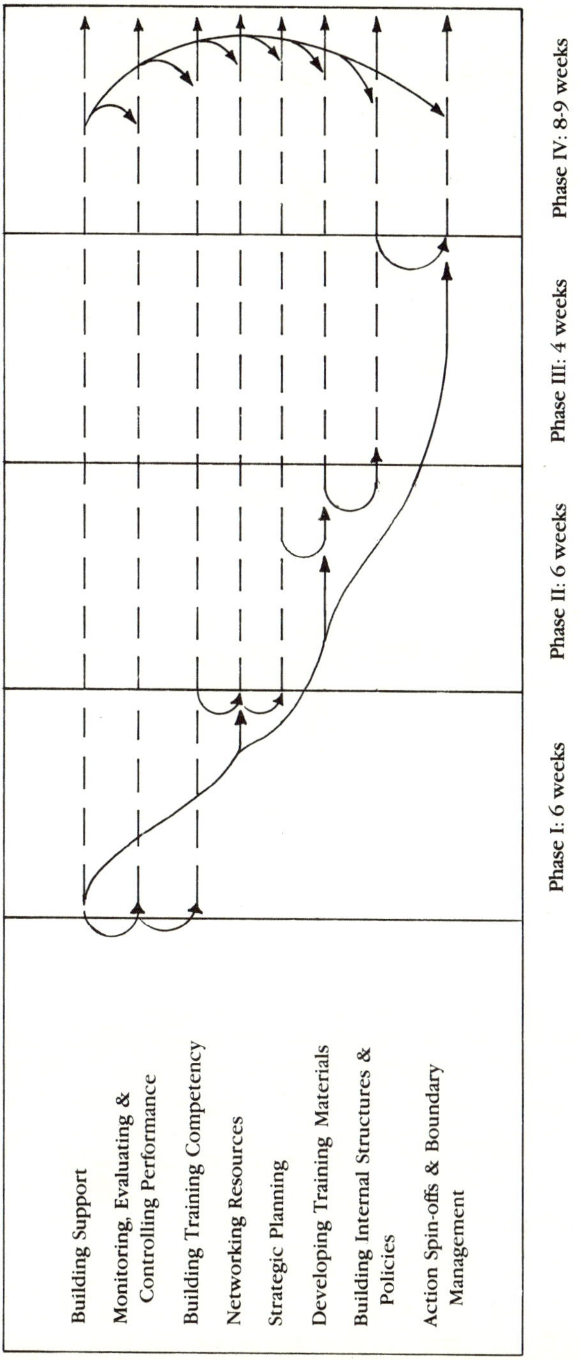

to enable system developers to go on to the next is happily easier to make in practice than to define in abstract terms. When the levels of performance in adjoining tasks repeatedly hinder further progress with the task in focus, attention should be shifted to the others. Even after attention has moved on, the momentum may well continue to carry the earlier task forward as information comes in about how well the work is progressing and hindrances to development are removed. So, for instance, there is no such thing as "total" acceptance and support "from the start"; "enough" is well short of that. Initially, especially when an organization's past experiences with training have not been encouraging, proposals for developing the training system may be merely tolerated, and extra resources for it, if any, come through minimal reallocations. Even small amounts of national or international funds can make a crucial contribution, in this first phase. But as developments get underway and some early training yields practical results and promise beyond expectations, tolerance changes to lively interest and on toward more active involvement. Later, additional resources (actually already available locally) are "found," commitment to the developments is publicized, and an active search by the organization for yet more resources produces notable results. In the Indonesian province this progression took six months. Progress with *any* task contributes to and reinforces progress with all the others.

As the training system continues to shift attention to different tasks in turn, round and round, with conscious, deliberate intent informed by orderly monitoring of progress and problems, the map of tasks and their interconnections becomes familiar and using it habitual. Thus, when all levels of the system are routinely receiving general attention, and the system is so organized that it can keep all under regular surveillance and servicing, specific concerns will move in and out of focus at different levels and at different times. When both overall surveillance and shifts in focal attention between components and between levels become routine, system development has been "learned" and become an integral part of operations. This can be said only for the system itself, but also for the organizations which it serves, and to a lesser degree, to its other constituencies.

As shown in figure 12.4, developing the training system in the Indonesian province in the initial six months moved through four phases. These can be characterized as follows:

> *Phase 1:* Getting acquainted. Getting sufficient approval and acceptance to proceed. Arranging some funds from outside. Monitoring, evaluating and controlling performance begins right here. Work with trainers on competence development (for one district administrator's program) was the legitimating activity at this stage.
>
> *Phase 2:* Competence development became the primary area of attention:

having proved its usefulness—even once—it could be built on. A special technical input program attracted additional trainers. The beginning of a provincial network of trainers and of their institutions came here.

Phase 3: Continuing success created criteria and motivation for reviewing the province-wide training strategy and budget for the next year. New choices were made. Many regular programs were refined and rescheduled. Implications for allocating staff time, funds, and facilities were worked out. Implications for longer-term plans for program and resource development then came into focus. These raised issues in improving system structure and processes and in strengthening formal system linkages to operational and service units in the organization.

Phase 4: The technical inputs had, from the beginning in phase 2, included practical exercises in participants' work situations, and several exercises had quickly proved of practical value to the work organization and so also contributed to the growing recognition and support there for developing the entire system. Within two months three of these "action projects" had been developed into major province-wide strategies for addressing strategic problems of the organization (a severe current and prospective shortage of hospital nurses; the unacceptably low standards of services management at the district level; and inadequate coordination between the two major provincial offices). The organization was then eager to invest its manpower and substantial amounts of other resources in working on these important problems and to involve in this, in preplanned stages, units at various levels of the provincial services. Since work on these problems had national priority also, the provincial government secured additional resources for two of the three projects from the national level.

Rapid success with training systems development is fertile ground for seeds of destruction also. What in good time would be very attractive onward developments can overstrain the planning and management capacities of a barely begun training system, leading to its collapse if undertaken too easily. Regular reviews of system boundaries and careful boundary management offer the best immediate protection. Behind it, the enlarging of resources, improving system structure, and firming program strategy can then receive attention. Top-level support from work organizations is essential for deliberate, orderly responses to demands for program expansion and diversification in line with growing system capacity.

By using the catchall word "system" to designate the partner responsible for training and associated consultation, we now have the setting for making three points. One is that the functions we have listed are composites, enveloping manifold variety and application in many possible situations. Second, to be used well and economically, the components required for any particular development effort need to be fitted together, that is, dovetailed into a single system. Any third, while the system may include one or more component units that specialize in training and consulting (e.g., have fulltime staff and constitute the training department in an organization or a training center outside) the other components carry out more, more continuous and, overall, more important "training" functions. If specialized training components in the system are not to spin off into self-serving irrelevance, they need particularly strong ties to the rest of the system and, through the system as a whole, vigorous roots in purposeful action.

Overall, this system perspective allows the same basic question about training resources to be raised at any level for decision and action. Is training—of all kinds and from all sources—of a sufficient scale and quality, and is it sufficiently well-paced and coordinated, to meet the requirements of planned projects, expansions, and technical and administrative improvements. "Temporary systems," as well as permanent units of training, are also included in the system and as specially arranged and staffed programs, serve better in many situations. Institutions elsewhere in the country or abroad can also be used. Meanwhile the less formal, altogether more extensive, unobtrusive programs also continue in the system, such as understudy, induction, apprenticeship, and effective on-the-line supervision. All these varied and widely dispersed avenues are integrated by an effective system into cohesive training for organizational purposes. The system also links training with public and private agencies that deal with work force planning and the provision of resources; with work organizations (the immediate "consumers" of training personnel); and with professional associations and resources centers, e.g., for quality maintenance and economies of scale in developing materials and for strengthening support in the general culture for good training.

The training goals, properly set by work organizations, guide decisions about training strategies (e.g., what training to provide in-house and what training to draw on from outside, what parts to provide through full-time programs and what parts part-time and/or on the job and/or at a distance), about the resources needed for training and their allocations, and—a very strategic consideration—what components to include in the system, i.e., where to draw boundaries. Issues internal to the system, such as task sequences, or development of the kinds and numbers of trainers and other system resources required for achieving the goals, likewise stem from the same set of estimates and considerations.

Chapter 13

Training Centers and Like Institutions

> Fragment to fragment clings; the things thus grow
> Until we know and name them. By degrees
> They melt, and are no more the things we know.
>
> —LUCRETIUS

A TRAINING system aims to comprise all kinds of possible arrangements by which people involved in a development effort can acquire the competencies necessary for it. In such a system, what place and function is there for full-time training centers, departments, and similar special places with "training" on their name plates? These places exist in the hundreds and figure prominently in training budgets and even more in technical assistance funding. They have full-time trainers, administrators, and staff. Many are located away from participants' work and families, "islands" unto themselves, wholly devoted to making training intensive, unremitting, and "around the clock." While other kinds of training can also offer the same scales of purposefulness, intensity, and trainer expertise, full-time training, especially when located away from work, family, and residence, signals a quantum jump, an arrangement of a different order. It is training in its purest form. Essential dimensions stand out most clearly under such conditions. Training intermixed with other activities strives in the same directions but stops short of those standards. So training centers are the institutional backbone of the whole field of training.

Delineating the contribution of specialized institutions in these theoretical terms is not difficult. It is for four constituencies in particular. The first is participants. Staffed by competent, flexible trainers and administrators under a responsive principal, the institution provides participants with a program and an environment that consistently promotes learning relevant to more effective behavior at work. It is a living model of organizational standards such as the participants hope will also shape their work at home. It is a setting that consistently motivates them to learn and to improve their performance, that offers stimulating challenges they can handle, that provides opportunities to discover effective responses, and situations in which to enforce them.

Behind the participants is the organization that selected them and expects to meet an organizational purpose through their training. For the organization the training institution is a major resource, clarifying what training can contribute to a development effort, proposing a training strategy, designing a program and carrying it out — all professionally and reliably with only minimal demands on administrators, supervisors, and managers while they carry on the organization's primary task.

For the third constituency, its trainers, the institution provides steady support: the collaboration of colleagues, where necessary; supportive, readily accessible services of many kinds; and a climate that is both stimulating and satisfying. These are all immediate and day-to-day. For the longer term, the institution provides trainers with opportunities for further professional growth, through a satisfying range and variation of roles in which they gain experience, through contact with colleagues in other institutions, and through special faculty development programs from time to time.

And finally, for the society in which it works, the training institution can be an agent for development. It permeates the social fabric with its own qualities of inquiry, active response, evaluation of effectiveness, and, above all, with its enthusiastic and skillful engagement in society and its tasks.

If this theoretical picture were even broadly descriptive of training institutions in practice, there would be little need for this book. As it is, the theory provides a framework into which we can order for consideration the main dilemmas encountered in practice, as well as some estimates of the main directions, the minimum support, and the working methods which would help training institutions to move closer to the model. Our presentation may appear somewhat patchy since we do not propose to dwell on theory while practical inadequacies delay strategic actions.

CHARACTERISTIC DILEMMAS

We will start by stating boldly the prevailing standards in training centers we know personally or through close colleagues. That nothing more general and organized is possible underscores the secrecy in which trainers and principals of training institutions shroud themselves. Studies of trainers in action are very few and these few mainly by outside researchers, not reflective studies carried out by trainers themselves for their own improvement. Data on the actual operations of training centers are fewer still. There are almost no descriptions of how training programs were decided, planned, and carried out: how trainers in fact operate in "teams," as they do according to many program announcements, or how a training institution rejuvenates itself. Given the size of the training effort, its cost, and the promise effective training holds for development, it is surprising that training has gone on year after year, even expanded fast with so little self-evaluation and deliberate improvement.

The most plausible explanation is that trainers and training institutions have been caught in the same vicious circle that circumscribes and enmeshes society at large: Change is threatening — it is wiser to leave the cocoon undisturbed; God knows what explorers might find if they unraveled it! But unravel it we must. It is certain that if we trainers are unwilling, severally and jointly, to learn from our experiences, we can hardly expect participants to learn from theirs.

Where training needs are great and skilled trainers few, as is true in developing countries, the individual trainer becomes entangled in the vicious circle first of all by an excessive workload of direct training activities. Regular loads of fifteen training sessions per week are quite common. Hardly has one batch of participants passed "through," the next arrives — a relentless stream. In many institutions programs involving the same trainers are separated by less than a week. Prevailing pressures urge ever larger numbers per session and more courses per year. They leave little room for improving the quality of training in terms of greater effectiveness on the job. Research, or even a minimum of professional reading, often goes by the board. Inevitably, it is not long before the training becomes obsolete and the wellsprings of creativity run dry. In such a situation any proposal to evaluate the work in terms of effectiveness is more than an added burden; it is a threat. This is one dilemma.

The same dilemma precludes closer contact among trainers as colleagues and consequently collegial work on developing the institution further. Colleagues tend to work as individuals, carving up the training pie into separate, though logically related, wedges. Each trainer pleads shortage of time when someone suggests going beyond this mechanical sharing. They do not expect collaboration to lighten their burdens, only to lead to risky and time-consuming displays of weaknesses and rivalry. The rare meetings between trainers usually confirm these dire expectations. For many trainers the lack of professional contact with colleagues symbolizes an implicit contract: "As long as I do not question your work, I expect you not to question mine." When pressed, trainers have even defended this separateness as academic freedom. Hence trainers work as teams in very few institutions, and any consistency in approach to training programs is by and large a matter of good fortune.

These dilemmas become disabling when full-time trainers are so scarce that most training is conducted by administrators or university lecturers hired for a session or two in their particular field. The latter have not been involved in planning the program. Their briefing, if any, is abstract: what the trainers have generally in mind for this or that session. Scheduling of guest sessions in the program usually reflects the lecturers' preferences more than the participants'. Guest lecturers rarely remain long enough for more than very immediate, superficial impressions about the effectiveness of their work. And very rare are the lecturers who participate in follow-up or in integrating their contribution with other aspects of the program. By and large, lecturers use their session to tell what they know. They are not involved in working out training strategies or developing the institution.

> Indonesia exemplifies countries that experience grave difficulties in putting training on a sound footing. For historical reasons, a severe shortage of trainers persists. Over ninety per cent of management programs in the government, for instance, a system with over 300,000 supervisors and administrators at various levels for a work force of over 3 million, are conducted by part-timers. They are paid fixed rates per session in accordance with their work status and not calculated to include preparation or follow-up. Because of the structure of training budgets and in order to obtain adequate personal income, the very few "full-time" trainers actually divide their efforts among many programs and agencies. Having one's base residence in Jakarta or in one of the larger provincial capitals is best for that. The Central Ministries have over sixty training centers, including four specializing in management training, but given present staffing conditions they are, with few exceptions, merely facilities for housing programs planned and staffed elsewhere; most are used less than half-time.

Some new centers and institutes have recently been established which embody attempts by consumers and well-wishers to help the field of training emerge from such dilemmas. They have been set up as autonomous bodies, separate from universities and all ongoing programs. This may be the best safeguard against the contagion of harmful traditions. But this hope has been purchased at a price: the price of isolation, of lessened contact with existing centers, and of possible rivalry. In these new institutes trainer working loads have been sharply reduced, in some cases to six or eight training sessions a week for nine months of the year, and trainers are encouraged to engage in research and consultation.

It is too early to assess the eventual outcome of such attempts to step out of the past. Meanwhile the difficulties these new institutions are experiencing reveal how broad-based and pervasive prevailing traditions really are. Reduction in work loads per se has not led to greatly improved programs or a corresponding upsurge in other activities. Collaboration between trainers, institute-wide agreement on training approaches and evaluation of effectiveness toward routinized take-it-or-leave-it teaching, and away from stress on participant self-motivation and independence. This assessment is cutting. We wish it were wrong.

Only by very deliberate and sustained efforts can institutions push beyond these standards. Even generally agreed policies and mechanisms for collaboration are insufficient. For instance, training staff meetings are certainly necessary for integrating the work of different trainers and for adequate forward planning. But these purposes are only served when deep understanding of the training process and determination to make it maximally effective prevail. How to spread this understanding and determination is the question. In their absence the same meetings tend to lose their professional direction and degenerate into excessively complicated and time consuming mechanisms for reaching administrative decisions. Time is spent on such matters as library procedures and program dates rather than on consideration of program designs and trainer roles. And where administrative concerns predominate, principals are functionally in charge and trainers often compete for their attention.

In addition to the establishment of some new institutes and their attempts to develop higher standards in crucial segments of the training process, three other, rather different developments are also taking place that hold promise. One is the mounting dissatisfaction among the consumers of training. It is important that this "divine" dissatisfaction of clients not be dissipated through lack of focus or simple destructiveness. Second, while a reduction in trainer work loads has not removed professional reluctance to change, some key institutions have freed resources for work on innovation and significant development. Third, our own experience and indications elsewhere suggest that unraveling the cocoon will reveal hidden strengths and talents enough for initiating institutional development.

Trainers can therefore proceed to institutional learning with good cheer—with the same trust and confidence, in fact, with which they recommend learning to participants and their organizations.

CONSISTENT LEARNING ENVIRONMENT FOR PARTICIPANTS

We have had earlier occasions to stress the importance of making every aspect of training activity and environment contribute to the attainment of training objectives. This is true even for individualized programmed instruction which is closest to immune to institutional influences; that method, too, needs a favorable institutional climate. "Truly individualized instruction", Thelen has concluded, "can be achieved only by a really major change in the context of teaching and learning.... [It] can't go forward with business as usual."[1] Otherwise, he has written elsewhere: "Procedures change with each new fad, but the attitudes—the spirit—that

[1]Herbert A. Thelen, "Some Classroom Quiddities for People-Oriented Teachers," *Journal of Applied Behavioral Science*, Vol.I, No. 3 (1965).

animate [learning] keep change from reaching any vital organ.... The new vocabulary merely promotes hypocrisy—the hypocrisy of schoolmen masquerading as educators."[2]

Participants are entitled to expect consistency in at least four facets of the training environment.

1. Between Trainers' Statements and Their Behavior

This is the most obvious consistency: trainers' behavior must be reasonably in line with what they teach, otherwise all their teaching is thrown in doubt. Since behavior has deep personal roots, the point for early action may be to avoid statements about what trainers will or will not do. This includes statements about trainer consistency.

Phrases like "always ready to help," "patient at all times," and the like invite trouble. The same consideration reinforces our view that it is risky and possibly harmful to ask trainers to use a training method that they do not find congenial. They may test new methods in the safe environment of colleagues. With participants their genuineness is of greater importance than their novelty. Genuineness avoids the recurrence of the classic lecture (behavior) about the value of frank and full discussion (statement); of the exhortation (statement) to participants to take their own decisions and act on them while in fact insisting on their own preferences (behavior); or of repeated assurances (statement) that nothing matters so much as that they get all the help they need, immediately followed by cutting short a discussion (behavior) in order to leave for home.

Participants depend on reasonable consistency between trainers' statements and behavior not only in the program, but everywhere they see them. They watch how they behave with each other, with staff, with their families. The higher the standards trainers recommend during a program, the more exposed they are to risks of disappointing and confusing participants.

Trainers in residence with participants, or out in the field with them full time, are caught in many unplanned situations and unguarded moments. Trainers need to be selected with this in view. Laboratory trainers who take participants farthest into experiencing personal stress and expressing angry feelings must be able to remain "true" under the consequent pressures. Many decide to limit their contacts with participants outside the laboratory lest they not be able to maintain their "training" orientation in other kinds of situations.

[2] *Four Case Studies of Programmed Instruction* (New York: Fund for the Advancement of Education, 1964).

2. Between Different Trainers in the Same Program

The program as a whole needs to display consistency of orientation and priorities. So long as trainers share this, they need not behave alike. In fact, being persons of different makeup they will express this underlying unity in many different ways. One comes through best in case sessions, another in field training, yet another in lectures. Trainers have different styles, and the closer these suit their different personalities the better. What they need to share and express consistently are genuineness and openness, and pervasive concern for the training task and for improved performance. Not unison but harmony is the outcome of this consistency.

Achieving this consistency in a training program is the outcome of sustained endeavor. It cannot be achieved once and for all, but progressively. Trainers should be teamed up with consistency in mind. Besides possessing the requisite knowledge and skills, team members need to feel basically compatible and ready to be drawn into close professional and personal relationships. This is important since inconsistencies among trainers may cancel out required learning and may soon confuse participants so much that they tune out trainers who differ.

The danger of inconsistencies among trainers is almost inescapable when training laboratories and other process-oriented training are mixed with knowledge-oriented sessions in the same program. Participants may then learn little from either one. This can be avoided by concentrating different orientations—and trainers—at separate stages of a program or by running separate programs for each.

When all possible allowances have been made in the design of the program, the training institution still faces the dilemma of how to promote each trainer's individual style and creativity—which make for good training—and consistent, integrated experiences for the participants across the program in its entirety. Much as trainers may want to experiment, and much as the institution may encourage them, participants are suspicious of radical differences in the behavior of different trainers. Innovative trainers are particularly likely to meet suspicion when they act counter to participant expectations. They are constrained within the limits of tolerance of the participants and also of the institution. They are not wholly free agents, for the simple reason that they are also an extension and carrier of prevailing institutional standards. Given a sensitive principal and an institutional climate favoring high standards, this dilemma can be addressed by varying trainers' roles and functions from time to time, and by a number of other specific steps we shall detail shortly.

3. Between Training Objectives and the Physical Environment

Not only the trainers by their behavior, but also the inanimate physical surroundings and administrative procedures of the institution convey signals to participants that are either attuned or at variance with the training objectives, and so help or hinder training.

> For instance, democratic values and participatory methods call for a new layout of session rooms. The traditional layout of a podium and table for the trainer, on the one hand, and participants' chairs in parallel rows, on the other, signal in advance that a trainer will speak rather than listen, that she will be personally distant from the participants, and that the training method will not include much discussion among participants. Chairs in a circle, with the trainer sitting side by side with participants, make a communication consistent with the new values.
>
> Luxury may be as inconsistent with the training objectives as spartan facilities. If a program for shop-floor trade union leaders is held in an expensive seaside hotel, participants (and their constituents) may conclude that the primary objective is to buy them over to the side of management. the centralized residential training program for foremen mentioned in chapter 11 harbored this kind of inconsistency.

Appropriateness is the relevant criterion, because it is consistent with training objectives. Since any training is intended to promote high standards of performance, every item in the training environment needs to perform well. Documents need to be well laid out and well typed, and physical facilities need to be neat and clean, but, above all, appropriate for their functions. It may be possible for trainers and administrators to allocate office space and facilities, such as secretarial services, transport or air conditioning, not in terms of hierarchical status in the institution but in accordance with job requirements. The Indian Institute of Management in Ahmedabad has done much along these lines. In countries where air-conditioning equipment is not widely available, it is not unusual to find it limited to the offices of foreign "experts" and "the administration." Functionally, it would be far better to air-condition some of the classrooms. Where office accommodation is tight, as it often is in rapidly expanding training institutions, the situation could be eased by allotting scarce air-conditioning to the typing pool or the duplicating room. By doing this the trainers will effectively underscore in practice the functional emphasis on organizational relationships and decision-making processes they talk about in the training program.

4. Between Training Objectives and Institutional Administration

If efficiency, personal concern, flexibility, and speed of decision and action are among the values to be promoted through the training program, then the administration of the training institution needs to exemplify these same values in practice. This, again, will avoid damaging confusion and delays and also underscore the relevance of these values and demonstrate their efficacy to the participants.

The need for consistency on this score is greatest at points where participants of the center come into direct working contact with administrative staff. This usually happens when travel and finances are to be arranged, training documents issued, and, in full-time programs, living arrangements and food provided. In residential programs training and administration intermingle so often and so closely that administrative contacts with participants can affect the progress of a program in major ways.

> The classic example is food. Food often becomes the subject for complaint at stages in the program when participants feel unsettled and deprived of their habitual landmarks and supports. They feel uncared for, wishing they were back home with their families and in surroundings they know. The unfreezing stage of the training process is characterized by pervasive feelings of this kind. Complaints about food are often their major expression. To handle complaints about food as a mere administrative matter would then miss their central meaning.

In their manifold contacts with participants, then, the administrative staff has a quasi-training function. Beyond this, participants notice administrative standards and the general climate at the center and draw conclusions that affect their learning. This makes it very important for trainers and administrative staff to associate closely in developing the institute's orientation and in designing living arrangements and "administrative" procedures consistent with the training objectives.

> Some institutes hold regular meetings of trainers and administrative staff to make the overall approach consistent. Others deliberately reduce to a minimum the working contacts between participants and administrative staff. They identify trainers to be liaisons for all administrative matters, in the expectation that they can thereby ensure due attention to training components in administration while the administrative staff can carry on its work protected against pressures displaced from the training program. Some centers turn over to participants large portions of the administration of "their" program. At Aloka for instance, when participants complained about the food provided, they were informed of the budget for food purchases and other limits set for catering, and encouraged to take over the planning, purchasing, and preparation of food.

Some of these steps may be too time-consuming in short programs. But the principle holds: to bring administrative concerns in line with training concerns. Participants can effectively take responsibility for library and documentation procedures, game equipment, and many other administrative items. The ensuing activity, besides providing direct practice in accounting, storekeeping, and other useful managerial competence, may have the additional benefit of developing the attitudes and skills of collaboration and leadership.

In residential programs, above all, a training center has both the wonderful opportunity and the taxing task of achieving consistency throughout the participants' stay, in session and out of session. The unscheduled time deserves special attention there, since it accounts for at least half of the participants' working hours. With one day off each week, the proportion of off-time may in fact be close to two-thirds. There is no doubt that conflicting influences during this time could markedly offset what is achieved "during training." Alternatively, off-time influences in line with training can powerfully reinforce the progress of the program.

The major limitations and wastages of part-time and nonresidential training in fact arise from inconsistent, perhaps conflicting, influences on participants from various sides: the training program, work, family, and social contacts. In training they may be treated as responsible, trustworthy people, but at work must limit themselves to carrying out instructions. Their family and friends may resent the time they spend on the program, and so belittle its importance. It is such inconsistencies rather than the mixture of work and training activities that constitute the problem in off-time, part-time, and even full-time but nonresidential training. Two steps forward followed by one step back may constitute good progress for the pilgrim-participant in such programs.

To sum up: A training institution has the function of aligning as closely as possible all the various influences on participants. Some part of this is achieved through contact with participants' organizations. In the program itself, an institution tries to offset the ill effects of other inconsistencies outside its control and its influence. For instance, it can prepare participants to expect some inconsistencies and encourage their discussion. Many more detailed points could be made. However, of all the possibilities open to appropriate action the most important is to ensure that the institution itself has one orientation and one voice for participants.

INSTITUTIONAL "CLIMATE" FOR TRAINERS

Because of specialization and economies of scale the private tutor or "guru" have been replaced by a training center or institute headed by a director or principal. Not only has the center now to do that tutor's job, it also needs, we have learned, an image, some distinguishing characteristics, what some call an organizational personality. More precisely, to do the job of training well, the center has to become personal and engaging. An institution is never finished with striving to develop such an orientation and character and to speak with one voice to participants and the society around it. The image must forever be achieved afresh, and renewed. For one thing, a center's very function requires it to have one foot in the future, and to that extent be ahead of the present and at variance with it. Twice before in this book we noted and commended such a split stance: first, in chapter 8, when we considered the conditions during the program that favor effective training, especially the close relationship between trainers and participants; and again, in chapter 10, when we visualized the participants' return to work after training and their attempts to initiate some innovation in their organizations. In every case, and this third is no exception, standing with one foot in the present and the other in the future calls both for individual initiative and also for collaboration with others. Both attempts flower and yield fruit only if a climate of support pervades the institution.

Box 13.1

INSTITUTIONAL STRUCTURES FOR A SUPPORTIVE CLIMATE

HERBERT A. THELEN

Specification 1: Improvement of teaching calls for improved performance of teachers in the classroom.

Specification 2: Only the teacher can change the performance of the teacher.

Specification 3: To do this, he requires the emotional support and technical help of a small, friendly group of colleagues.

Specification 4: Resources will be needed and should be available to the small training groups.

Specification 5: The total faculty group, with the help of a steering committee, provides the members for the groups, creates expectancy for performance, and assimilates the results of the training groups' experience.

Specification 6: To do this, the total faculty must itself be a group with shared purposes and outside demands or expectancies to be met.

Specification 7: The "outside" must be composed, for this purpose, of responsible citizens representing the community as a whole, or defined groups such as parents, merchants, civic leaders, etc.

Specification 8: Teachers must maintain interactive contact with the outside, so as to get necessary feedback for the faculty as a whole.

Specification 9: As the program rolls along, the faculty must be able to identify its shared needs for further training and make use of faculty-wide workshops and other devices to meet these needs.

All the above specifications and the suggested plan itself (with slight changes in wording) can be seen to apply to in-service training in hospitals, engineering firms, libraries, and other institutions.

SOURCE: Herbert A Thelen, *Dynamics of Groups at Work* (Chicago: University of Chicago Press, 1954), pp. 91-93.

The institutional structures for a supportive climate have been summarized by Thelen. His nine specifications range over emotional as well as technical support from collegiate groups, the provision of additional resources, links with the community, and faculty-wide workshops. The list is reproduced in full in box 13.1.

In a training session the climate depends primarily on the trainers. In the work situation it depends primarily on the participants' superiors. So in the training institute it depends primarily on the principal. This is most unreservedly so in developing countries where tradition favors hierarchical authority and where organized training is still new and has as yet no deep-rooted traditions of collegiate responsibility.

Even in other countries principals have a very important and often dominant effect on institutional climates. Their direct influence seems to be greater even than that of the heads of some other types of organizations. Although many industrial and commercial organizations, for example, reflect the personalities of their heads, they are also shaped very directly by the impact of technical and commercial requirements. The external demands on training centers are more diffuse and indirect, and a principal's influence is correspondingly more insistent. We may wonder in passing about the satisfaction that this unquestioned importance may give to principals of training centers. The prevailing reluctance to evaluate the effectiveness of training on the job may well draw support from that high quarter. Very likely, effective evaluation would suggest sharing authority, at least the facts of the situation and potential demands for institutional change.

There are other reasons, too, why a principal in a training center is accorded undue importance. The difficulties inherent in evaluating the work of trainers leave their reputations — and often advancement — at the mercy of their principal's opinion; there is usually no other overriding criterion. A principal thereby wields great power in the eyes of trainers. And this, in turn, reinforces the characteristic personality trait noted earlier in trainers; as a group, they tend to be just as dependent on signs of approval from a principal as they themselves want participants in their sessions to depend on similar signs from them. This interlocking pattern of dependence—principal-trainer-participant—is most difficult to break, even under highly favorable circumstances. Where authoritarian roles and structures feature prominently in the general culture outside the gates, very few principals are disposed to open their traditional role to questioning and to possible change.

We will differentiate below centers that offer an unfavorable, tolerable, or favorable climate for their trainers. We have treated principals as the people primarily responsible for the climate and traced their influence via the trainers on the outcome of the training effort.

1. Unfavorable Climate

The principal is against changing the traditional pattern. The center, then, instead of playing a significant part in development, strengthens the status quo. We do not know how many institutions in developing countries belong to this unfavorable category, but the percentage is bound to be high. In U.S. grade schools this type predominates. Together with principals who "tolerate change but do not initiate it," it reportedly describes four out of five.

Two specific functions reinforce the general drag toward the status quo. One is the grave shortage of principals due to the training explosion in developing countries. Hence many centers operate for long periods without a principal or with successive principals occupying the position only temporarily. Some are headed by principals whose interests and experience lie not in training but, say, administration. Logically, this weakness at the top could leave trainers as a group freer to shape the center according to their needs. Actually, it leads to uncertainty so severe that any attempts by trainers to move ahead prove divisive and raise prevailing anxiety still further.

The second factor to reinforce the status quo operates strongly in centers that are part of a work organization — the training department in an industrial company, or a government department, for example. In developing countries governments are particularly active in establishing departmental staff colleges and training centers of many kinds. We noted the scale of some of them in the introduction. Many other formally autonomous institutes are so dependent on official finance and other support that their freedom to innovate is restricted within narrow limits. The problem posed by this structural arrangement can be delineated sharply: training in that situation represents a secondary function, since the organizational and funding arrangements of training usually have to conform to those serving the primary production or service functions. That is what holds the attention of the top management on whom training utterly depends for support, often for its very inception and continued existence. In that setting any training activities that appear to interfere with the performance of "the work" are likely to be restricted within narrow limits or even suppressed.

Whatever the origins for an unfavorable climate, centers that have it are characterized by a series of disabling features which coalesce in the absence of development.

> Nearly all the energy of trainers and administrators goes into current operations and maintenance.
>
> Principals insist that they cannot get additional financing and staff for the diagnosing, planning, and innovation that institutional development calls for.

Principals say that the bodies to which they report will not approve innovation; that they are powerless to act.

Departments and sections in the center stand apart in suspicion and tend to ever greater distance from one another.

Evaluation, if any, is not in terms of total effectiveness of training on the job—that would mix up the contributions of different departments and sections—but in terms of parts only, and those parts confined to the training program. Evaluation proceeds by loops within each department. It is self-confirming and stabilizing, not innovative. Development in one department tends to be "written off" by another. It may be ignored as insignificant or it may be belittled as no better than what has been done long since elsewhere in the institution without any fanfare. Or it may lead to real interdepartmental troubles. It may give the participants opportunities to play off some trainers against others, aggravate existing rivalries between trainers and departments, and provoke additional interference from principals and higher bodies. The innovating department is then seen as "causing" difficulties, and attempts are made to correct this by attacking or eliminating the offending part of the institution. Such "correction" does not lead to lasting improvement.

Lest this list seem too discouraging in its relentless direction, complicity, and lack of promise for action, this may be the place to recall that institutional developments in other fields face the same difficulties. Moreover, and more importantly, this moribund trend can be reversed—by a principal motivated to act, and able to act with skill.

The scientific approach to any field involves important social problems. Medicine provides a well-known example. Many nineteenth-century physicians bitterly resisted such scientific innovations as Semmelweiss' statistically supported plea to surgeons to wash their hands to save childbearing women from death. Other innovations, based on inadequate research, created medical "fads" and contentious schools which resisted rational correction. As medical science developed more adequate research methods and knowledge, it still required a heroic effort to reform the institutions of medical training and the standards of admission to medical practice. These changes were introduced only by calling upon strong professional organization, strict government controls on admission, outside support from very wealthy foundations, and a public willingness to pay for competent medical care. Despite this progress, there remain to this day serious problems in the organization of medical research and the transmission of scientific knowledge to medical students and practicing physicians, to say nothing of medical economics. Out of these problems has grown a new field of study, medical sociology.

Principals determined to change their institutional climates will, as the saying goes, find a way. As a first step they will probably separate fantasy from reality. Some of the disabling features in the list may prove minor. For instance, although financing and staff may be required for a change, they are almost certain to find enough of both available in the center to make a start. To cast principals as the victim of the budget is misleading. True, the budget limits them and change might well be easier if there were more money and more trainers. But principals also shape their budgets and have much to do with channeling the energies of available trainers and other resources. Nor are they powerless before their governing bodies. American studies have shown that structural relationships do not determine the rate of innovation. Farmers or physicians, who are quite independent of work organizations, change no faster than managers or principals. We have never met a principal who maintains that he or she is at the mercy of a governing body. Very likely they quitely secure the support of the members of that body, severally and jointly, for what they wish to do.

But who are these principals who are likely to set about improving an institutional climate and how do they get appointed? Matthew Miles has analyzed a series of studies of these questions and formulated a set of generalizations.[3] The set includes the following pointers:

> The major impetus for change in institutions comes from outside. In the case of training departments and staff colleges, "outside" means other parts of the organization. The "consumers" of training, participants and their organizations, demand greater effectiveness of training on the job. Such outside pressures can be blunted by inadequate evaluation and by inadequacies in linking the effectiveness of trainers' work with their advancement in salary and status.
>
> The degree and duration of change are directly proportional to the intensity of the outside pressure for change. So, "consumers," don't stop pressing! But if the initial response is slow, followed by an excessive response, these are signals that an institute has become too dependent on outsiders for effectiveness, perhaps even for survival.
>
> Improvement is more likely to be started by principals selected from outside an institute than by one promoted from inside.
>
> The change will proceed from the top down.
>
> The rate of change will slow down after an initial burst. This is as it should be, for, as a new principal takes hold, an institute develops a more effective climate for its trainers.

2. Tolerant Climate

A more promising situation exists when principals, though they do not take the initiative, tolerate some change. They are willing to step out of

[3] Matthew B. Miles (ed.), *Innovation in Education* (New York: Teachers' College, Columbia University, 1964), pp. 431–35.

the prevailing system, at least for a try, perhaps to go along with trainers eager for a change. Officers from the general civil service placed as principal of a training center often belong to this category; also others who do not personally depend on the traditional system and have had no experience of any other; and likewise the many who have no clear urge to take the initiative and strike a new direction.

In a climate tolerant of change the initiative generally lies with a few trainers bent on innovating. Their success depends on how accurately they assess the principal's tolerance for change. His or her tolerance matters in deciding the particular directions of change and also the disturbances created by it in the institution. The latter is particularly difficult for innovative trainers to assess. It involves close contact with many colleagues who may prefer to keep their anxieties and resentments to themselves. Silence is a safer protest when the principal is condoning, perhaps supporting, change and seems quite anxiety-free. Introducing change under such conditions is risky. And if the predictions are inaccurate, or an unforeseen event overtakes them, the trainers' attempt may fail.

The safest course of action is what Kenneth Rice calls "a protected experiment."[4] The trainers secure agreement for going ahead with a limited change and for letting it run for a while without interference or interim judgment. If the change affects a marginal area and can be isolated from the rest of the institution or program, this agreement is easier to secure. The difficult problems of integrating the change, should it prove successful, with the rest of the institution are postponed to later. While the experiment is on, close contact between the innovating trainers and their colleagues is perhaps the most important preparation for dealing with the problems of integration.

> The lid blew off an unstable situation such as this in one institution over the discontinuation of laboratory training as part of the regular residential training programs. With the departure of the principal who had supported this (and other institutional developments), anxieties and resentment which had accumulated in the general training staff over many issues erupted and were focused on laboratory training. The innovating trainers were accused of having forced changes down their colleagues' throats by using the last principal-director as a ramrod. They were seen as hungry for power and, at last, could be stopped and punished. When the trainers suggested that the effects of laboratory training be evaluated on the job, it was treated as their bid for restoration of "power." Unlike the outgoing principal, the new one came from a closely related organization. He dealt with this turbulence by isolating "the offenders." Sensitive to any insinuation that he might be "used" by trainers, these or others, he made it a point to remain personally distant from all trainers.

Effective use of a tolerant climate for innovation is easier if the

[4] A. K. Rice, *Learning for Leadership* (London: Tavistock Publications Ltd., 1965), pp. 184-85.

principal can be convinced that the change will benefit the center as a whole and the work it carries out. Verbal persuasion, even facts and figures, may not be of much help in this. Such conviction comes from personal experience followed by insight and informed understanding. This could be the main objective and promise of advanced training programs for principals. Such programs offer opportunities for sharing experiences with principals of centers in the same country or new experiences in the different conditions of a foreign country. Many such programs enhance a principal's status and sureness, especially when held abroad.

3. Favorable Climate

Finally, there are the principals who are eager for change and both willing and able to take the initiative to develop the center in significant directions. They certainly have a large and continuing task, and one that is potentially very effective and personally satisfying.

These principals' contacts, like those of effective trainers, are characterized by openness and genuineness. As far as they are concerned, any question can come up for discussion. Tasks and better ways of carrying them out are the dominant points of reference. They encourage explorations for more effective and economical methods of work, whatever the unfamiliar directions they may take. In this sense they favor a functional point of reference and play down differences in age and status between trainers. They are genuinely personal. To them, people matter. They openly express their feelings, feelings of dissatisfaction and anxiety as well as of pleasure and excitement. By doing so they free trainers to express *their* feelings. That is the climate created and these are the ways in which it permeates the whole institution.

This favorable climate is reflected in at least five areas of specific action by principals:

i Sharing Routine Responsibilities, Including Discipline

Principals increase their trainers' responsibilities. They refuse to take certain decisions themselves or even to check on, let alone interfere with, decisions reached by trainers in the areas delegated to them.

Problems of discipline among participants may offer an early opportunity of this nature. One principal informed the trainers soon after his arrival that he considered them well able to handle most disciplinary problems and that, therefore, he would prefer not to deal with these. That sufficed to bring the number of referrals down sharply. It stayed down. Even in major cases, calling for action by the principal, he or she can insist on a specific recommendation for action from the trainers concerned and usually follow it.

The need for flexible behavior by trainer and the delegation to them by the principal of maximum responsibility and training concerns intermingle, this delegation needs to include some administrative decisions. With this freedom and support, trainers, in turn, are enabled to share freedom and responsibility with participants. As part of their interest in avoiding dysfunctional formality, principals also encourage direct professional contacts between trainers and their colleagues in other institutions.

ii Gearing the Internal Organization to Function Efficiently

Most centers have functional departments below the principal. Each department is headed by a senior person: economics, sanitation, accounting, management, research. Like professors in the academic world, these department heads ensure the continuity and development of their specialties in terms of personnel and program. There are signs, however, that this type of organization no longer suffices, even in academic institutions. Interdisciplinary programs and centers are sprouting with increasing speed. The older type of organization is proving particularly inadequate in training institutions directly concerned with improving participants' continuing and undifferentiated behavior on the job.

Designating some trainers as course and project directors — leaders or coordinators are other titles common for this position — suggests a useful direction to pursue. Trainers team up for a particular task, with one in charge. The team as a whole is responsible for all aspects of the work. Full-time and part-time trainers may be included as required. Designated program directors each head "their" course. They may at the same time be a member of one or more teams working on other programs. The functional emphasis is clearest where the principals themselves join their institute's pool of trainers drawn along with others into programs and projects. Trainers then work in various combinations that are collaboratively set up to accommodate the needs of the work, on the one hand, and their individual interests, competence, and personal and professional development, on the other.

Such an arrangement runs more smoothly if the program directors are designated well in advance. If they are appointed prior to the commencement of a similar program, they have both a direct interest and opportunity to study that program with an eye to instituting improvements in their program. They have time to study the problems in the field, make contacts to secure applications, and to compose "their" training group. To ensure adequate evaluation, reflection — and also rest — after "their" program is over, trainers ought not to be the director of successive programs.

The program or project form of organization ensures widely shared responsibility. It distributes source of initiative throughout the institution. And it is very flexible, a doubly important consideration when demands on the institution change rapidly and will continue to do so.

> The Indian Institute of Management in Ahmedabad uses a matrix structure for sharing responsibilities among all faculty members. It has three dimensions, and every faculty member has some responsibility in each at all times: a substantive area (e.g., finance, policy, quantitative methods), an area of application (e.g., industry, health services, agriculture), and some duty in academic administration (e.g., admissions, doctoral programs, executive development programs, publications). Irrespective of seniority at the Institute, faculty members take three-year turns heading a function and are accountable to the group of colleagues working on it with them. The matrix design maximizes interactions among faculty members and helps to distribute power widely rather than allow it to be concentrated in a few points in the institution.

Some institutions have gone further, to rotate also formal administrative positions, such as departmental chairmanships. A welcome result of all these types of sharing is the rapid development of trainers capable of heading long-term developments. In this way experienced new principals are being developed for the increasingly numerous training institutions required today and tomorrow.

iii Diversifying Trainers' Functions

A third large area for concern and action by principals eager to develop the institution they lead is the organization of work for individual trainers. If, like mechanics, trainers consider their job so routinized they could handle it "in their sleep," they are no longer trainers who communicate the values of inquiry, inventiveness, enthusiasm, and high standards through their activities. Their training sessions will very likely be outdated as well, both in content and certainly in the examples used. In short, training is not a good full-time job by itself.

Trainers need to keep at least two facets of their competence fully alive. One is their first-hand experience in using research results and providing services under operating conditions, for example, of plant managements or area development. The other is continued growth in their professional field: they must be in the mainstream of their field through professional contacts, reading, reflective practice, and periodic participation in programs for professional upgrading.

Reducing the training load may be the first step toward keeping these competencies alive and up to date but it does not guarantee this result.

Nor need work-loads invariably be cut. Trainers may not need relief from work so much as a broader range of activities and roles. The academic world offers sabbaticals for this purpose. One year off after five or six years of teaching. For trainers, changes ought to occur more often, probably in a major way every year. They need time for research studies in the field and for consultation with operating organizations. Some institutions have found ways of offering their staff occasional temporary assignments for managing an industrial unit. It is difficult to imagine a better way than this to help trainers regain their feel for the real work situations of participants in all their complexity and conflicting demands, and the pressures for action to strict specifications.

The principal's task here is not to propel trainers into set series of activities but to arrange opportunities for trainers over the years to develop and express their inclinations and competencies. This task also includes ensuring that no trainer rates his or her capabilities too low, including the capability for change.

The provision of some of these opportunities has structural and financial implications, e.g., the institution of regular sabbatical leave. The provision of other opportunities requires only indirect action. For instance, the principal may draw the attention of a department head to some desirable or undesirable limitations in the activities of a particular trainer.

> For instance, trainers who prefer highly interactive group methods sometimes find themselves virtually participants in terms of their role and their complete preoccupation with the ongoing program. Other tasks, usually the long-term may suffer, it is the responsibility of their colleagues to draw attention to such neglect.
>
> At the Aloka International Training Center junior faculty members had to live with another type of conflict. By age and experience as well as by residing in the same buildings with course participants (though in separate rooms), they were closer to the latter than to other trainers. This was part of the training design. The young trainers who performed this function were then often torn between the confidences participants shared with them and the contribution they could make to improving the program by sharing these confidences with other trainers. To safeguard their closeness to the participants, the principal made sure that these trainers took no part in the most emotionally demanding training sessions. Later, he located two trainers with the participants in every program so that they could at least share wth one another the stresses of their conflicting roles.

The trainers' formal role should ideally embody six major functions:

1. Training participants, using at least two major types of training methods regularly.
2. Directing a program or project.

3. Research, enough to feel fully abreast and acknowledged in their professional field.

4. Self-development through participation in systematic programs for this purpose. (We shall return to this below).

5. Consulting with the types of work organizations from which participants are drawn. This is important partly "to keep one's hand in," partly to sustain the severely practical bias of training. Beyond this, consultation provides trainers with a valid check on their continuing competence. When an organization asks — and pays for — their services, trainers have a measure of their standing with some influential people outside the institution. So consultation can increase trainers work satisfaction and self-respect, in addition to their income.

6. Managing an operating unit, or project. The values of this are readily evident but arrangements outside the institution usually difficult. The same values can be realized to some extent by placing the trainers in charge of some administrative or developmental tasks right in the institution itself. A residential institution — a society in miniature — can readily offer a wide range of opportunities for management by trainers. It needs, for instance, routine purchases, budget and inventory control, materials management, building maintenance perhaps new construction, certainly organization and staff management, and forward planning. It also has to relate itself to other organizations in the locality, market its services, and deal with public relations. Th size of the unit to be managed matters less for the purpose under discussion here than giving the trainers full responsibility for its efficient functioning.

Some institutions do more. At least one sends a trainer to manage an industrial unit while the regular manager comes for training. Principals of other centers encourage trainers to start and run enterprises of their own, a rural clinic, for instance, or a commercial establishment, such as a restaurant.

In terms of time allocation the following rough division has proved useful for full-time trainers.

Training (sessions and preparation)	50%
Research and writing	20%
Administration and professional development	10%
Consultation and services outside	20%

Experiences in some centers come very close to suggesting the employment of part-time trainers. This puts the rotation of roles on a regular basis. Or managers and other kinds of practitioners may be employed as full-time trainers for limited periods. Part-time employment can work well as long as the training function does not, for reasons of declining interest or external pressures, become the least favored activity. While industrial consultants, for instance, can usually control their time to function regularly as trainers if they so wish, industrial managers generally cannot. Full-time employment of practitioners as trainers for short periods carries other severe problems and, in fact, is only worthwhile in very rare circumstances.

The main problem with employing practitioners is that they usually lack training skill in serious measure. They have little understanding of how people learn. Developing them into trainers is not simply a matter of helping them acquire some new training techniques. They may possess a good working knowledge of their subject but not the ability to generalize about it. They are not likely to be familiar with developments since the time of their own formal education. By attitude and personality, too, practitioners may not have the markings of a good trainer. Most are not satisfied with the indefinite, hard-to-measure, and longer-term results a trainer works toward, and not at ease questioning habitual perceptions and normal ways of working, which is part of the trainer's function. Even if they wish to do so, developing appropriate attitudes and skills may demand more time and skilled effort than practitioners can repay the institution in less than two or three years. Only few organizations (outside the military and police) allow leaves this long.

For these reasons and others, the continuing base had best be the training center. Trainers' roles and functions are better expanded and diversified into the world outside than vice versa. This diversification may well include providing trainers with operational assignments of several months' duration.

The principals' task goes beyond general encouragement to trainers to diversify their functions periodically. They need to ensure that time and opportunities are made available for this on a regular, accepted basis. Unless they do this rigorously, the immediate demands of training programs will surely push other functions aside or not allow adequate concentration and intensity of experience. For these reasons it is doubtful that a principal should encourage trainers to shoulder more than two major functions at one time. It is better that they be engaged in different functions in turn.

iv Improving the Professional Competence of Trainers

Trainers can enhance their professional competence through many day-to-day activities. They can join and learn from each other's sessions, collaborate on joint projects, read, and so forth. Their principals can facilitate professional contacts outside their institution and encourage special programs for their further development. They can encourage trainers to be members of professional societies and to contribute to meetings and journals. Studies of innovation show that widespread professional contacts characterize innovative institutions in many fields: education, agriculture, industry, medicine. Trainers in these institutions are more cosmopolitan and also more widely read than trainers in other institutions.

Figure 13.1

COMPARISON OF LEARNING PERIODS OF COMPARABLE GROUPS OF PARTICIPANTS

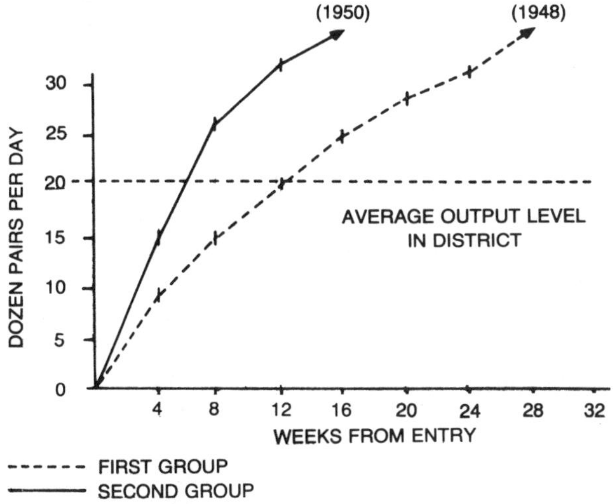

SOURCE: S.D.M. King, *Training within the Organization* (London: Tavistock Publications Ltd., 1964), p. 241.

Principals can give particular attention and facilities to trainers who try out new ideas and methods. They can help them secure necessary outside assistance, for example, supervised practice of a new skill until the trainer can use it independently. Substantial improvements can result from a combination of methods. The performance of successive groups of participants learning an operating skill from the same trainer is depicted in figure 13.1. Early groups hit average output levels after twelve weeks of training and full output after twenty-eight weeks. Later groups reached the average level in six weeks and full output in fourteen weeks. The groups were similar in composition. True, many influences affect training results, but the trainer's greater skill in this instance undoubtedly accounted for the very rapid improvement.

At SIET Institute newly recruited trainers start by taking one of the regular courses as full participants. They thereby gain inside familiarity with the kinds of people who come for training and also with their reactions to the training program. When the course is over, the new trainers have notebooks full of ideas about what they would like to do differently in their turn—questions about course design, timing, specific sessions, training methods.

To develop a specialized skill for limited application, several Indian Institutions collaborated in a faculty program. In 1965–1966, for instance, trainers from six institutions first joined a sixteen-day training laboratory and training skills session. Subsequently, twelve proceeded through a four-stage internship program for laboratory trainers, practicing at various institutions periodically over the course of one year. At the end of the program a two-week laboratory was organized in which trainers collaborated on the specific needs this kind of work revealed in different institutions.

Special programs for trainers carry a significance beyond the sharing of new information and experiences. They signal that the center and its principal are interested in the trainers' further development and in ensuring the highest quality of work possible. Where trainers are as few and inexperienced as they still are in most developing countries, such programs are especially important. We do not mean programs abroad, which, at best, can cover only a small fraction of what is needed, but regular programs, some within different institutions and others organized by several institutions in collaboration. All can be parts of systematic plans to upgrade the quality of training through raising the motivation and competence of trainers.

The shortage of trainers and the prevailing low standards of training make it very difficult to introduce such programs as a regular and permanent feature of the life of any one center. The heavy pressures for quantity, even at the cost of quality, and the requirements for unfamiliar kinds and degrees for collaboration lead to this dilemma. This makes the principal's task heavier and more important.

v. Developing Center-wide Responsibility For Plans and Programs

The principal's most difficult task may be to combine encouragement of individual, team, and departmental initiative and responsibility with encouraging trainers together to assume responsibility for developing plans and programs for the center as a whole. Emphasizing individual initiative and flexibility at the cost of institutional responsibility would blur overall orientation and effectiveness. It almost certainly would lead to destructive internal rivalries. On the other hand, emphasis on institutional responsibility at the cost of widespread initiative and responsibility lowers effectiveness in operation and stifles morale. Happily, the two directions, contrary though they sound, actually spring from the same source. The same favorable climate that encourages the freedom to explore and to take responsibility also engenders a readiness to work closely and jointly with other people on tasks that require collaboration and joint responsibility. The problems lie in balancing the two sides.

Primarily three tasks require institution-wide collaboration and joint responsibility.

1. Periodic redefinition of the institution's objectives and review of the range of organizations it seeks to serve. This involves agreeing on priorities.
2. Planning the main lines of training, research, and service activities, and the facilities required for them.
3. Defining the criteria for selecting new trainers, and setting standards of work.

The introduction of a new program can illustrate center-wide responsibility and the processes by which a principal can foster it. The principal would take no action alone on a program not included in plans already agreed to. It would first be discussed and agreed upon by the trainers meeting as a body. Irrespective of its points of origin—an individual trainer, a department, the principal—a new program is acceptable only if it is sufficiently central to the main objectives and methods agreed upon for the period in question. If so, agreement on it must clearly command requisite priority for time and other resources. If not central, it may still be accommodated in the standing provision that departmental budgets have for additional exploratory work. Should this not be possible, it may still go ahead under the institution's auspices, provided only that it meets accepted standards of work and is designated as an individual, departmental, or for that matter, an outside contributor's responsibility.

The main point is that principals, far from regarding the making of plans as their special responsibility by virtue of their position, involve trainers in all stages of the process. They thereby secure access to the whole range of their ideas and understanding. At the same time, they also secure the sharing of views and closer interaction that occurs in the process of working for agreement on joint plans. The end result, the agreed-upon plans and programs, then carry more weight on several scores. And their execution commands trainers' energies more readily because responsibility and satisfactions are shared.

By way of summary, exhibit 13.1 juxtaposes some major facets of institutional climates that favor or detract from development. The point of view is the principal's.

TRAINERS' LANGUAGES OF RESISTANCE

To promote a favorable climate for development principals assume functional roles and divest themselves of authority and power sanctioned by tradition. In doing so they meet the same kinds of initial difficulties that trainers experience when they move in a similar direction with participants. The first reaction of trainers is usually defensive, full of distrust and suspicion. They feel manipulated rather than freed. They see principals' endeavors to draw them closer as a clever and hence more frightening exercise of arbitrary power. What is genuine is seen as technique.

Exhibit 13.1

INSTITUTIONAL CLIMATES FOR TRAINERS: PRINCIPAL'S POINT OF VIEW

The Principal's	*Favorable Climate*	*Unfavorable Climate*
Self-image	Influential innovator, needs others' support.	Powerless, overworked, self-sacrificing. Disciplinarian, toward self and others.
Image of trainers	Capable of self-motivated work of high standard and of collaboration in joint activity and responsibility. Will enjoy development.	Need continuous prompting and guidance. Disinterested in conflict with colleagues.
Areas of attention	Diagnosis of current activities, long-term plans. Developing sound relationships within the institution and between the institution and its clients and the locality.	Current operations, rules, checks on individual performance.
Behavior	Listens, encourages expression of feelings and views on all aspects. Encourages innovation. Joins in making joint plans which commit trainers to heavy work.	Works separately, makes plans alone. Works through impersonal logical rules and orders, keeps trainers and departments distant.

The first murmurings may well arise over the greatly increased number of meetings required to establish the new climate and to reach general agreements on broad outlines of development. "All right," trainers say to one another, "so we have to meet. It is all a waste of time. We will carry on afterwards as we always have, you'll see." Or "She is asking us to speak only to test us out, to see who is with her." Listening to the trainers discuss institutional issues among themselves one might conclude that the principal is an obstacle, not a help. "She's not doing her job"; "He's the one who needs training!"

As principals persist in the new direction, an inevitable period of incredulity sets in. "It's all a gimmick. It can't be true." The trainers continue to experience the change as an imposition and resent the extra burden placed on them—basically, the burden of reaching agreement among themselves and of living with the consequences of joint decisions.

Then trainers test the principal. "Let's see if he really means what he says. I bet he doesn't." This is perhaps the first recognition of the possibility that they might mean it after all, contrary to all expectations. Such testing out can take many forms. For instance, when principals delegate to course coordinators not only more functions but also the corresponding authority to take action their behavior is open to several negative interpretations. Trainers may regard it as an attempt to stay out of trouble, to save themselves work, or as confirmation that they are totally uninterested in the impact on participants; they are "just an administrator" when trainers view the transfer of responsibility negatively, they assume new functions without enthusiasm, with a wary eye, with frequent glances over their shoulder. This period is characterized by a strong ambivalence that is difficult to dislodge. A very important set of experiences and expectations is in question. Like other people, trainers would prefer their earlier expectations confirmed instead. So this twilight stage may last some time. And right through this period, it is the principals who have to carry the burden of change, if necessary, alone. Hardest for them may be the emotional strain of remaining friendly and engaging, open and patient with the trainers, even while their endeavors seem little appreciated and results so slow in coming.

The authors have talked and corresponded with principals of a variety of centers and programs in several countries about the ambiguities and disturbances of establishing a favorable climate. Two descriptions are reproduced here at length. The one in box 13.2 came from the principal of a well-known experimental school in a developing country. The second, in box 13.3, is from A.K. Rice, when he was director of an annual leadership training program organized jointly by the University of Leicester and the Tavistock Institute of Human Relations in London. Every principal mentioned the trainers' proclivity for viewing the principal either as *the* authority or as *no* authority, as being too distant or too close to participants. In short, at the outset of any major institutional development trainers feel thoroughly insecure, quite at sea. For their part principals see trainers as "listless" on important questions, "as if neither the questions nor

Box 13.2

A SCHOOL PRINCIPAL AT WORK IN A DEVELOPING COUNTRY

How does one get people to link their hands together in joint effort? Why do teachers in some groups seem so insensitive to the problems of the young? What is it in me that seems to block the perception in others? I

Box 13.2 (Continued)

suppose the order of my questions should be revised, but I ask them this way.

From what I gather from my staff, I constantly confuse issues that others seem to see clearly in black and white terms until I enter the scene. I can live with error but my colleagues can't live comfortably with error in me.

As one of them stated it, "I hated you that time I knew I was right and you were wrong." Another put it, "Why aren't you consistent? You make a decision and later change it." When I replied, "I thought the new facts we gathered were sufficient cause," the answer was, "When there were already so many variables that made the decision difficult, you doubled the difficulties many times over when your changed it." "Sometimes you are like a General in the army fraternizing with us, the unlisted men, and sometimes you are just the General."

The teachers in one school feel I am too close to the children and "*know too much* about individual children to be an impartial observer of their [the teacher] work!" They see me either as The Authority or as No Authority. This is my constant dilemma.

There are two schools, with about the same enrollment in each. One school moves along with children, with a minimum of acute behavior problems. Children and teachers alike radiate a happiness and a quality of reaching out toward others which is noticeable enough to be mentioned even by strangers entering the gate. The other school, with a much better physical plant and facilities, is full of problems, yet I can't spot *why* this difference should exist. I can list a number of possibilities, such as space which limits the number of face-to-face contacts in day-to-day situations, the difference in social class and the pressure on a rising middle class. But why these situations give rise to the particular problems and what can be done about it requires more provisions and not less concern! But free teachers are less active in the interests of children.

I use the word *awareness* often in disussion with the teachers, yet they seem resistant. I admit to being more aware of child needs than teacher needs and I suppose I'm impatient to get at crucial conditions affecting the *child.* I think about the teacher and try to, I suppose, manipulate her into doing that which I see as needing to be done. But if the teachers in school A can do it—why don't the teachers in B?

I feel the heaviness of so much I don't like to see and so little of what I want to see at B. Yet, as teacher personalities, as managers in the class rooms, as subject matter specialists, they are an exceptionally well selected group.

In a New Education that can help children to go forward on their own, teachers, too, have to move forward on their own. What training can help do this? Teachers need help to gain insight into the significance of the process by which a child comes into an active awareness of the world around him. But how does a teacher achieve this awareness? Can teachers identify their own "intentions" with respect to their work? Can they see the

Box 13.2 (Continued)

necessity for total effort yet accommodate wide difference among themselves? Can they accept me in my role as a co-worker without damage to their own security on the job, or do I need a "strong" administrative assistant to hold the teachers in line while I play among the variables!

Considering the problem of staff turnover, of the effects of rapid expansion and the mixing of untrained, newly trained, and overtrained on the job, the difficulties arising out of missed cues in communication among such groups, and from and to me, are very painful. Perhaps, I'm just assuming too many roles at one time to deal effectively with any one of them. What kind of training do I need to serve in the process now called inservice training? How can I handle the details of a school day that often gets mixed into the training process to mould the "goals" we find so annoyingly elusive—now you see them, now you don't?

SOURCE: Private Communication.

the answers mattered much." Trainers seem personally involved only in discussions of administrative questions that directly affect them: hours of work, salaries and benefits, physical amenities, leave.

Another principal considered discontinuing professional meetings because "only I and a very few others wanted them." He kept them going because of two slender possibilities. One possibility was that the listlessness of the trainers might be expressing some accumulated resentment against earlier authority figures. By their listlessness they were able to deny the principal something he obviously wanted. If the trainers had such resentment to express, he concluded, it had better come out in the open, if necessary through this listlessness and denial. The second possibility was that the trainers found the changes the principal proposed so unsettling that they needed to hang on to concrete, measurable, short term issues, mainly to steady themselves. Issues at hand for this purpose tended to be administrative. This possibility looked the more plausible whenever trainers toyed with simple solutions to delicate problems, as if almost any solution was preferable to continued worrying. They displayed inordinate eagerness to accept a "solution" proposed by the principal, even when he had only put forward a suggestion or an idea. This principal concluded that if he could just keep going steadily in the same direction for a while, the anxieties and resentments would eventually be expressed and exhausted, and the trainers would then be ready to join him in a fundamentally different kind of relationship. But he was unsure whether the next stage could be initiated without more institutional control from the general environment, in particular without more institutional control over some key areas which now required decisions by his board of directors.

Several principals mentioned "very disquieting" declines in the

Box 13.3

A PROGRAM DIRECTOR AT WORK

A. K. Rice

Though I was appointed director by my colleagues who formed the conference staff, and though I continue to hold office only with their sanction, I have directed in my own way; and as director I have been in a privileged position when decisions about design and method have had to be made. My colleagues have not always agreed either with my approach to, or with my actions in, the conferences. But they have not disagreed so much as to make our disagreements intolerable or their support impossible. They have influenced not only conference design but also my own conduct in more ways than I can make explicit or even know about. We still disagree on some points of theory and on more of practice. At this stage of our understanding of problems of interpersonal and intergroup relations, I believe it to be right and healthy that we should continue to differ, provided we can also continue to use our differences constructively.

This is not therefore an agreed account, and I have to accept responsibility for it. I am nevertheless writing it now because developments are continually taking place, and if we wait until we are all agreed about what we are doing and how we are trying to do it, I doubt if an account will ever be written.

[In a later passage he poses the problem of separating fantasy from reality and notes the illusion that administrative questions can be at all clearly separated from professional ones].

When I am involved I have to ask whether my own anxiety about my performance is making me even more obstinate than usual. How far is the difficulty due to my capacity for blackmailing my colleagues by threats to resign the role of director? How far am I using in an inappropriate way the authority delegated to me? How far is the quarrel due to the intransigence of the colleagues with whom I am in dispute? Is the disagreement based on genuine technical differences or does it arise mainly from different views of the conference and its events? These questions are not peculiar to conference direction, they are inherent in any discussion about policy in any group that is responsible for leading and managing. What is important for a staff group running a conference that is itself about leadership and management is that the group's attention to its own difficulties should sufficiently differentiate fantasy and reality for the result, as it affects the members, to enhance learning opportunities.

One of the difficulties of separating reality from fantasy is the toleration of uncertainty of outcome demanded of the staff. In a staff meeting, anyone who expresses a point of view with sufficient strength, or seems sure in his prediction, tends to wield more influence than either the point of view or the prediction sometimes deserves. One consequence is that when I exercise decisively the authority delegated to me, I can sometimes do so with more

Box 13.3 (Continued)

power than I was intended to have. The very demonstration of power makes it more difficult for others effectively to oppose the decision. In addition, because of the need to make drastic economies in the time (and money) spent in preconference planning, almost all administrative decisions have been left to the conference secretary and myself. But "administrative" decisions, particularly those that have to do with what is sent out to inquiries and to members, are frequently found, like administrative decisions elsewhere, to have modified or even predetermined the policy they were intended only to implement. In solving some problems we have now to beware that our solutions do not serve to suppress other problems that need equal attention.

Yet even with all the meticulous training and years of experience Rice and his colleagues have had consistently in this orientation, Rice is still conscious of his colleagues' need to hide things from him and propitiate him with token gifts.

It appears to be assumed that though the director need not be told anything important, he should be told all that is unimportant. He needs, in other words, to be treated with respect and consideration, and a way of doing this is to propitiate him with token gifts. Behind the respect and consideration, however, is the hope that providing him with useless information may keep him from finding out anything useful, and hence make it easier to discredit him. The major communications to management are inferential, they have to be deduced not from what is said, but largely from what is not said.

Source: A. K. Rice, *Training for Leadership* (London: Tavistock Publications Ltd., 1965), pp. 3-4, 150-52.

motivation for work and the efficiency of many trainers during the early stages of major changes. For instance, joint responsibility initially seems to mean no one's responsibility. As a result, participants receive less supervision and help from trainers than before. Trainers preoccupy themselves with questions about how far they can afford to get ahead of their colleagues. A principal's personal commitment to effecting significant change can itself become a block to change if she becomes impatient for visible progress and intolerant of other people's difficulties.

Innovative principals often seem weary and a little discouraged even when, to the outsider's view, they are making notable progress. Trainers express some resentments more freely and directly, there is altogether far more openness, more frankness than before. The principals themselves talk of being newly able to proceed by agreements to differ. "We still disagree on some points of theory and on more of practice—[this is] right and healthy...provided we can also continue to use our differences constructively."

The fullest picture we have of a principal and a group of trainers engaged in close collaborative work is in Lynton's *The Tide of Learning: The Aloka Experience.*[5] Just the statistics reveal something of the great amount of work involved in establishing and maintaining collaboration. During the week preceding the start of this program, the whole faculty met for at least two hours a day. During the first four weeks of the course, faculty meetings were still almost daily, then every other day during the remaining eight weeks of the program. On the average, meetings during the program lasted over an hour, substantially lengthening an already long working day. The meetings were tape-recorded. Content analysis reveals that fully three-quarters of the meeting time during the initial four weeks was taken up by reports on individual participants, building up a picture of each. That done, preoccupations shifted to how to handle the most active and the most silent participants; how to accept the hostility that came as the relationships between trainers and participants changed; how to adjust the program to take into account needs becoming newly clear, in the later stages; and finally what the principal and the trainers were learning that would be of use in future programs.

What comes through the statement and descriptions of every innovative principal is not a particular outcome labeled "success" versus something labeled "failure," but the difficulties and excitement of professional people collectively becoming more and more involved in their work and improving its quality. They do not leave things alone. They worry over them and churn them until further improvement results. There is a continuous endeavor toward greater effectiveness, a need to concern oneself with better and better questions. This atmosphere in the training center, of the principal, trainers, and administrators all struggling to learn, is not lost on the participants. In fact, it may be the most important and pervasive communication of all that the process of training is continuous and that it engages everyone, certainly the principal and the trainers. It is this that puts the training institution really on the road to development.

CRISES, DILEMMAS, AND RESOLUTIONS IN INSTITUTIONAL DEVELOPMENT

From our work in new training centers and institutions and from watching sister institutions start and grow, we have become conscious of important similarities in the "life cycles" of all—to adapt the term Erik Erikson uses for individual maturation.[6] Rough though the analogy may be, even a brief systematic description of the uniformities may interest those

[5](London: Routledge & Kegan Paul, 1960), pp. 182-95.

[6]In e.g., *Identity: Youth and Crisis* (New York: W.W. Norton & Company, Inc., 1968), pp. 92-97.

charged with setting up new centers as well as innovative principals who are attempting to move existing centers toward greater maturity.

Exhibit 13.2

CRISES IN THE LIFE OF AN INSTITUTION

Crisis	*Characteristic Features*	*Dilemma*	*Resolution*
1. *Birth*	A few individuals full of ideas and zest. Frenzied activity. Attention oriented outward—power points, sister institutions, customers.	When should the institution be born and how large? Planning for every contingency or have a crash program?	Strong continuing leadership.
2. *Identity* a) Seeking identity	Search for main focus or foci. Conflict and uncertainty. Internal competition for attention.	Perfection of one thing or value all comers?	Clearly explicit long-range objectives as a priority system for decision making.
b) Seeking acceptance	Search for relationships with existing systems. Inter-organizational jealousies. Attention outward.	Stress likeness and conformity or stress novelty and differences?	Moratorium to establish standards, largely in isolation.
c) Seeking balance	One or two activities have made a quick start, now threaten to dwarf or belittle others. Jealousies within.	Curb fast starters or let them run loose?	Focus on lagging functions to encourage their momentum.
3. *Growth*	Great demands for services, mostly short-term. Temptation to take on too much load. Meeting demands increases demands.	Consolidate and develop slowly or expand in all promising directions?	Moratorium to reexamine objectives and priorities Publicize long-range plans.
4. *Maturity*	Success revives inter-organizational jealousies, even threatens sponsors. Attacks on autonomy and independence.	Forego identity and submit or revolt and break away?	Develop interdependent relationships focused on tasks.
5. *Develop-- ment*	Self-satisfaction. Temptation to rest on laurels. Reluctance to work out new ideas.	Fossilize or break up into progressive and conservative, young and old?	Check objectives against changing situation, rejuvenate institution, build in indices of relevance.

The uniformities are systematically set out in exhibit 13.2. They are ordered into three concepts. One is the crisis, not in the sense of an emergency, but of a constellation of forces internal and external that insistently pose a dilemma—the second concept. The dilemma is not a problem to be solved, once and for all, the constellation of forces does not dissolve. The alternatives it offers are tempting but a false choice. What the dilemma demands is resolution—the third concept—but one sufficiently deep to embrace both. Working out such a resolution calls, in the first place, for quiet pause from day to day activities, a disengagement for reflection, a turning inward. For this disengagement Erikson uses the word "moratorium."[7] The moratorium is not itself the resolution but sets up a condition for discovering it.

The crises occur in a certain predictable order. We have called them birth, identity, growth, maturity, development. Each has characteristic patterns and issues. They overlap, and occasionally there may be a regression, but the sequence broadly stands. Only after the current dilemma is resolved and the crisis passed is the institution ready for the next phase of its development. This phase will likewise shape towards a crisis. Characteristically unresolved, any crisis persists and prevents further development. So every phase carries the seeds of institutional death. "Doom" would be a better word: growth stifled, an atmosphere of death. The institution may continue to exist; institutions usually do. But it is at a halt.

Regular self-renewal processes built into a center's on-going life are the antidote to institutional doom. It is a principal's primary task to ensure that they are properly instituted, workable, and also used. Like a steadily revolving radar screen that picks up signals from all 360 degrees of its surroundings, effective mechanisms for self-renewal regularly scan all aspects of institution building. Recent studies enumerate six sets of signals of greatest significance. *Leadership*, primarily for holding all parts together and focusing them collectively in the desired direction; *doctrine,* the direction desired which governs also the style and image of the institution; the *program* of activities through which the institution expresses its doctrine; the *resources* and *internal structure* which make programs possible; and the *linkages* through which the center interacts with the sectors of its environment that matter to its existence.

THE TRAINING CENTER IN ITS ENVIRONMENT

Studies to date tell us very little about the amount of general support an institution requires to tolerate, sustain, or promote a major innovation in its development, or how strong and active an institution has to be in order

[7]Ibid.

to initiate changes in its environment. Certainly all the people at the institution—the principal, trainers, administrators, and staff of all kinds—no less than the participants, are children of the surrounding society and prevailing traditions. They bring "the outside" in. In reverse, through outgoing participants and direct contacts with work and professional organizations, the institution conveys to the society outside what is going on within. Further ripples of this two-way influence include everyone's family and friends and their myriad contacts with others.

The general conceptual picture of the relationship between the institution and the world outside is therefore clear: it is that of any subsystem within the larger systems to which it belongs, the immediate and those beyond. What studies on innovation have yet to clarify are the operational demands of this relationship—the sequences, weights, and priorities involved. Meanwhile we shall use the general indications available.

Simply stated, the overriding consideration is that the relationship between purposeful, active, innovative training center and its environment matters. We have already seen how training departments and staff colleges that form part of work organization may not be allowed to develop in significant directions if top management is preoccupied with early "concrete" results or fearful of possible disturbances to production and services "caused" by the training wing. A similar situation exists when an institution though autonomous in intent, formal position, structure and resources, is so small and weak that its efforts are swamped by traditional influences. Any changes within may then be offset by forces outside. We do not know what is "so small" or "so weak;" we only know that many training centers struggle valiantly but vainly with this constraint. Often only the principal's determination has prevented a center from sliding back into the undifferentiated thoroughly human trend to randomness.

If institutional development can be so smothered by general forces, the answer may lie in combining institutional autonomy with independent strength. Many new institutions have been set up as autonomous bodies but without sufficient support and hence are faced with the same danger, only indirectly. Autonomy and strength are not synonymous. An autonomous institution normally starts with more and better national contacts than local ones, but because its independence often spells separateness, it has additional difficulties in developing strong local links. A stand-off ensues: traditional forces in the locality may not be able to swamp the new institution; because it is too strong, but without strong local links the institution is deprived of the opportunity to act effectively as an agent for accelerated development in its own backyard. The same dangers to effectiveness lurk beyond its backyard but are more dispersed. Over a wider area—a state, region, or country—the institution's contacts may be too scattered to affect general development. It is the scattered participants and their diffuse network who are then in danger of being swamped by the enveloping traditions in the various localities and organizations in which they live and work. It is a matter for anxiety that national institutions, e.g., in India, which draw participants from far and near, often have only a few or one from the very localities in which they are located.

Effective contact between a training institution and its environment raises questions of structure, of what makes for strength in the institution and in the environment, and of the kinds of relationships that might be effectively built. As to structure, the historical development of professional bodies may suggest ways of combining optimum autonomy for effecting change with local relationships for achieving influence. Universities in many countries consist of autonomous "schools"—medicine, architecture, public administration, and so forth. They profit from sharing skills and facilities. Yet they profit most from sharing an atmosphere in which learning is the primary task. Many have local roots. Whatever the formal relationship, studies show that close contact between various centers and institutions in the same locality goes hand in hand with sustaining and spreading development in general. Geographical proximity—clustering of institutions—is the most obvious condition for local contact and collaboration.

> In studying the diffusion of new teaching materials, Miles reports that clustering of institutions was the dominant condition for quick diffusion. Four out of five early users were geographically close to other users. Those cut off from other users either forsook the innovation or stimulated colleagues to use the new materials and thereby introduced other users. More often, the materials were used in tightly knit groups and in clusters of institutions. That the institutions were of different kinds was not important, only that they were geographically close. What happened, apparently, was that principals and trainers, after seeing the change in operation in a nearby institution, decided to implement it themselves. Only after reaching the decision to use the new materials did they try to develop the necessary skills and material resources. Direct observation or firsthand reports tipped the balance.[8]

Training centers tend to cluster in large towns. It seems important to encourage similar clustering in smaller towns, for example, market towns in rural areas. The wisdom of this is confirmed by another observation: innovation feeds on innovation, no matter what the subject or field, through the generation of an atmosphere of development. People become accustomed to change and to seeing institutions develop. Development creates the climate for further development. Thus, development can become a self-perpetuating process (as stagnation can, likewise).

We have already noted that institutional development depends heavily on who is at the helm. A principal eager for change, with the skill requisite for creating a favorable climate is mandatory. Trainers with wide

[8]Matthew B. Miles (ed.) *Innovation in Education* (New York: Teachers College, Columbia University N.Y., 1964), pp. 262-65.

professional interests and contacts come next. And then, to complete the prognosis for development, we must add financing just as innovative farmers tend to operate larger farms and have higher incomes and saving than other farmers, innovative doctors tend to have richer patients, and innovative companies tend to have larger operations, so innovative training institutions tend to serve organizations and localities with higher levels of income and expenditure.[9] The process is an interlocking one. Development often starts in an institution that has some extra resources. Foundation grants can play a key role in priming the pump. Once development is under way, it becomes easier to raise funds independently.

The localities in which innovative institutions prosper are also characterized by certain strengths. The institution's objectives are widely known and understood, and expectations of the contribution to the locality high. Understanding and expectations of this sort are associated usually with education, socio-economic class, and the distribution of political power, but they are also open to deliberate influence by the institution.

Rendering a service to the locality may be an excellent first step toward developing a sound local base for a training center. A small factory that trainers help to run well, a new community health service that is both an additional facility and one distinctly more effective than others run on "normal" lines, a modernized farm operated with the same physical resources available to local farmers—these are examples of effective services. They mark the institution's goodwill and interest in the locality. They show what training can produce by way of patently useful results. They make the point that effective training develops in participants new attitudes, knowledge, understanding, and skills that can transform other resources, whatever they be, into contributing streams to development.

Maintenance and further development of linkages with the outside world may distinguish most reliably between training centers with promise and those in decline. Centers in decline tend to activate their linkages only spasmodically (and usually with dread), notably at annual budgeting time, or when something urgent and unusual is required. Otherwise they are passive, anticipate antagonistic or at least unreasonable demands from outside, and are hence most willing to postpone such interference. Centers of promise handle their linkages quite differently. They are active on behalf of their work and making it effective. They present resource providers with realistic estimates. They keep information flowing routinely to large networks of contacts, build constituencies, and alert important people and agencies in their environment of impending difficulties as well as successes. They reach out for collegial and inter-institutional contact. In this process they come to be seen as open, creative, purposeful, and reliable.

[9]Ibid., p. 314

Chapter 14

Action Research for Better Training

Perfect as is the wing of a bird, it never could raise the bird up without resting on air. Facts are the air of a scientist. Without them you never can fly...

But learning, experimenting, observing—try not to stay on the surface of the facts. Do not become the archivists of facts. Try to penetrate to the secret of their occurrence, persistently search for the laws which govern them.

—Pavlov's Bequest to the Academic Youth of Soviet Russia, February 27, 1936

Training for development has been addressed primarily to practicing trainers, consultants, center principals, institution builders, planners, and decision makers in training. They are engaged in the challenging task of increasing the effectiveness of organizations through developing the people working in them and shaping the systems in which they work. All are practitioners, yes, but not thereby amateurs. On the contrary, our theme throughout has been that training is a profession with goals and methods and ethics that can be stated and generally deserve recognition and respect. We have supported the theme on two pillars. One pillar is our own experience of developing, administering and conducting a variety of training programs and institutions, and includes the experiences of others. From this have come the illustrations and examples to make the theme come alive with the kind of signs that practitioners recognize as their language. But the second pillar is important, too, and deserves particular attention because it tends to be neglected, even in this age of science. This pillar is research and onward study. From research in training and education, and wider fields of the social sciences, have come the concepts and theories, i.e., the framework, wherein myriad experiences are ordered toward serving a general purpose. Research, too, is essential to a profession; it goads the continuous improvements in practice that high professional standards demand.

If trainers in the time-honored tradition of practitioners impatiently brush aside the idea that research deserves their attention—and we shall indeed urge that they themselves engage in it—research workers are partly to blame. All too often research connotes the esoteric and impractical. This is not what we mean. By research, we mean, first of all, a desire for improvement followed by action. But this action, second in order, is not off the cuff or based only on a hunch or on intuition. Intuition has its place at the creative moment where research has as yet no guidance to offer, yet action has to be taken into the unknown. Research is at the moving frontiers of knowledge, and we want trainers to actively engage in pushing them farther and farther back. Research is systematic action to enhance knowledge and understanding. It need not be abstract and erudite, but does need to be systematic and planned. We would like to conclude this book on the note of improving training continuously through research.

The formulations presented in this book are valid, at best, for now. If they inspire training in general, it will surely become more effective and economical than it is. Yet, there is always more to know about improving training strategies and methods, and more to understand about how training plays its part in general designs for development.

Maybe research will look more practicable if we consider several levels short of high-level abstractions, rigorous hypotheses, and statistical models. These can be left to the specialists, although only safe with them if the questions addressed are rooted deep in practice. At the other, most practical, end of the range is that research into individual experience usually termed reflection. What happened? why? how do I do better next time? What are the indicators for assessing my progress? These are questions for this level of "research." As seen earlier in this book, reflection is the difference between a passing event and an experience for building on. And practitioners are quite right: we learn only from experience.

The next level of research looks for data beyond the immediate experience, from similar experiences in the past and those of other people. It seeks to generalize more widely, and to note commonalities and variance. It tends beyond individual learning to checking and sharing with others.

The third level of research commences with extracting from these more or less tentative generalities some experiments in which to test them. Nothing very rigorous yet, but essentially akin to testing a hypothesis. What will happen in that situation, if I do X? I rather think the result will be Y. I will try it and see.

ACTION RESEARCH BY TRAINERS

Improvement comes from a concerted effort to face squarely questions that need answers, to search systematically for these answers, to test these answers rigorously, and to accept the tested solutions for action as the best available now and as a basis for further research if required. This approach assumes another, new discipline for trainers, one to use side by side with their intuition guided by experience. It is the discipline of action research, i.e., research to improve action.

Action research is a way of approaching problems or questions. Four beliefs underlie action research:

1. Solutions to problems are more effective and enduring when they emerge from systematic search rather than from the dictates of authority or solely from a practitioner's intuition.
2. Research done by practitioners themselves on the problems contributes more to the solution of these problems than research done by others.
3. Research consists in analyzing problems, searching for solutions, and testing and evaluating the solutions. It consists of skills which can be learned and developed by practitioners. Research is not the prerogative of experts.
4. Development of people's capabilities, for example through training, is basic to improvement in practice.

Action research is the application of the scientific method to problem solving and involves the same steps: identification and focusing of the problem, diagnosis for probable cause, selection of one or a few causal relationships for formulating hypotheses, formulation of an action hypothesis which can be tested, designing an action plan based on the hypothesis, evaluation of the action, and generalization and formulation of further questions. Figure 14.1 shows these components built into a complete feedback model for action research.

Figure 14.1
FEEDBACK MODEL OF ACTION RESEARCH

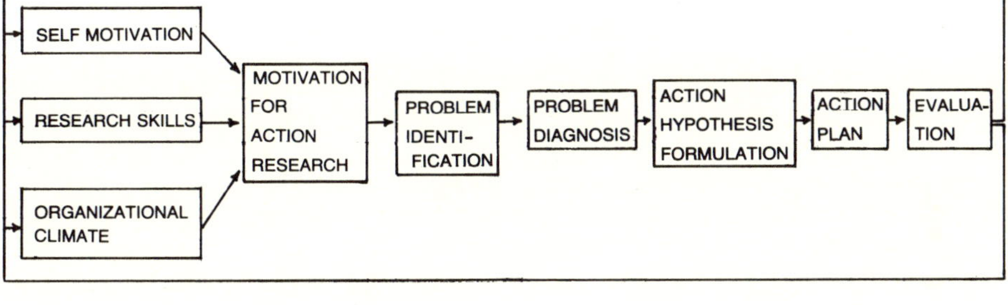

The process starts, quite simply, with trainers' desires to improve their work in some respect. Every subsequent step follows without much difficulty. Shaping the "problem" into a researchable question and collecting and analyzing data so that they provide useful guidance require only minimal research skills; trainers who lack these or feel they have rusted through neglect will find that acquiring them involves diligence rather than difficulty. Pointers emerge quickly, even from minimal starts. Trainers engaged in action research find that the prerequisites—motivation, skills and organizational climate—grow strong in the process. Concepts, too, may be redefined to suit a situation.

> In Indonesia a program on organizational effectiveness was planned for midlevel health managers of a province. Instead of extracting standard criteria of excellence and effectiveness from foreign texts, the participants developed fresh criteria of excellence in Indonesia by selecting some from known excellent Indonesian organizations and deriving from them their own. The criteria thus derived were: long survival, adequate resources, high performance, financial efficiency, and social relevance and awareness. The search for characteristics of organizational effectiveness in Indonesia yielded the following: collaborative and cooperative working, nurturing and effective leadership, realistic and detailed planning, effective human resource management (acquiring good people, proper placement, utilization, and training), high performance, and properly used control systems. These criteria were then used to design a program that proved highly effective.

Essential for action research are ready questioning and openness to alternative answers based on experience and information. Various devices can be used to stimulate, develop, and use this basic research spirit. Field research for case to be used in training exemplifies research of the clinical kind. There, in an ongoing working situation, an issue emerges that calls for understanding and decision. Whose responsibility is it to attend to it and act? Who are involved in its generation or implications? How do the main actors and others affected view the issues and options for decision? Researchers familiarize themselves with a situation and its background, interview participants, and collect relevant documents. They draft a "case" that sufficiently describes the situation and the happenings to make them "real" to readers who must understand the situation and think their way through to what they would do under similar circumstances. The original participants in the case modify and, usually, flesh out the draft to convey more accurately how it actually was. This is a meticulous, often protracted recess. Trainer-researchers develop through it and the result is a potent vehicle for training, precisely because the case is full and realistic enough for new participants "to the see themselves in it."

Another way to generate data is to tap the cumulative experiences participants in a training program bring to some focal situation. This can generate a realistic "simulation" to be used in training. Such self-generated simulations are more engaging and productive than standard "exercises" which tend to close out any search for potent questions and the generation of relevant data.

In a program on organizational effectiveness in Indonesia, midlevel managers were set the task of constructing an effective organization from their experiences of working together in the program and then, individually, to rate their organizations back home on dimensions in the simulation that they considered relevant. Eight dimensions stood out, and rankings on a simple four-point scale produce the following results (mean values):

Mission orientation	3.4
Social benefit	3.4
Leadership	3.2
Client orientation	3.0
Innovation	2.8
Use of data and feedback	2.8
Expansion and growth	2.5
Competitive spirit	2.5

With the more general, abstract dimensions already so much better developed (in the participants' assessment) than innovation, achievement, and instrumentalities for them, the remaining program focused sharply on the latter dimensions.

Data currently generated by participants can also be usefully combined with already published formal research.

In one seminar on Indonesian culture and management, thirty-three managers of central and provincial health systems first rated Indonesian culture individually on the eight dimensions that major formal research had found significant. They next worked in small groups, discussed the dimensions and individual ratings, and worked out group ratings by consensus. Thereafter, published research data were made available. The two sets of findings were closely similar, and validated each other. Later work on these dimensions, to strengthen the functional and undermine the dysfunctional, was very meaningful to the participants. Their evaluation confirmed that having generated the list and analyzed the functional and dysfunctional dimensions themselves was a valuable experience for them.

Another way to generate meaningful data is through "instruments." Valid instruments can help participants look at data about their own orientations, attitudes, values, behavior, etc. The main instruments are available in research and training literature but few have been standardized for relevance and use in cultures or settings in specific developing countries. Involving participants in developing simple instruments can therefore serve a double purpose.

Exhibit 14.1

STEPS IN PREPARING A LOCUS-OF-CONTROL SCALE

1. Trainer explains concept of locus-of-control (internality and externality).
2. Participants divide into groups. Each group brainstorms and generates proverbs in the local language, showing internality or externality (a total of 204 proverbs were collected).
3. A team of participants works through the proverbs, edits them, and eliminates duplication and those vague and irrelevant (reduced the list to 93).
4. Each proverb is read aloud to the entire group and each member votes (by show of hand) on the proverb to indicate whether it shows internality or externality, or neither. The votes for each proverb are recorded.
5. Proverbs receiving at least 80% agreement (in our case, 12 votes) are selected (43 proverbs qualified).
6. A team of 3 pairs the proverbs, so that internal and external control are covered for the same dimension (17 pairs resulted, each requiring a respondent to choose one item from each pair).
7. "Filler" items are added to complete the instrument (17 + 8 = 25 pairs).
8. Reliability index is prepared for each item (from 55 responses).
9. Validity and norms are established.

Pairs	1	2	3	4	7	8	9	12	13	16	20	21	22	23	25
Reliability Index	.79	.56	.58	.47	.87	.74	.21	.01	.53	.32	.19	.31	.46	.56	.58

To make management training more relevant in Indonesia, several instruments were developed with the help of participants. One instrument measured internal and external loci-of-control. Fifteen participants worked on this; exhibit 14.1 details the steps. The participants were quite rigorous in judging the items.

Development of another instrument, on leadership styles in Indonesia, was much more complicated but even more exciting and educative. Its purpose was to test the possible usefulness of "situational leadership" (Hersey and Blanchard's theory) in Indonesian health organizations, and, if useful, to develop an instrument based on Indonesian experiences of effective leadership. Exhibit 14.2 lists the steps. This instrument, called "Survey of Problem-Solving Strategies" (or SPSS) was then used in other management training programs in Indonesia.

Exhibit 14.2

STEPS IN PREPARING A SURVEY OF PROBLEM-SOLVING STRATEGIES

1. Decide on theory of leadership to use as framework for survey, e.g., Hersey-Blanchard's.
2. Collect critical attributes of effective and ineffective leader behavior of a) task-oriented and b) people-oriented health administrators in Indonesia from 20 respondents.
3. Collect written descriptions of 6 typical situations that a leader encounters, 1 description from each of 6 groups of participants. In situation 1, the leader is new, and is effective; in 2, the leader is new, and is not effective; in 3, the task is simple

Exhibit 14.2 (Continued)

and the leader is effective, in 4, the task is difficult and the leader is not effective; in 5, the group is mature, and the leader is effective; and in 6, the group is mature and the leader is not effective.

4. Collect from 3 persons for each situation critical incidents of effective and ineffective leader behavior in situations where:
   1) group has low maturity, 2) medium-low maturity,
   3) medium-high maturity, 4) high maturity.
5. Test the (Hersey-Blanchard) model by analyzing the critical incidents.
   Having found the model suitable for Indonesia,
6. Edit the situations described, and select 12 situations, 3 each for 4 levels of group maturity.
7. Edit the critical attributes and prepare 4 alternative responses for each situation.
8. Translate the instrument into local language (Bahasa Indonesia). Administer the instrument to several groups (totaling about 100 health administrators).
9. Design an answer sheet to facilitate quick scoring and calculation of final scores on styles and adaptability.
10. Test reliability and validity and establish norms.

In addition to cases, simulation, and instruments for collecting or generating data, considerable other data, records, and information are commonly available for use in researching training issues. Secondary source data and unobtrusive measures for evaluating training are examples (see chapter 11). By involving participants in the search and identification of indicators for assessing, say, management qualities, their insight into organizational dynamics is sharpened and research into organizational problems is also made more fruitful. Critical incidents and other observations can be collected from a large number of persons at very little expense.

As a general rule, it is useful simply to request participants to bring relevant (perhaps specified) information and data from their organizations with them when they come for training. The request itself underscores that training and work will be closely related and that the participants' training will focus on live issues so that they can return to their jobs with action proposals. When combined and studied together during the program, these materials also generate appreciation beyond the particular organization and situation. The indices and priorities developed from them can become far reaching action strategies. In this respect they resemble the use made of epidemiological data. Just as medical records are examined for incidence, prevalence, severities, and patterns of health conditions of particular cohorts (age groups, sex, occupation, location or other characteristics) and the findings collated to concentrate efforts where most needed and promising, so participants in training, individually and collectively, can establish organizational patterns and become sensitized to characteristic ones. In addition to carrying away from training some specific action strategies to use at work, they will also have developed greater familiarity, sensitivity and alertness to common patterns. These are qualities that characterize competent practitioners in any field.

SOME QUESTIONS FOR TRAINERS TO STUDY

Action research starts with "framing the right question," or, better still, "framing an important question aright." No sophistication later—in method, sample size, or instrumentation—can compensate for irrelevance or loose formulation. As the proverb states, the right question is already half the answer.

Below is a short list of questions which, in our opinion, call for research by trainers and lend themselves well to action research. They are illustrative only; many more could be listed. They are ordered in sequence with this book and so allow us to walk over the same ground again—this time with questions.

General

1. What are the different uses of the word *training*? What are the implications of each for a) training practice, and b) organizational development?

2. How can the costs of training be calculated accurately? Direct and indirect costs? Costs per session? Above all, costs for various outcomes: e.g., immediate, medium- and long-term; direct, i.e., improved performance by participants; indirect, i.e., participants in turn improving the performances of others?

3. When is an organization ready for training? What are the characteristics of a client system most likely to benefit from training?

4. What happens to participants during training? What is a useful model for participant learning? For example:

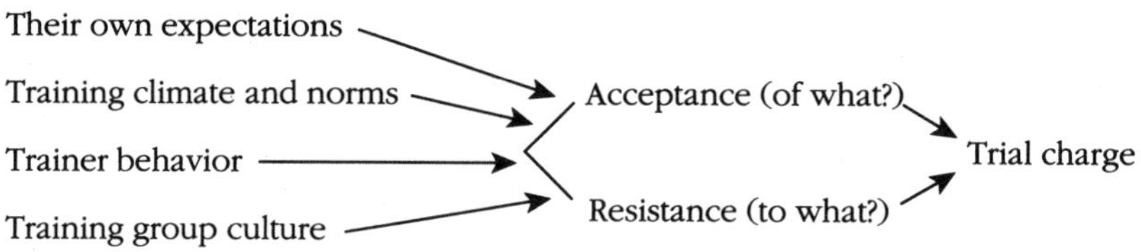

Training Strategies

5. Besides purpose and costs, what conditions favor certain training strategies over others? What operational (quantitative) data can be made available to assess them?

6. Which strategies can be effectively combined? For what purposes? With what stresses?

7. What are the lead times for introducing specific strategies? What is the minimum concentration of skilled trainers, etc., for changes in strategy?

The Training Process

ESTABLISHING OBJECTIVES AND PREPARING THE PARTNERS

8. What indicators are practical and useful in assessing an organization's commitment to a development effort in which training figures?
9. How can training needs for organizational change be assessed? How can we evaluate the effectiveness of various methods for this?
10. What are the ratios of people benefiting and not benefiting from training? In general, apparently, one-third receive no benefit at all, one-third benefit a little and one-third benefit greatly. How do these ratios operate in reality?
11. What are useful indicators of individual readiness for training? Which kind of training, when, and under what conditions? Do people ready for training have distinct clusters of personality characteristics? Expectations? Motivation? How can these be measured? How can we spot such people?
12. What are useful indicators of individual "unreadiness" for training?
13. How might trainers deal with those in the category of "not likely to benefit"? Any special pretraining work? Special work with them during the training period?
14. What can be done to prepare (pretraining work) participants for a training program? Feedback on behavior? Pretraining laboratories? Shifting responsibility for selection to participant, i.e., voluntary versus nominated participation?
15 What is the role of participants' organizations in pretraining work? Does the role vary according to the type of organization?

DESIGNING THE PROGRAM

16. Program mix: Which sequences are most effective? Modules? Parallel series?
17. How much flexibility is required in different programs? How can it be provided effectively and efficiently?
18. How can outside part-time resources be integrated in the program?

TRAINING METHODS

19. Different methods and their effectiveness: Under what conditions are particular methods effective?
20. What training sequences are most effective for what purpose?
21. Research questions in each method: For example, what are the purposes and places of field experience in training? Is field training effective when it is concentrated? Or phased? When?

THE TRAINING GROUP

22. Group composition: Within what ranges of age and experience can participants be effectively combined for training? For what purposes? What methods?

23. What are the cycles or phases in the development of a training group? How can the maturity of a training group be measured? How can it be enabled to develop at certain stages?

THE TRAINER

24. What values in trainers contribute to what kinds of behavior in participants?

25. What are the different roles of trainers? What are the role congruencies? Role conflicts?

26. What different systems of expectations are trainers expected to meet? How can they be helped to integrate these into their perception of their role?

27. How are role conflicts resolved? What are adequate and inadequate coping mechanisms for the resulting stress?

POSTTRAINING SUPPORT

28. How can participants be helped to avoid or offset losses in transferring new learnings from training to work situations?

29. How can training institutions assess more accurately the effects of training on (a) participants and their growth, (b) the use of new knowledge by work organizations, and (c) the range and speed of changes of various kinds?

30. What effective roles can training institutions play to support change produced by training in different kinds of organizations?

31. What are the various methods and their comparative effectiveness of involving work organizations in posttraining work?

EVALUATION

32. What are the costs/benefits of different methods for helping work organizations and policymakers to evaluate training in line with their responsibilities?

33. How are evaluations by the various constituencies best related and how can training institutions help do this?

34. What are useful roles and functions of training institutions in administrative and financial evaluation?

35. What role and functions can training institutions play to ensure timely attention and provision for future training?

THE TRAINING SYSTEM

36. For training systems of different sizes and degrees of complexity, what criteria and mechanisms are useful for reaching decisions about system boundaries (i.e., inclusion and exclusion), internal differentiation and integration, and quality control?

37. What issues of governance and leader characteristically arise at various stages of systems development and how are they best handled?

38. What administrative apparatus—and funds for it—do different systems minimally require and how is it best provided for?

39. How can provisions be built into systems for maintaining responsiveness to new needs and conditions, and inclusion, cohesion, and other aspects of renewal?

40. What characterizes effective network management, e.g., information flow, identification and interlinking of resources, costs, and fee arrangements?

41. What are the cost/benefit ratios for various types of temporary systems under different conditions and how can they be improved?

THE TRAINING INSTITUTION

42. What are effective role mixes for trainers and how can an institution organize itself for their systematic performance?

43. What are effective specializations within a training institution? For example, administration and training, training and services?

44. What contributes to a favorable climate for change in an institution? What are the advance indications of climatic change?

45. What are the phases in the life of an institution? The crises? Dilemmas? How are these generally resolved? Effective and ineffective behavior? By whom?

46. What are effective ways of building and maintaining morale in training institutions?

ACTION RESEARCH

47. What proportion of trainers now engage in action research? What are their personal characteristics? Academic and/or professional preparation? What time and other resources do they spend on it? Individually and with colleagues? Interinstitutional projects?

48. Are there any patterns to their output and its use(s), e.g., papers for conferences or publication or training materials? Effects on their professional standing, on institutional rewards, e.g., promotion?

49. What are effective institutional supports for action research? How can they be built into (a) new, and (b) existing situations?

TRAINER-RESEARCHERS

Let us say that a group of trainers has chosen a question for action research. The next step is to work and continue working, open-eyed and attentive to detail, and to record data about problematical experiences in meticulous detail: both quantitative facts (for example, how many participants borrowed books from the evening library), and qualitative facts (for example, about human relationships, and feelings; sequences and other linkages of facts; records of meetings, dialogues; anything, in short, that may throw light on the problem in hand). As they begin to record experiences in detail, the trainers find their world enlarging, as if the courtesy of their attention brought to life many aspects of the problem that had not existed for them before. They will also discover that their capabilities for observing, listening, and recording expand with practice, and concomitantly, their sense of being more fully alive. They develop a (gently) questioning attitude into personal traits, finding interest in myriad things around them.

The trainers will need this curiosity to strengthen them for the rigor and discipline and, let us be realistic, often troublesome routine of collecting data of sufficient quality, quantity, regularity, and duration to elucidate a problem. This is the second step. Sound evidence is needed at all steps of problem solving, right from the first step of problem identification. Indeed, with awesome regularity important known problems of long standing are redefined in the light of evidence accumulated for problem identification. Evidence is needed at every stage to evaluate the effectiveness of an action, even the action of collecting more data. General impressions by themselves are not sufficiently reliable for detailed action, certainly not for significant evaluation.

Thus, one series of steps takes the trainers toward collecting adequate data for analysis and understanding. Another series takes them toward increasingly closer relationships with each other, and also to the environment outside the institution. Action research ideas, designs, the formulation of hypotheses and methods—all profit from frank examination with colleagues. More basically, more problems that call for action research extend beyond the purview and competence of a single trainer. Our list contains numerous examples of this general trend. Finally, worthwhile research results and processes should be shared.

A training institution's contribution to action research is a favorable climate. The crucial evidence for the existence of this climate is the allocation in plans and budgets of regular and substantial time for research by trainers. Additional resources are secondary and often minor, and can never take the place of professional time. Further evidence of the climate is the respect and advancement offered to trainers who continue to improve themselves and their training practice through research.

Throughout this book we have seen effective trainers as the kind of people they want participants to become. Their engagement in action research is one more aspect of this theme. Like participants, they also must be involved in a permanent process of learning, of becoming. Thereby they become a part—a changing, viable part—of the life they study and influence.

Index

Index

D

E

F